14
steps
to
FINANCIAL
FREEDOM

Disclaimer

This book provides financial education only and is for financial empowerment. Please, therefore, talk to your advisers before you make any decision relating to your financial affairs. This book does not guarantee financial success in that each person's situation and dedication to change are different. The author takes no responsibility for any loss incurred by anyone who has read the book.Furthermore, the views and opinions expressed are those of the author and not those of any of the entities he represents.

The author uses a number of stories throughout this book. The names and sometimes elements of the stories have been disguised to protect the identity of the individuals without changing the essence of the stories. Any resemblance to persons alive or dead is entirely coincidental and unintentional.

To my late grandmother, Ms. Olive Shepherd, the cornerstone of our family; my mother, Ms. Janet Shepherd, who sacrificed her all to secure the best future for me and my siblings; my wife, Suzette, my biggest cheerleader; and our sons, John, Justin, and Jared—three streams of joy in our lives.

To my brother, Corey, and sisters, Shelly-Ann and Nadine, who knew me before I ever got any public accolades or awards.

BOARD
HORSE
PRESS

13 West Lake Ave., Kingston 10, Jamaica
bruce@14stepstofinancialfreedom.com

ISBN: ISBN 978-976-96959-1-7 (paperback)
ISBN: ISBN 978-976-96959-2-4 (ebook)
ISBN: ISBN 978-976-96959-0-0 (hardcover)
ISBN: ISBN 978-976-96959-5-5 (audiobook)

Ordering Information:

Special discounts are available on quantity purchases by corporations, associations, and others. For details, contact bruce@14stepstofinancialfreedom.com and 14stepstofinancialfreedom.com

table of contents

14
steps

to

FINANCIAL
FREEDOM

Simple Strategies to **G**row, **P**rotect,
and **S**ow Your Money at Any Age

BRUCE SCOTT
CPA (COLORADO), FCA, FCCA, MBA

INTRODUCTION

I wrote this book for you, working adults and full-time students who were never taught how to manage money at home or in school — only 21 of the 52 states in the U.S. require high school students to take a course in personal finance before graduation[1]. I also wrote the book forthose struggling with their personal finances e.g., people who are living paycheck to paycheck — meaning, if you did not receive one month's pay, for whatever reason, it would cause you serious financial distress due to a lack of savings [2].

In 2019, according to *Charles Schwab's 2019 Modern Wealth Index Survey*, 59 per cent of adults in the U.S. were living paycheck to paycheck[3]. This statistic means that for approximately 60% of you working adults who will read this book – it is likely that you are struggling with your personal finances (i.e. living from paycheck to paycheck) and should therefore

---

1   Sharon Epperson, "Teaching Financial Education in Schools Finally Catches On," CNBC, last modified February 5, 2020, https://www.cnbc.com/2020/02/04/teaching-financial-education-in-schools-finally-catches-on.html.

2   Julia Kagan, "Paycheck to Paycheck", Investopedia, updated May 23, 2022, https://www.investopedia.com/terms/p/paycheck-to-paycheck.asp

3   Ibid

find this book a source of wisdom and hope in helping you to improve your financial health.

I used personal financial data and statistics primarily from the U.S. and some from Jamaica (e.g., annual household incomes, average house prices, and average investment returns) to illustrate many of the financial concepts in the book. I used U.S. information because (1) it was readily available through online sources, (2) the wide influence of U.S. culture in many parts of the world and, (3) the U.S. dollar is the global currency of commerce[4] that most people can relate to. Accordingly, I have used U.S. dollars primarily to describe numbers and figures throughout the book. I live in Jamaica, so it is only natural that I also illustrate and write with a Jamaican flavor.

In an effort to demonstrate the practicality of the concepts presented in the book, I have used stories of people I have coached during my one on one financial mentoring sessions, stories of people who have attended my financial webinars, stories and wise sayings from the Bible and personal stories (including my life changing conversion to Christianity at age 14 and how I was able to buy my first apartment at age 23). My hope is that you will find these stories helpful in cementing your understanding of the concepts taught as well as to inspire you to move further along the road to financial freedom.

Finally, notwithstanding my use of U.S. and Jamaican financial information in the book, the principles articulated are universal and neutral. Learn and apply them, and they will work for you regardless of your geographic location or postal code.

---

4   Kimberly Amadeo, "Why the US Dollar Is the Global Currency," The Balance, updated March 16, 2022, https://www.thebalance.com/world-currency-3305931.

chapter 1

THE GREATEST FINANCIAL INVESTMENT YOU WILL EVER MAKE

If you give a man a fish, you feed him for a day. If you teach a man to fish, you feed him for a lifetime.
—Proverb

There are three compelling reasons you should read this book:

Reason 1: It is a road map out of your financial rabbit hole.

"Dear Bruce,

I became depressed after the [financial] webinar because I realized we [Judith and her husband] are terrible stewards, and financially my family is falling down a bottomless rabbit hole with very little hope of getting out. We knew we had been falling for a while, but we ignored it and refused to have a conversation about it because of fear of what it might do to our marriage."

—Judith, from California

Judith sent this message to me after participating in one of my financial webinars. I went on to coach her and her husband on using the 14 steps that I recommend in this book on how to climb out of the "bottomless financial rabbit hole" she mentioned. This cry from Judith represents the cry of millions around the world who are in financial depression and distress. Such dire straits have been confirmed by statistics from the 2019 GOBankingRates Survey, which states that 50 percent of Americans have less than $600 in savings, and 57.4 percent of Americans have less than $1,000 in savings.[5] These statistics shout stress and distress — they are one of the leading contributors for divorce (which ends approximately 50 percent of marriages in the U.S.)[6] and serious mental health problems in the world today.[7] Judith said she was depressed.

Do you see yourself in Judith? Do you want to make a 180-degree turnaround in your financial situation? I think I heard you just scream, "Yes!" The windows in your house just shook. Then this book is for you. It will give you the steps, the road map you need to navigate out of your financial rabbit hole.

There were many years in my life, like Judith's, where I had big struggles with money. Bear with me as I tell you a bit about my humble beginnings. I grew up in the low-income and volatile inner-city community of Southside, located in Central Kingston, Jamaica, in the late 1970s and 1980s.

The crime rate was high, and rival gangs were constantly at war. In 1980 alone, around the time of the national polls (election), over 700 people died in Jamaica as a result of gang violence leading up to the election.[8]

5   Yaël Bizouati-Kennedy, "Americans' Savings Drop to Lowest Point in Years," GOBankingRates, last modified May 21, 2021, https://www.gobankingrates.com/banking/savings-account/exclusive-covid-report-40-americans-less-300-savings/.

6   Shellie R. Warren, "10 Most Common Reasons for Divorce," Marriage, last modified September 30, 2021, https://www.marriage.com/advice/divorce/10-most-common-reasons-for-divorce/.

7   "Debt and Mental Health," Mental Health, last modified August 10, 2021, https://www.mentalhealth.org.uk/a-to-z/d/debt-and-mental-health.

8   Howard Campbell, "Flashback: 1980 General Election, Ballot, Blood and Bullets," *The Gleaner*, October 30, 2010, https://jamaica-gleaner.com/gleaner/20101030/news/news5.html.

The first of two of the bloodiest incidents happened at a dance party on Gold Street in Central Kingston, where five people were killed.[9] I lived on a road parallel to Gold Street. We heard the gunshots, and I know someone who got shot during the incident.

I lived with my mother and three siblings. My mother worked at a garment factory and later on worked from home as a dressmaker. She learned this craft from my late grandmother, who had 12 children, and we all lived as one big family in tenement yards in different parts of Southside.

My family was financially poor, however, we were rich in spirit and ambition. My family taught me the value and power of education, which was pushed and emphasized. Consequently, I did well academically. I attended Holy Family Primary and InfantSchool in Central Kingston, and from there I earned a place at a prominent Jamaican high school, Jamaica College. In September 1990, I went to work as an audit trainee in the Kingston office of PricewaterhouseCoopers (PwC) Jamaica, a member firm of PricewaterhouseCoopers International Limited, one of the largest professional services networks in the world. Fourteen years later, I became one of the youngest partners in the history of the firm at age 32, and years later, on July 1, 2022, I became the territory leader (senior partner) of the PwC Jamaica firm.

I worked and studied while at PwC, becoming a chartered accountant (a professional accountant) through the Institute of Chartered Accountants of Jamaica (ICAJ), of which I became president years later, having sat for and passed the examinations of the UK body, the Association of Chartered Certified Accountants (ACCA), at the age of 21. Qualifying at age 21 was a national record at the time, and it brought a lot of good publicity for me and my family. I was still living in Southside when I became a chartered accountant in 1993 and therefore had to navigate violence and tension in the community over the years while I worked and studied. I moved out of Southside around 1995. In the mid-2000s, I also went on to become a certified public accountant (CPA) through the State of Colorado. I am

---

9   Campbell, "Flashback."

a recognized professional accountant in Jamaica's ICAJ, the UK's ACCA, and Colorado's State Board of Accountancy—a powerful application of the lessons I was taught by my family about the value of education.

I have said all of this so that you can see where I am coming from and to show that I can relate to Judith and her financial rabbit hole. You should also take note that I was able to invest in myself through my accounting studies and employment at PwC—two strategic and important moves. Those two investments or moves laid the foundation for increased earnings and hence my financial freedom success later on. You may not study accounting or work at an international accounting firm, but making similar moves will pay you a handsome return.

Reason 2: They don't teach you personal financial management in high school and college, but they should!

"Bruce, my only regret in life is that I didn't learn these golden rules of financial freedom before leaving high school or college. Otherwise, I wouldn't be in such a financial storm today."

—Marlon, young engineer, Jamaica

Marlon made this statement to me during an in-person coaching session with him and his wife. Marlon is only one of millions of young people in the world who leave high school, college, and their parents' homes each year without the knowledge required to manage their money. Although the U.S. has made improvements in that deficiency, and as stated earlier, only 21 of the 52 states require high school students to take a course in personal finance before graduation.[10]

I wasn't taught personal financial management in school in Jamaica. I can safely state that no such mandatory requirement exists in the wider Caribbean and in most of the world. I wrote this book to help to reduce not only the number of Marlons out there, but also the number of category-five financial storms that are raging in homes across the globe today.

Even if you are currently in high school or college, it is not too early to

---

10   Epperson, "Teaching Financial Education in Schools Finally Catches On"

start preparing for your financial future. For example, you should seriously consider undergraduate or graduate studies, because higher levels of education generally put you in a position to earn more, which then puts you in a stronger position to attain financial freedom sooner rather than later.

Your friends and companions matter in your path to financial freedom. Choose them wisely. Realize that they can help or hinder you on your financial journey. Take heed of Napoleon Hill's advice, author of the best-selling 1937 book *Think and Grow Rich*:[11] "Deliberately seek the company of people who influence you to think and act on building the life you desire."[12] Young people, let this book be one of your companions as you trod the dusty road of financial freedom over the next 25-plus years.

Reason 3: It will inspire you to believe, that you too can achieve financial freedom – yes you can!

I know the joy of climbing to the top of a physical mountain. Yes, I was one of a group of staff members from PwC Jamaica who went on a hiking trip over 25 years ago to Blue Mountain Peak, which stands as the highest point in Jamaica at 7,402 feet. The feeling and the vistas were surreal.

Even more surreal and exhilarating, however, was conquering my debt mountain to become debt-free! The debt my wife and I had accumulated was a high number, driven by what was a large mortgage on our newly acquired residence, but we were still able to live comfortably based on my earnings as a young partner in my mid-30s. Nevertheless, by the time we were about seven years into a 25-year mortgage, becoming debt-free became a priority after analyzing our financial health and soaking in the reality of (1) the amount of interest we would be paying for years to come on our home and (2) wanting the psychological and practical benefits that come with not having a home mortgage. Five years later, we conquered our mountain of debt. There was no more debt— no mortgage, credit card, personal loans, or other forms of debt. Do not think for a minute that I'm

---

11   Napoleon Hill, *Think and Grow Rich* (Meridon: Ralston Society, 1937).

12   Napoleon Hill, *The Prosperity Bible: The Greatest Writings of All Time on the Secrets to Wealth and Prosperity* (New York: Penguin, 2007).

saying borrowing is bad—I'm saying use debt wisely. Later in the book, I deal with leveraging low-cost mortgage debt as a means of acquiring investment properties and how debt can be used to wisely acquire important items such as your car or your home.

I talk about conquering my debt mountain not to brag or boast but rather to say that if I can rewrite my financial boundaries, notwithstanding my humble beginnings, then I believe you can do it too using the principles outlined in this book!

If you want to (1) navigate out of your financial rabbit hole, (2) become more financially intelligent, or (3) conquer your debt mountains, you should seriously consider reading this book. You may either read from the beginning through to the end or go directly to your topic or chapter of choice. I encourage you to work on the money journal assignments at the end of each chapter! Those two actions will move you like a magnet toward the land of financial freedom. They will put legs on your desire for financial independence, regardless of your age. They will "teach you how to fish." They will represent your greatest financial investment—an investment in yourself, in your family, and in your financial legacy.

I now invite you to start taking the 14 steps on your financial freedom journey, with me as your copilot, by moving swiftly to the next page!

part 1

THE FOUNDATIONS

chapter 2

FINANCIAL FREEDOM—WHAT DOES IT MEAN?

Do you now ask, "Bruce, what is financial freedom? How would you define it?"

I believe there are three main stages.

1. Total Financial Freedom

Total financial freedom means having enough money to generate sufficient income for you to live without working if you don't want to. Total financial freedom, therefore, has two components:

1. You are able to give up your nine-to-five job, if you want to, and let your money work for you.

2. You can use your time to do the things you want to do.

Both prospects mean you wouldn't have to drag yourself to a job that you don't like! Such is the power of total financial freedom.

How difficult is it to attain total financial freedom?

The path to total financial freedom is much easier than you may think. Given my definition above, I will share with you a very straightforward way to achieve it. Keep on reading.

Let's say you are a 22-year-old college graduate. If you do what I am about to share, you could attain total financial freedom by age 52. That feat would put you in a special category, since most people have to continue working even after reaching the full retirement age of 66 years and two months in the U.S.[13]

The method I am about to share with you does not involve you learning to be the world's greatest foreign-exchange trader, becoming a real estate mogul, or starting a new line of clothing or shoes. One or more of the foregoing could potentially get you to total financial freedom—but I am not even talking about any of them. It is so straightforward, yet many people don't even seem to be aware of it. Here we go, as I share this straightforward route to total financial freedom with you.

If you earned an average of $35,977 per year—the average (median) annual individual income in U.S. dollars in America in 2019[14]—over the next 30-year period, and you invested 15 percent of it per year (i.e., $5,397 or $450 per month) in shares at a 10 percent return, that investment will grow to a total of $1,025,696 at the end of 30 years. Taking just 4 percent of that total per year would be $41,028 per year. Did you notice that this $41,028 is more than the $35,977 per year that you earned? However, we must not ignore the fact that over a 30-year period the cost of living would be rising annually (inflation), so one would need more than $35,977 per year to reach financial freedom over and up to the end of the 30 years. The cure for this quandary would be to increase the $450 monthly investment by the expected annual inflation rate, which in general, though not always,

---

13   Erik Haagensen, "Full Retirement Age (FRA)," Investopedia, updated July 20, 2022, https://www.investopedia.com/terms/n/normal-retirement-age-nra.asp.

14   Alex Kopestinsky, "What Is the Average American Income in 2022?," PolicyAdvice, last modified March 12, 2022, https://policyadvice.net/insurance/insights/average-american-income.

falls below 5 percent per year in the U.S. In fact, the annual inflation rate between 1960 and 2020 in the U.S. for the most part was less than 5 percent.[15] You could apply an inflation rate that is appropriate for your country.

It is also reasonable to assume that over the 30 years your income would be increasing due to career progression and salary increases (although some persons don't enjoy salary increases for many years), and from such increases, you could increase the amounts invested each year to deal with the effects of inflation.

Let's now do the same analysis using household income instead of individual income. The U.S. average (median) annual household income in 2020 was $67,521;[16] investing 15 percent per year under the same assumptions as above would grow to $1,923,751 at the end of 30 years. Pulling off 4 percent per year would yield $76,950, which would be higher than the annual household income of $67,521. Again, remember the discussion about cost of living and likely salary increases over the 30 years. If you don't have time on your side—for example, say you are in your 50s or 60s—then you would have to be saving much more than the 15 percent and likely may have to work part time during retirement.

Why take 4 percent? I answer that question, and more, in chapters 10 and 11 that deal with retirement planning and investments respectively.

So, I believe you would agree with me that the method I just showed represents a straightforward route to total financial freedom for an individual as well as for a household.Remember that my definition of total financial freedom is having enough investments that can generate the income you need to live and not working if you don't want to. I believe I successfully demonstrated that outcome above. Agreed? I hear a resounding *yes*.

Your next question should be "Why are so many people in the U.S., Jamaica, and around the world struggling financially?" An excellent ques-

---

15 "U.S. Inflation Rate 1960–2022," MacroTrends, accessed June 7, 2022, https://www.macrotrends.net/countries/USA/united-states/inflation-rate-cpi.

16 Kopestinsky, "What Is the Average American Income."

tion. Recall the low savings statistics I quoted earlier. I just showed you the math above about how one can get to total financial freedom—the math is not the problem. The problem is how we behave as human beings. We are not always disciplined enough to ensure that we save and set aside the 15 percent of our income as I advised earlier. Dave Ramsey, the famous personal finance expert, summarized it this way: "Winning with money is 80 percent behavior and only 20 percent head knowledge."[17]

Personal financial management is, ultimately, about behavior and not numbers! If you can remain disciplined and follow the 14 steps in this book, you will be on your way to the land of total financial freedom.

Isn't 30 years a long time to wait to get to total financial freedom?

Again, I hear you shouting out, "Waiting thirty years seems an eternity!" My response is, first, you will be enjoying the journey as you move through the various stages of financial freedom. I am not asking you to put your life on pause while you wait for the magical moment when you are able to afford giving up your regular nine-to-five job. You will have many opportunities along the way to have some fun and enjoy your life as you move toward the ultimate state of total financial freedom. More to come on this.

My second answer is that 30 years will creep upon you like an armed bandit. Yes, the time will fly like a Concorde. I can't believe that I have been working for almost 32 years. Remember I told you that I started working and studying at age 18.

So, don't delay in starting to put aside that 15 percent of your income, or whatever you can manage, to start saving—start with what you have.

If you feel strongly that my 30-year plan is too long, and you want to live it up now, show me a better plan than trying to save and invest 15 percent of your income each year. Do you have a plan that will ensure that you will have a source of income if you choose not to work or if you are

---

17   Dave Ramsey (@DaveRamsey). "Winning with money is 80 percent behavior and only 20 percent head knowledge. What to do isn't the problem; doing it is." Twitter post, January 3, 2022, 8:42 a.m., https://twitter.com/daveramsey/status/1356280884836630528.

forced to stop working when you reach normal retirement age? If you can't produce a better plan, then I suggest you think of working with the plan I have presented and will be developing further as we go through this book.

The FIRE Movement

Those of you who want to reach total financial independence faster will need to save and invest a lot more than 15 percent of your income per month to accumulate the amount of money you will need to live each month. For example, people in the FIRE (financial independence retire early) movement are good examples of that ambition. Their aim is to retire in 10 to 15 years after entering the world of work and are willing to make tremendous sacrifices in order to save up to 50 to 60 percent of their income. Guess what? They often do it, and many have retired in their late 30s and early 40s. Amon and Christina Browning demonstrate this quite well. They were federal government employees in the U.S., but they set a goal to retire early, and through flipping (buying and selling) houses and exercising serious financial discipline, they were able to accomplish that goal at age 39 and moved to Portugal.[18] Another inspiring example is Roshida Dowe. Roshida lost her job while working as an attorney in the U.S., but with a new mindset and by leveraging great saving habits she always exhibited, she was able to amass enough money to retire at 39 and moved to Mexico.[19]

I believe you must be earning a minimum amount of money to be in a position to reach such aggressive goals, because you must still be able to live at a minimum standard after saving 50 to 60 percent of your income, even if part of your minimalist lifestyle includes eating bread and butter every day. You will still need to pay for transportation, housing, and similar basic items. So, if you aspire to be part of the FIRE movement and live in the U.S., you should be making *at least* the average annual individual income of $35,977 or $67,521 for average annual household income. You can extrapolate what the equivalent figure would be if you live outside

---

18   "Hello! We're the Brownings," Our Rich Journey, accessed June 7, 2022, https://www.ourrichjourney.com/about.

19   "How I Retired Early at 39 in Mexico City with $660,000," CNBC Make It, YouTube video, September 23, 2021, 9:34, https://youtu.be/8SPEwzAXLs8.

the U.S. Take note that key elements of becoming financially independent include how obsessive you are about achieving it and the sacrifices you are willing to make. Some members of the FIRE movement chose to move from the U.S. or their home country to another country that would afford a comfortable lifestyle based on the income they can generate from their accumulated investments. This apparently was part of the strategy of Amon, Christina, and Roshida.

2. Partial Financial Freedom

You must work or be self-employed in order to earn an income (or have a fabulous inheritance that will generate some form of income). Most likely, however, you don't spend more than you earn, and you are able to save 5–10 percent of your income each month. You contribute toward a retirement plan, and you are also able to invest a consistent amount of money each month either toward your children's education fund or in a personal investment portfolio that will boost your overall lifestyle and legacy. You might expect that people who have been in the workforce for, say, 10-plus years have achieved partial financial freedom given the number of years they have been working. Based on the low savings rates and high debt burdens that the typical working adult faces in places like the Caribbean and the U.S., however, many adults (late 30s and above) are, unfortunately, in financial bondage instead of qualifying as having attained partial financial freedom. Recall the dismal savings statistics I quoted earlier.

3. Financial Bondage

Financial bondage is a real "place" where people live from hand to mouth, or paycheck to paycheck. Their monthly expenses exceed their income, they struggle, or are unable, to save money, and they have a mountain of high-cost debt. Many young people who are in their 20s and early 30s tend to find themselves in this category, having been in the workforce for a relatively short period of time and having the burden of heavy student loans that take a big bite out of their monthly income and relatively low starting salaries.

Unfortunately, I have observed that not only those in their 20s and early 30s are in this category, but also people in their late 30s, 40s, 50s, and 60s. Every age group is represented in the financial bondage category. Most, but not all, of the people in my one-on-one coaching sessions start off in the financial bondage category and span all generations and age groups.

I have defined what I mean by financial freedom by arguing that there are three stages involved. As you go through this book, you will get the opportunity to identify your current level of financial freedom, and the rest of the book will take you through the other steps that will get you to total financial freedom (which, of course, is subject to your personal circumstances and attitude), if you are not already there.

Why is attaining total financial freedom such a big deal?
It changes your life.

It is a big deal for three reasons. The first has to do with the fact that it will completely change your life! You can move from being part of the 78 percent of people who worry about money[20] to those who don't, and hence, enjoy better financial and mental health. Everybody will agree that when the bills are paid, you sleep better, and there are fewer quarrels about money in your house. It changes your life, also, in the sense that you can do the things you want to do, which brings a lot of personal satisfaction and peace. You can take a nice vacation, buy the golf clubs you really want, and most importantly, take care of your loved ones. How many times have you heard young people who have achieved success, through sports, music, business, or other fields say, "I am going to buy my mother a house." Those types of things are possible when you achieve financial freedom. Your life will change!

It changes your legacy.

The second reason is that financial freedom will change the legacy you leave your children. If managed properly, your financial resources will en-

---

20   Vivian Manning-Schaffel, "Most of Us Live Paycheck-to-Paycheck. This Is What It Does to Your Health," NBC News, November 2, 2017, https://www.nbcnews.com/better/health/most-us-live-paycheck-paycheck-what-it-does-your-health-ncna816411.

sure that your children get a solid education, participate in extracurricular activities, and enjoy overseas travel and a range of other activities that will help in their personal development. Your children will also see you as a model of good money-management skills. If you teach them how to manage money, they will also become financially savvy, increasing their chance of having their own financial success.

It changes your community.

The third reason why financial freedom is a big deal is that it allows you to change your community. You can affect generations of people by using your financial resources to help those in your community. It could be paying for the tuition of a low-income youth, donating tablets or computers to a school, giving to a church, or addressing just about any real need. You can send your money to places where you can't go but where others can go and achieve great results (e.g., supporting overseas missionaries doing work in communities in need). Financial freedom allows you to have more control over your time so that you can spend time mentoring and coaching young people who are desperately searching for role models. More on this subject of influencing your communities to come under part 4, "Sow Your Money."

You don't have to earn a huge salary to achieve total financial freedom.

I was listening to a talk show when a lady, a school bus driver, called in to say she was approaching 60 years, and her total net assets were close to $1 million. When asked what the secret was for amassing so much money, despite her relatively modest salary, she simply and calmly said that her mother had taught her to always live within her means and to save money! School bus drivers in the U.S. are not among the highest paid workers—their average salary is much less than that of other well-known professionals such as doctors, lawyers, accountants, and engineers. The average salary of a school bus driver in the U.S. in 2022 is $41,951.[21] The point is that she did not earn a huge salary compared to others, yet she was able to amass a huge amount. I can't recall the state she lived in to get a sense of her cost

---

21   "Bus Driver Salary in the United States," Salary.com, accessed June 16, 2022, https://www. salary.com/research/salary/benchmark/bus-driver-salary.

of living or whether she was married, single, or had dependents, among other personal details. For sure, she could move to a state with a lower cost of living or a country like Mexico, where the cost of living is 110 percent lower than in the U.S.![22] This bus driver's story drives home the message that it is not how much money you make; it is what you are able to save and invest that really matters!

To achieve financial freedom, use only honest means.

Proverbs 20:17 says, "Bread of deceit *is* sweet to a man; but afterwards his mouth shall be filled with gravel" (KJV). In the King James Bible, King Solomon teaches that doing things illegally carries a thrill, and the persons involved normally boast about their ability to, seemingly, get ahead. Solomon, however, also quickly points out that such gains are only short-lived—sweetness turns to toughness (gravel). The message is that, notwithstanding the desire to be financially independent, only honest means should be used to gain wealth. Shortcuts and illegal means will end in disgrace and embarrassment. Think of Bernie Madoff, who lured people to give him their money to invest. He was found guilty of fraud and operating a Ponzi scheme and was sentenced to 150 years in prison. Honesty is the best policy, always![23]

To achieve financial freedom, emulate the money habits of millionaires.

If I want my car to be fixed, I will go to the car dealership or the garage. If I want to stop the leak in my bathroom, I will call the plumber. So, as we are on the road to financial freedom, it makes sense to understand the money habits of those who have already achieved financial freedom and who have the experience in getting there. Various studies have been done on this subject, and in essence, all the research has, more or less, landed on the following five key habits of the financially free.[24]

---

22   "Cost of Living in United States Compared to Mexico," Expatistan, accessed June 7, 2022, https://www.expatistan.com/cost-of-living/country/comparison/mexico/united-states.

23   "Madoff Gets 150 Years for Fraud," CBC News, last modified June 29, 2009, https://www.cbc.ca/news/business/madoff-gets-150-years-for-fraud-1.784066.

24   Elizabeth Gravier, "10 Common Money Habits This CFP Says His Wealthiest Self-made Millionaire Clients Have That Normal People Could Copy," CNBC News, last modified January 26, 2022, https://www.cnbc.com/select/money-habits-of-self-made-millionaires/.

1. They manage debt wisely, which includes avoiding high-cost debt.

2. They live within their means (on a budget) and try to save up to 20 percent of their income.

3. They seek financial advice.

4. They have multiple streams of income.

5. They invest for the long term, and hence, they accumulate their wealth over relatively long periods of time, averaging two to three decades.

How many of these habits are you currently practicing? Don't worry if your answer didn't match this list—the 14 steps outlined in this book are in alignment with the habits of such millionaires.

In chapter 3, we will address the cultural influences to avoid in your pursuit of total financial freedom.

chapter 3

FOUR CULTURAL INFLUENCES TO AVOID

The Four Deadly Horsemen of the Global Savings Crisis

When I use the word *culture*, it means how we do things around here. The world is one big cultural village made borderless with modern communications technology and the internet. Consequently, financial behaviors and practices in one country are easily exported to others. In today's world, there are at least four horsemen (cultural influences) that, if not managed, will derail your attempt to achieve total financial freedom. The derailment will come primarily because these four influences all serve to reduce your ability to save money! Savings is one of the key pillars on which the house of financial freedom is built. These four influences are as follows.

1. A Culture of Instant Gratification

Instant gratification is not new. It's the idea that tomorrow is not guaranteed to anyone, and hence, you should live in the moment. This ideology goes against the grain of one of the fundamental requirements for achieving financial success in that saving requires deferred gratification and patience. It is a necessity in order to generate the money for investment.

Instant gratification demands a good or service in the present. It is like a four-year-old screaming and shouting orders at his parents, screaming out for wants and not the things that he needs in life. To become financially independent, you can't afford instant gratification. It is the archenemy of savings.

Please become like the bamboo tree. The bamboo tree steadily and patiently sends down roots, and for a long time, it looks as if nothing is happening until one day it blossoms and becomes a mighty tree. Such is the behavior of those who attain financial freedom. Instant gratification is the opposite of the bamboo tree and should be totally discarded except when your budget allows you to have some "fun money." Notice I said, "if your budget allows." More on budgeting later on.

2. A Culture of "How Much Is the Monthly Payment?"

Many suppliers of goods and services market their products on the basis of how "small" the monthly loan repayment is rather than emphasizing what the up-front cost of the item is if it is paid for in cash. Many people don't seem to realize that waiting and saving to purchase an item is quite fine and will be much cheaper in the long run. Instant gratification plus the ability to get access to credit over a long period creates a combination that, for those who don't fully understand the cost implications, ends up draining their financial resources. The point here is to wait and buy with cash or go for the shortest loan repayment period you can afford. More on this topic in chapter 9 on managing debt.

3. A Culture of Failing to Teach Money Management in Schools

I repeat here that I wish I had known the things I am writing about in this book when I just left Jamaica College, my high school alma mater. It would have helped me to make fewer money mistakes in the earlier years of my financial journey. Why isn't money management taught in schools? My research suggests it results from a combination of school administrators not being able to find time in an already packed school curriculum and not finding enough people who can credibly teach this course. Whatever the reason, the result is that millions of students around the world leave school and their parents' homes every year without the knowledge of the need to win with money in today's complex financial world.

4. A Culture of Keeping Up with the Joneses

We live in a culture where impression management is the order of the day. Social media platforms fuel the ability of persons to see how lavishly others are living. Too many people feel as if they have to keep up with their neighbors' children who have the latest gadgets, their neighbors' home expansions, and a host of other things. You have to rid yourself of what I call Joneses disease—a feeling of jealousy and or rivalry based on what you see others have. Otherwise, you will fail to achieve financial freedom.

I had a session with one of my financial mentees—let's call her Lisa—who recounted that she would go to the homes of her son's elementary school friends for birthday parties. She admitted that during many of those visits, she would often be infected with Joneses disease when she observed the beauty and grandeur of some of the homes. She then went on to share how she cured herself, as follows:

1. She would tell herself that she is not aware of how these beautiful homes were acquired (i.e., whether through heavy debt, inheritance, or hard work) and that whatever the source, she said she just started to celebrate and be grateful for the parents of her son's friends, the fact that she was invited to enjoy their homes, and how much of a blessing that was.

2. She observed that about two weeks after these visits, she would not remember these homes. Somehow, with the passage of time, the symptoms of Joneses disease would slowly disappear.

The story confirms the reality of Joneses disease, but also that we don't have to be taken over by this malady. Tell yourself that the Joneses left town a long time ago, and you don't know where they are living these days. Tell yourself you don't even want to know. Stay in your own lane and your own budget, and you will be one step closer to financial freedom.

Now that I have shone the light on these four influences, please avoid them like the plague as you travel the road to financial freedom. In chapter 4, I will introduce you to the first step on the road map that leads to financial freedom.

part 2

GROW YOUR MONEY

chapter 4

STEP 1: DIAGNOSE YOUR CURRENT FINANCIAL HEALTH

A doctor cannot treat you until they ask you a series of questions and perform certain basic checks on your general state of health, such as checking your blood pressure, temperature, pulse, and so on. It is the same with growing your money. There are tests that can be done from a financial perspective that will help to establish your current financial health.

Specifically, I recommend you start this financial health check by preparing two very important statements: your statement of net worth and your statement of income and expenses. After completing these two statements, the next move is to drill down further, like an MRI examination, by looking at 10 financial indicators that give a clearer picture of your current state of financial health. We will address these items in this chapter.

Statement of Net Worth

This is a list of all you own (assets) minus all you owe (liabilities). Your net worth is a single indicator that gives you a snapshot of your entire financial position. It's like your end-of-term average score of all your subjects taken in high school for a term or semester. This number is what people use to determine whether someone is considered wealthy or not.

The aim, ultimately, is to own more than you owe, which is referred to as a positive net worth. Having a positive net worth also means that if you were to sell all your assets at their current market values, you would be able to settle your liabilities and have money left over!

If, however, your liabilities are more than your assets, you would have a negative net worth, which means that you would still owe your creditors. Having a negative net worth usually means that you are currently spending more than you are earning, and hence, you borrow each month to pay for the extra spending. Such borrowing is what helps to bring about the negative net worth and is exactly why we should never attempt to judge how rich or financially strapped someone is based solely on their income or the car they drive. You can have a high income of, say, $150,000 per year, yet if you like to wear the latest of everything, drive the biggest of everything, and spend more than you earn each month, you will have a low net worth. On the contrary, someone who makes $35,000, lives within their means, and saves, say, 10 percent of their income each month will have a higher net worth than the person who makes $150,000. Remember the story of the school bus driver who was a millionaire by age 60, although she made far less than many other professionals. Do you see why the measurement of your wealth is based on your net worth and not on how high your income is?

Spending more than you earn is a vicious and deadly cycle, and it is the reason most people end up with their liabilities being greater than their assets! The statement of income and expenses will tell you exactly how you are spending your money and by how much you may be overspending each month.

Below, I have an example of what a statement of net worth looks like for a fictional family called the Goldsons. I want you to use it as a basic format to complete what could be your first official statement of net worth, now or after you have completed reading this chapter. The Goldsons consists of a family of four living in the U.S. Mr. Goldson, age 36, is a junior sales manager at a small private manufacturing company. Mrs. Goldson, age 34, is an elementary school teacher. They have a seven-year-old son and a five-year-old daughter.

In your list of assets, include everything that you own such as the amount you have in your retirement or pension account, the current market value of your house, car, jewelry, television, and so on. You can use rough estimates to arrive at the values if you don't have recent valuation reports. For your liabilities, list all the institutions and individuals that you owe.

The Goldsons' statement of net worth shows they have a negative net worth of –$33,999. This is not good. The question, then, is how do you, or households like the Goldsons who have found themselves with a negative net worth, turn your financial situation around? Keep on reading to see how the Goldsons improved their financial position.

TABLE 4.1: GOLDSON FAMILY STATEMENT OF NET WORTH AS AT DECEMBER 31, 2021

Assets (Own)	$
House	293,000[25]
Savings	
Retirement account	
Car	20,000[26]
Total:	313,000
Liabilities (Owe)	
Mortgage	286,333
Car loan	18,666
Credit card debt	21,333
Loan sharks	14,000
Personal loans (family and friends)	6,667
Total:	346,999
Net Worth	(33,999)

25   Lyle Daly, "Average House Price by State in 2021," The Ascent: A Motley Fool Service, last modified August 5, 2021, https://www.fool.com/the-ascent/research/average-house-price-state/.

26   Replace with: "Used car purchased with debt"

Statement of Income and Expenses

Below is an example of a statement of income and expenses, which I already referred to, for the Goldsons.

TABLE 4.2: GOLDSON FAMILY STATEMENT OF INCOME AND EXPENSES THE MONTH OF DECEMBER 2021

December	$
Income: Salary (After Taxes)[27]	4,133
Expenses:	
Mortgage	1,159
Food	620
Transportation (includes car loan payment of $352)	550
Other	248
Insurance (health, life, and disability)	
Consumer debt (credit cards and line of credit)	1,873
Entertainment	150
Charitable giving	233
Total expenses before savings	4,833
Savings/(Shortfall)	(700)

This statement is compiled based on your monthly income (how much you earn each month from all sources after taxes—salary, child support, side hustles, investment income) and your expenses (how much you spend each month). At this point, you can use estimates of these figures from memory or actual figures if you keep good records. I cover in more detail the mechanics of how to go about actually coming up with these numbers in a more precise way in chapter 7, which deals with budgeting. You can start now, though, by using estimates from memory.

The statement reveals that the Goldsons are spending more than they are earning by $700 (or 17 percent of their after-tax income) each month, which means they are borrowing to pay that amount each month. This monthly borrowing is a major contributing factor to the Goldsons' negative net worth of –$33,999, as shown in their statement of net worth. Not to cast judgments

---

27   Monthly gross household income before taxes is $5,417, or $65,000 gross annual household income.

here, but these numbers do not show a pretty picture for the Goldsons. More to come on how they can budget to save better in chapter 7.

Your Financial Health: 10 Basic Signs

In addition to the financial insights obtained from the two statements above, we now need to do a deeper examination (the MRI equivalent) by looking at the 10 financial indicators I mentioned earlier. I will continue to use the Goldson family to illustrate these points.

The actual results for the 10 financial indicators for the Goldsons' household have confirmed the seriousness of their financial condition, as was strongly indicated by their negative net worth. The Goldsons' financial indicators fall below the recommended best-practice targets in all instances. The table and the analyses below give further details on each of their 10 financial indicators. As you go through, I want you to gather the information for your 10 financial indicators so that you can see how you are doing financially. A number of financial sources recommend or discuss specific best-practice targets as a measure of good personal financial health. I have included the references for a number of these sources in the table below.

TABLE 4.3: GOLDSON FAMILY 10 FINANCIAL HEALTH INDICATORS (FHI)[28]

No	FHI	FHI Indicator Targets	The Goldsons' FHI Actual Performance	Ratings[29] (Danger, Caution, or Safe)
1	Savings ratio	10%–25% of monthly income (after taxes)	(17%)	Danger
2	Rainy day fund	3–6 months of expenses	No "rainy day" fund	Danger
3	Total debt-to-income ratio per month	43% of gross income[30]	62%	Danger
4	Credit score	>670 (Good)	400 (Very Poor)	Danger
5	Monthly retirement investments[31]	15% of gross income	No monthly retirement investments	Danger
6	Personal investments per month[32]	Flexible	No personal investments	Danger
7	Health insurance coverage[33]	Coverage to pay for major medical events or sickness	No health insurance coverage	Danger

28   Sabrina, "35 Personal Finance Ratios to Help You Crush Your Goals," Finance Over Fifty, accessed June 9, 2022, https://financeoverfifty.com/5-personal-finance-ratios/.

29   A rating of *safe* is given if the target is achieved, *caution* if the target is marginally off, and *danger* if the target is way off. *Danger* means immediate action should be taken to improve the particular financial area. *Caution* means action should be taken within one to three months to improve the area, and *safe* means no action is required.

30   This is income before taxes and any deductions from gross income ($65,000 per year or $5,417 per month). Total debt paid per month is $3,384 and is made up of $1,159 (mortgage), $1,873 (consumer debt), and $352 (car loan).

31   This would be taken out of amounts that are saved each month. See savings ratio above.

32   This would be taken out of amounts that are saved each month. See savings ratio above.

33   Brian Collins, "Why Insurance Should Be Part of Your Financial Plan," Hippo, accessed June 9, 2022, https://www.hippo.com/blog/insurance-part-financial-plan.

No	FHI	FHI Indicator Targets	The Goldsons' FHI Actual Performance	Ratings[29] (Danger, Caution, or Safe)
8	Life insurance coverage[34]	At least 6–10 times annual gross salary	No life insurance coverage	Danger
9	Estate planning[35]	An up-to-date will	No will	Danger
10	Net worth	Expected net worth: based on age and gross income of working head(s) of household: $227,500	($33,999)	Danger

Savings Ratio

The savings ratio speaks to the percentage of your income (after taxes) that you save each month. The best practice is for households to aim to save a low of 10 percent to a high of 25 percent of their monthly income. The Goldson family has a negative savings ratio of –17 percent—put differently, instead of being able to save money each month, they are spending more than they are earning by 17 percent! This is not a good sign, as one has to have savings to start the journey toward financial freedom.

Let me say very quickly that the 10 percent end of the range is for people in their 20s or early 30s who have not been in the workforce for a long time. Interestingly, though, many individuals, not just those in their 20s, struggle to save 10 percent of their income each month. Statistics show that in the U.S., only 40 percent of Americans would be able to cover an unexpected expense of $1,000.[36] In Jamaica, *37 percent of Jamaicans would*

---

34 Andrew Beattie, "How Much Life Insurance Should You Carry?," Investopedia, last modified May 25, 2022, https://www.investopedia.com/articles/pf/06/insureneeds.asp.

35 "Estate Planning: A 7-Step Checklist of the Basics," NerdWallet, April 18, 2022, https://www.nerdwallet.com/article/investing/estate-planning.

36 Annie Nova, "A $1,000 Emergency Would Push Many Americans into Debt," CNBC, last modified January 23, 2019, https://www.cnbc.com/2019/01/23/most-americans-dont-have-the-savings-to-cover-a-1000-emergency.html.

not be able to find $186 (JA$28,000) to deal with an emergency.[37]

I explained earlier the four cultural influences that contribute to people not saving money. Here's a reminder of these influences:

1. Culture of debt that asks how much the monthly payment is instead of the real cost of the item up front.

2. Households attempting to keep up with the Joneses.

3. A culture of "living today, for tomorrow we die" (a.k.a., a culture of instant gratification).

4. Failure to teach money skills at home and in schools in the same way that math and science are taught.

The implications are staggering as you cannot reach financial freedom without the ability to save money consistently and, ideally, start at 10 percent each month!

In his book *The Richest Man in Babylon*, George Clason argues through the character, Arkad, that saving "10% of thy earnings" is one of the fundamental requirements for financial freedom.[38]

While saving 10 percent of your income is the recommended minimum (although you should start with whatever you can, however small) toward getting to financial freedom, the more you are able to save, the faster you will get there. Therefore, you should aim to move from saving 10 percent, to 15 percent, to 25 percent, and even beyond 25 percent as your earning power increases over the years due to career progression and by increased financial intelligence by reading books like this.

The thought of saving 25 percent or more of your income may feel like climbing Mount Everest, right? Have no fear; in this book, I explain that it is possible by developing simple, but powerful, habits such as living within your means, avoiding carrying high-cost debts (like carrying credit card

---

37 *National Financial Inclusion Strategy 2016–2020*, National Financial Inclusion Council of Jamaica, March 2017, 15, https://boj.org.jm/wp-content/uploads/2019/07/Jamaica_NFIS_Final_Draft.pdf.

38 George Clason, *The Richest Man in Babylon* (New York: Signet Books, 2008).

balances), and having multiple streams of income. Such habits will keep more of your money in your pocket.

Another factor that leads to low savings is simply the relatively high cost of living that many people experience in their countries. For example, the U.S. is ranked 112 out of 138 countries in terms of most affordable nations,[39] which means that only 26 other countries are more expensive to live in than the U.S. Jamaica was ranked 90th.[40] High cost of living combined with low or no salary increases and limited career progression for many over years create a dangerous combination that can make it really hard for people to save money—hence the reason for books like this to help to show how to save and invest despite these challenges. Keep on reading!

Emergency Fund or Rainy Day Money

This financial indicator checks how much money you have for an emergency. The recommendation is for you to have three to six months of your monthly expenses in this fund. I explain in chapter 8, which deals with emergency funds, why that amount is a good size to have. The Goldsons' statement of net worth shows them having zero savings, which means they have no rainy day money. My dear readers, therein lies the beginning of financial sorrows for so many, many people that I have spoken to.

Yes, the absence of an emergency fund is the trap door that flies wide open to a life of spiraling debt and escalating misery. When you don't have rainy day money, and it rains hard—say you need to repair your car or roof—you will have to borrow money to deal with the emergency because you don't have a rainy day fund. Oftentimes this borrowing is done with a credit card, as it is easy access to money. Given that you used your credit card, as you never had the cash, you won't be able to pay the credit card debt when it becomes due. Then you are faced with interest and possible late charges each month, which make the debt snowball into a massive amount.

---

39   "Cost of Living in Jamaica: Can I Afford to Retire There?," Retirepedia, accessed June 7, 2022, https://retirepedia.com/cost-of-living-in-jamaica.html.

40   "Cost of Living in Jamaica."

My financial-mentoring sessions have confirmed that this vicious cycle (triggered by the lack of an emergency fund) is one of the main reasons why individuals end up with such great mountains of debt. The cycle I described above demonstrates that it is critical to have an emergency fund in place.

Do you have an emergency fund? Does it cover at least three months of your expenses? You may be one emergency away from spiraling into a sea of debt!

Total Debt-to-Income Ratio

This ratio shows how much of your income goes toward debt repayment each month and is calculated by taking all your monthly debt payments as a percentage of your gross monthly income. The DTI is used by lenders to determine if you qualify for a mortgage or consumer loan. Most lenders in the U.S. will approve your loan if your DTI is 43 percent or lower;[41] however, some lenders will go up to 50 percent.[42]

The DTI for the largest non government mortgage lender in Jamaica is 40 percent,[43] which is not far from the range used in the U.S. I have used 43 percent throughout this book as a number that falls within the 40–50 percent range discussed here.

The Goldsons' statement of income and expenses shows that they spend $3,384 per month of their gross income of $5,417 repaying debt. Their ratio is therefore 62 percent compared to the target of 43 percent. This is serious and tough. Such a high monthly debt repayment leaves them with little money to pay for utilities, transportation, food, and other basics.

How does your debt-to-income ratio compare to the benchmark DTI in your country or to the 43 percent if you live in the U.S.?

41   Chris Murphy, "Debt-to-Income (DTI) Ratio," Investopedia, last modified May 30, 2022, https://www.investopedia.com/terms/d/dti.asp.

42   Miranda Crace, "Debt-to-Income Ratio (DTI): What Is It and How Is It Calculated?," Rocket Mortgage, March 18, 2022, https://www.rocketmortgage.com/learn/debt-to-income-ratio.

43   "What to Know When Buying a House," JN Bank, February 26, 2021, https://www.jnbank.com/what-to-know-when-buying-a-house/.

Credit Score

Credit bureaus take your credit information from banks and other lenders to determine your credit score. If you are good at repaying loans, you get a good credit score, and people will want to lend you money at attractive interest rates. If you are not good at repaying loans, this will contribute towards a bad credit score and the related consequences.

The best practice is to target a score of 670 (good) or higher.[44] The Goldsons' score is 400 (very poor), which means they have a lot of work to do to turn this score around. Do you know your credit score? If you have loans, you have a credit score. More to come on credit scores in chapter 9.

Retirement Investments as a Percentage of Monthly Income

This ratio deals with how much money you are putting aside per month specifically toward retirement—whether in tax-friendly accounts or other forms of investment.

Studies show that saving and investing 15 percent of your income over your career will generally allow you to accumulate enough to live comfortably by normal retirement age (60–65).[45] This scenario assumes that you start to save and invest early (20s or early 30s). I also illustrated this concept in chapter 2, where I introduced the concept of how straightforward it is to achieve total financial freedom.

Individuals who start to build their retirement funds later in life (40s and 50s) would need to save and invest more than 15 percent to make up for their late start.

The Goldsons' statement of income and expenses reveals that they are not saving anything at all toward their retirement. They, therefore, have a lot of catching up to do.

Note that the money you would put toward your retirement fund

---

44   "What Is a Good Credit Score?," Equifax, accessed June 7, 2022, https://www.equifax.com/personal/education/credit/score/what-is-a-good-credit-score.

45   Judith Ward, "Reasons Why You Should Aim to Save 15% for Retirement," T. Rowe Price, April 11, 2022, https://www.troweprice.com/personal-investing/resources/insights/save-15-percent-for-retirement.html.

would come from the money that you are able to save each month. That fact highlights why it is so important to save money. See, again, the discussion above under "Savings Ratio." How much do you contribute each month toward investing for your retirement years?

Personal Investments as a Percentage of Monthly Income

This investment is separate from what you are investing for your retirement years. I am not aware of a specific benchmark around this financial indicator. This money can be used to secure your children's college tuition, to build up your net worth so that you can leave a good inheritance for your children, to enhance your lifestyle to a higher level, and for major charitable gifts. The Goldson family is not securing funds for their children's college studies or lifestyle activities they want to pursue, which is another tight spot for them. Again, they are not investing monthly because they have no savings. Already you can hear my refrain ringing loud: You must learn to save to move toward financial independence! How much are you investing per month outside of your pension plan? More to come on investments in chapter 9.

Insurance Coverage
Life Insurance

The basic recommendation is that you have at least six to 10 times your gross household income in life insurance coverage to protect your family's income if one of the breadwinners in the family were to die.[46] I write more about life insurance in chapter 13. The Goldsons have no life insurance. Do you have life insurance? If so, is it enough?

Health Insurance

This is similar to life insurance except that this is money you would get from a health insurance company to pay for medical bills. The Goldsons have no health insurance coverage—not a pretty picture and, hence, perhaps Mr. and Mrs. Goldson, knowing that a major illness could further decimate the family's already fragile financial position, aren't sleeping well at night. Do you have adequate health insurance coverage? More to come

---

46   Beattie, "How Much Life Insurance Should You Carry?"

on health insurance in chapter 13.

Estate Planning

Estate planning speaks to the plans you put in place today about how you want your assets to be transferred to others when you die. A basic way to do this is to write a will. The breadwinners of the Goldson family have no will in place, which means that the courts (the laws of the country) will determine how their assets will be distributed. That is scary. But that is how it works when you don't have a will! Do you have a will? More to come on estate planning in chapter 14.

Expected Net Worth

We discussed the concept of net worth when we spoke about preparing the statement of net worth. A relevant question is whether there's a way to figure out what your expected net worth should be. The answer is yes. I was introduced to this concept in the book *The Millionaire Next Door* by Thomas J. Stanley and William D. Danko.[47] They explain that your expected net worth can be estimated based on your age and your income by using this simple formula: age × gross salary / 10.

The Goldsons' expected net worth is $227,500 (35 × $65,000 / 10) compared to their actual net worth of –$33,999. They are well below their expected net worth, which should not be a surprise given how heavily in debt they are and that the family spends more than it earns each month.

One caveat is that the formula assumes you have been working for a number of years. So, if you are relatively young (less than 25 years old) or just entered the world of work, the expected net worth figure computed by the formula is generally going to be greater than your actual net worth, given your relatively short time in the world of work.

Notwithstanding this caveat, I am imploring all readers to calculate your expected net worth, and if your actual is below your expected, see it as a challenge that will help to push you to increase your net worth. How

---

47   Thomas Stanley and William Danko, *The Millionaire Next Door: The Surprising Secrets of America's Wealthy* (Exeter: Longstreet Press, 1996).

does your actual net worth compare to your expected net worth?

The Goldsons' Overall Financial Picture

The Goldsons do not currently enjoy good financial health given that all 10 financial indicators are in the danger zone. They failed all 10. They should proceed to develop a financial plan and implement it aggressively. But believe it or not, though, many people do nothing. When you are struggling with your finances, it can bring on a range of negative emotions such as feelings of shame, sadness, and guilt, all of which may leave you unmotivated. One thing is for sure: A bad financial score card will not just turn around on its own. The Goldsons will need to face this giant if they are to stand any chance of moving their ten financial health indicators from the "danger" zone to the "safe" zone.

Your Financial Picture

If you are reading this analysis, and your financial health card is looking great, meaning you have exceeded all, or most, of the targets for the 10 financial indicators, then congratulations. Keep on doing what you have been doing, or try and take it to the next level. The rest of this book will either reinforce what you have been doing or challenge you to make some adjustments to achieve even greater financial success.

If your financial health card is not looking good, keep reading! The upcoming chapters will show you how the Goldsons used the principles of the 14 steps to financial freedom to turn around their bad financial situation. Their actions should then serve as a blueprint for you to see how you can do the same with your finances!

Your Money Journal Assignment: Are You Financially Fit?

WORKING ADULTS: 18 YEARS & OLDER

1. Complete your statement of net worth.

On a blank piece of paper or spreadsheet (best estimates are fine), list the value of all you own (market price):

- Home

- Car

- Retirement account (call your HR department)

    ○ Put it at zero for now if you don't have the information, but continue on with the computation.

- Investments

- Savings

- Then, list all you owe, including the following:

    ○ Mortgage

    ○ Car loan(s)

    ○ Credit card(s)

Calculate your net worth, which is all you own minus all you owe. Is it a negative or positive figure?

2. Complete your statement of income and expenses. Use table 4.2 as a guide.

3. Compute your financial health indicators.

Use the 10 financial indicators that were used for the Goldsons in table 4.3 as a guide. Complete one table for yourself and or one for your household.

4. Calculate your expected net worth.

Calculate your expected net worth by the formula of gross salary × age/10.

- How does it compare to your actual net worth?

- If the actual is less than the expected, use this number as a motivational tool to push you along your financial journey.

Note: If you have been working for fewer than five years, the expected net worth figure will be a bit skewed based on the formula assumptions. And if you are a two-income household, use the average age and average income to do the calculation.

5. Reflect on Your Financial Health Scores/Ratings.

- What emotions did you feel when you assessed and saw what your financial health ratings or scores were for each of the 10 financial indicators?

- If you were in a negative emotional state, write down what mindset shift you need to make to move out of that emotional state.

FULL-TIME STUDENTS: 14–24 YEARS

- Write down at least three habits or behaviors of millionaires that you learned in this chapter that you plan to *exhibit* consistently over the next five to 10 years to ensure that you have a strong positive net worth by the time you reach age 30.

chapter 5

STEP 2: SET FINANCIAL GOALS AND BECOME OBSESSIVE ABOUT ACHIEVING THEM

Financial Goals

What are we really talking about here?

Financial goals are targets that you set to achieve certain financial outcomes, such as saving $25,000 to buy a car in three years' time. A financial goal should be specific, time-bound, and achievable. It should flow directly out of the results of your financial health check. In the case of the Goldsons, their financial goals should revolve around trying to fix the 10 financial indicators that all fell below the expected benchmark levels. For example, given that their debt-to-income ratio was 62 percent, their goal should be to develop a debt-reduction plan to bring that ratio to at least 43 percent in a reasonable period of time. The timeline is going to be determined by how much they are willing to sacrifice in terms of cutting expenses and increasing income to pay down their debt mountain. Chapter 9 has been dedicated to managing debt.

Three Types of Financial Goals

Financial goals fall within categories, in my view, depending on the time-line within which they are to be achieved.

1. Short term (to be achieved within one year—e.g., to build a one- or two-month emergency fund).

2. Medium term (to be achieved within one to 10 years—e.g., to be totally free of consumer debt in three years).

3. Long term (to be achieved after 10+ years—e.g., to save $90,000 for my child's college fund).

Obsessive Desire for Your Financial Goals

It's not just about setting goals. You must be obsessed with making the goals become realities. In my motivational speeches, I say that "only ob-sessive desires rewrite boundaries," which is the intensity of desire you will need in order to rewrite your financial boundaries and to become finan-cially free.

Mark 10:46–50 (KJV) describes a beautiful story about Blind Bar-timaeus. One day, Blind Bartimaeus heard that Jesus, Son of David, was passing by and shouted "Jesus, thou Son of David, have mercy on me." The crowd proceeded to tell Bartimaeus to be quiet. Some persons may even have shouted at him and chided him to stop disturbing the Teacher. However, this impoverished, blind beggar, who obviously had no powerful network or friends in high places, did not back down. The powerful throng could not thwart his obsessive desire to see the beautiful sunset and his grandchildren. Instead, he shouted louder—so loud, I imagine that the windows in the area shook. Jesus stopped the crowd, went over to Blind Bartimaeus, and gave him back his sight.

That, my friend, is obsessive desire. Obsessive desire leaps over walls and mountains. Do you have it like Blind Bartimaeus? If you don't, you will not—in my view, at least—break free and move swiftly along the road to financial freedom.

As I mentioned previously, I grew up in Southside in downtown Kingston, Jamaica, and my family is from very humble beginnings. I used to take the country bus with my grandmother to sell school uniforms and clothing at markets in Spanish Town, St. Catherine, and on Heywood Street, in West Kingston.

Remembering those struggles to make ends meet helped me to decide from when I was a teenager to want to "bruk out a brukness" (to not continue a life of being broke) and to achieve financial independence as soon as I could. This obsessive desire led me to pressing hard with my professional accounting exams, and this rock-solid, bulldog-like, obsessive desire was the foundation for my qualifying as a chartered accountant at age 21, a record at the time, as indicated in chapter 1. This set the foundation for my earning power and, hence, was a strategic move for my financial freedom journey. It was an obsessive desire that drove me. It is a real thing. Do you have it? If not, you must find it!

How badly do you want to change your financial situation? Only you can tell. Renowned motivational speaker Zig Ziglar had something to say about mindset and goal setting. He said, "If you want to reach a goal, you must 'see the reaching' in your own mind before you actually arrive at your goal."[48] He is right. I should let you know that I could see the top of the PwC building from where I used to live in downtown Kingston. I used to climb on a little wall in my yard, and I would just stare at the top of the building, dreaming of and visualizing getting the job I ultimately got, while I waited for PwC to respond to my job application. Yes, I visualized myself working in the PwC office before I started working there.

Such is the power of visualizing your goals (and putting in the hard work, of course) and manifesting your goal in your mind. All the foregoing is supported by scripture: "For as he thinketh in his heart … so is he" (Proverbs 23:7, KJV). You, too, must visualize and see yourself as financially independent while having an obsession with seeing the goal becoming a reality.

---

48   Zig Ziglar, "If You Want to Reach a Goal," Ziglar, accessed June 9, 2022, https://www.ziglar.com/quotes/if-you-want-reach-goal/.

Benefits of Setting Financial Goals

I now turn to formally capturing three benefits of financial goal setting.

1. Financial Control

Setting financial goals puts you in the driver's seat of your financial life. It gives you control of your money. When I am leaving my house in the mornings, and after I get in my car, if I turn the steering wheel left, it means that I will be taking route A to work. If I turn it right, it means I will be taking route B to work. I am in control just by setting the steering wheel in one direction or another. So it is with setting financial goals. It gives you control over where your money goes and lets you stop wondering about where your money has been going. That control then leads to the second benefit of setting financial goals: achieving financial focus.

2. Financial Focus

If your financial health check showed that you didn't have adequate life insurance coverage, and you know you are the main breadwinner for your young family, it is imperative that you set a goal to get the right insurance coverage. The value and importance of this goal, alone, should be enough to push or keep you focused like a blinkered horse in order to earn and save the money required to get the necessary insurance coverage. I heard the example given that if you had to raise a certain amount of money, say $30,000, to pay for a life-saving surgery for your only child, you would have laser focus. That attitude must be applied to your financial goals to, literally, save the financial lives of yourself and your family. You must, therefore, set your financial goals today.

3. Financial Joy

I see sports fans go wild with joy when their favorite team wins a crucial game or championship match. I am here to tell you that there is such a thing as financial joy. In my opinion, it can rival even the joy of seeing your team win a championship title. Financial joy comes when you set a financial goal and see the goal come to life. I indicated in chapter 1 that it took us five years to pay off all our debts from the time we made becoming debt-free a priority. When that goal was achieved, we felt an amazing sense of joy. Such joy then becomes infectious and motivational. It spurs you on to achieve other goals. It becomes a virtuous, not vicious, cycle—before you know it, your financial joy and peace are in abundance.

My Red Fiat Uno Car

I close this chapter with a story that further confirms the power and significance of setting goals and being obsessive about your goals.

I remember shortly after I became a chartered accountant in the '90s, I was driving a small red Fiat Uno, which I got as a company car as a young, newly minted accountant. I was still living in Southside, downtown Kingston, and I would park the car on the street outside my gate. By that time, I had already been on Ian Boyne's *Profile*, a prestigious national TV program,[49] based on having qualified asone of the youngest chartered accountants in the Caribbean at age 21 at the time. I became like a little rock star in Southside. My fellow Southies were very proud to have seen me on national television! Consequently, when some of them saw me driving an unassuming small red Fiat Uno, they said, "Bruce, a man like you should be driving a BMW, weh di Bimmer, deh?" (Where is the BMW?)

They had my best interests at heart and genuinely wanted me to be driving what they called a "big man" car. I calmly and respectfully explained to them that I wasn't focusing on a car. I had other plans for my life.

So, why didn't I go out and buy the big man car? Why was I willing to sacrifice and keep a low profile by keeping my relatively ordinary Fiat Uno? My goal was to buy an apartment, so I was saving up a storm. An apartment was a real asset that would increase in value over time. I bought the apartment when I was 23 and then sold it years later. That asset was a major part of my financial independence journey! Eventually, I also got one of the so-called big man cars, and today I continue to drive one of these. I was in control, and I wasn't swayed from my target. I kept my focus on the goal, and it brought great joy when I got the keys to the apartment.

---

49   Ian Boyne, "Mother's Day and Family Values," *The Gleaner*, May 8, 2015, https://jamaica-gleaner.com/article/focus/20150510/mother%E2%80%99s-day-and-family-values.

This story underscores my point about making sacrifices, putting in the work, and reaping the rewards later. You can't continue to spend and live for the here and now and expect to reach financial independence. You must do something differently to get a different result. Set some financial goals and give up some of the luxuries and the impulse of spending today for a better financial future tomorrow!

To grow your money up to this point, you first need to run the 10 financial indicator tests to diagnose your current financial condition. Then based on the diagnosis, you must develop treatments. The treatments are the financial goals, such as developing a debt-reduction plan to deal with a high debt-to-income ratio and so on. We also spoke about the control, joy, and focus that come when you set and achieve financial goals. The next chapter will deal with the third step of how to grow your money: discovering your money personality.

Your Money Journal Assignment: Conquering My Financial Goals

WORKING ADULTS: 18 YEARS & OLDER

Based on the weak areas (those that fell below the best-practices targets) in your financial health check results, write *at least* one financial goal that when accomplished will fix that particular area of weakness. Here are some examples you can use as a guide:

- Short-term goals (<1 year)
  - Weak area: zero emergency fund
    - Build a starter emergency fund of $2,000 over the next six months
  - Weak area: no written will
    - Write my will and identify all my assets over the next four weeks
- Medium-term goals (one to 10 years)

- o Weak area: debt-to-income ratio is high (62 percent)

  - ¤ All credit card and unsecured loans to be repaid within three years

- Long-term goals (>10 years)

  - o Weak area: no retirement fund

    - ¤ Start contributing at least 5 percent of my salary to an approved retirement scheme or fund so that I can retire with dignity in 20 years' time[50]

Pick at least one of the goals above, close your eyes, and visualize what life would be like if you achieved this goal. Let the feeling soak in, and let it help to drive you toward conquering all your financial goals.

FULL-TIME STUDENTS: 14–24 YEARS

This is the best time to set your financial goals, as you have a clean slate. You have not yet racked up any debts (except student loans perhaps). More importantly, you have youth on your side. If you start following the 14 steps now, you will be able, with commitment and dedication, to achieve your goals. Please write down your answers to the following questions:

- Where do you see yourself in five to 10 years? Will you be seeking scholarships? Are you planning to take out a student loan?

- Where do you see yourself in 20 years? Will you have an apartment or house? Will you have a family? Which of the 10 financial indicators will you have achieved?

- Where do you see yourself in 30 years? Will your retirement plan be in place?

- Where do you see yourself in 40 years? Will you be able to retire comfortably?

---

50   This time period will be dependent on how old you are. If you are in your 60s or 70s, then this particular exercise is likely not applicable to you.

chapter 6

STEP 3: DISCOVER YOUR MONEY PERSONALITY

Everyone has a money personality, whether we realize it or not, and it was formed over the years (from childhood) based on our exposure to money.

It's our attitude toward money. It is what we think of and do with money. It is important to discover your money personality if you want to become financially independent, similar to figuring out the personality and attitudes of your future spouse in order to have a successful marriage. If your spouse does not want to have children, and you dream of having four cute little ones tugging at your legs, your spouse's stance will pose a huge problem. In the same way, you need to know yourself in terms of your money personality.

The idea here is not for you to change your natural money personality overnight but for you to be aware of your natural tendencies toward money and to guard against those areas of weakness while shoring up those areas of strength. Several views exist on the various types of money personalities and names that have been given to these personalities. Below, I have distilled those views into what I consider to be the four key money personalities.

Four Types of Money Personalities

1. *Investors:* These individuals are not afraid to take risks and be exposed to losses, knowing that the rewards could be great.

2. *Savers:* This group likes to feel a sense of security and therefore likes to hoard money to provide that feeling of security.

3. *Moguls:* They are big spenders. They splash out the credit card and just simply pay for everyone's food and drinks. They just want you to be reminded that "yeow, boss, mi rich." (Hello, sir, I am rich.) Many moguls grew up in poverty and tend to demonstrate this type of behavior to show they have moved up into a higher money class.

4. *Ostriches:* Like the attribute with which ostriches are associated, these individuals are afraid to face their financial realities, especially if there is a mountain of debt and difficult conversations are needed to improve the financial situation. They would prefer to bury their heads in the sand.

The question, then, is which one of these personalities is most dominant in you? You are very likely to exhibit more than one personality, but you are also very likely to exhibit one more than the others in the list. This is a key step along the road to financial freedom. Socrates said, "Know thyself."[51] Self-awareness will allow you to see your financial blind spots and then take protective action.

Are you comfortable investing your money and knowing you could lose, say, 30 percent, and it doesn't make you nervous? Maybe that's a sign that your natural money personality is that of an investor. Do you run like a cheetah when the topic of how much you owe on your credit card comes up? If you start to sweat, and your stomach turns, maybe you're a natural ostrich. Talk to a friend or someone you trust about these four personalities and try to settle on which one is your most dominant personality.

51   Xenophon, *Memorabilia*, trans. Amy L. Bonnette (Ithaca: Cornell University Press, 1994).

What do you need to safeguard?

Savers need to realize that hoarding money, say under their mattress, is not good, although it provides a feeling of security. It is not good because there is something called *inflation*—increases in the price of goods and services each year—which will eat away at the value of your money like termites who take over a building. Let's assume that a loaf of bread that cost $2.50 in 2021 now costs $2.63 in 2022, a year later, representing a 5 percent increase. That is inflation. Because the value of the money now under your mattress is stagnant, you will be able to buy less bread. To keep the purchasing power of their money, savers need to learn and understand the importance of investing in order to protect the value of their money against inflation. When you invest your money, and we will talk a lot more about investing later on, the opposite happens—after, say, one year, your money will have grown by a certain percentage depending on what you invest in. At the end of that year, the new total (original amount plus the returns earned) will grow again until the figure grows to massive sums over long periods. In a nutshell, that increase is the law of compound interest at work. Savers must learn and apply that law to enjoy the full rewards of saving money and to protect their money from the ravages of inflation. More to come on compound interest.

Investors need to understand that while it is good to be willing to be exposed to losses as a result of their investment decisions, they should not put all their eggs in one basket. They need to appreciate and apply the principle of diversification, which means putting your eggs in multiple baskets and investing for the long term. Those two simple principles will allow the investor to reap massive rewards. More to come on investments.

The ostrich needs to be reminded that a money problem ignored is like a small, infected wound on a leg. If unattended, one day the leg might have to be amputated. Money problems don't just disappear like steam from a rising pot. They must be confronted and addressed head on. In his book *The Road Less Traveled*, Scott Peck talks about the concept of "life being difficult." He counseled persons for over 25 years as a psychiatrist, and he concluded that those persons who are willing to face the pain of their realities heal faster than those who refuse. It is painful to accept the difficulties of your financial problems, but it is even worse to ignore the problems. It will be twice as deadly in the end.[52]

Moguls, you will need to work on learning that a "man's life consisteth not in the abundance of things which he possesseth," to quote Jesus (Luke 12:15, KJV). Money can't hug or talk in times of need and crises. Big spending to impress others does not attract real friends. Moguls cultivate friends based on trust and loyalty, not on the sandy foundation of big spending. There is a time to "flask," "braf," and "splurge"—life is a balance. Don't let throwing money around be your way of winning friends and influencing people.

How is your money personality formed?

In her book *Broke Millennial*, Erin Lowry writes, "Your relationship with money started years before you took out your student loans or got a credit card."[53]

What I believe Erin is saying is that our money personalities today are shaped by all our conscious and subconscious money influences over the years. The money personality experts have concluded, therefore, that our money personalities are influenced by three basic sources:

1. Childhood experiences

2. The communities in which we grew up

3. The habits of those around us, like parents and friends

I heard the story of a man we'll call Akeem who told me that his money personality is that of a saver, and he believes it was influenced by his particular childhood experience. He did not live with his father as a child, so his mother would send him to his father's house for money to help with food and school supplies. When he visited, he was never sure if (1) his fa-

---

52   M. Scott Peck, *The Road Less Traveled: A New Psychology of Love, Traditional Values, and Spiritual Growth* (New York: Touchstone, 2003).

53   Erin Lowry, *Broke Millennial: Stop Scraping by and Get Your Financial Life Together* (New York: Penguin, 2017), 13.

ther would tell him, "I have no money," (2) he would see his father at all, or (3) he would get less money than he asked or hoped for. Akeem strongly believes the level of uncertainty he experienced with his father and money pushed him to be a saver today. He does not want to relive those feelings of uncertainty about money, hence saving money became a safe haven.

Which money personality type are you?

So, the question is "Which of the four money personalities that I have described is most dominant in you?" What are the forces that you believe shaped your money personality? You will have an opportunity in the money journal assignment to assess your dominant money personality.

Marriage and Money

As we close this chapter, I also want to go back to something I mentioned earlier: the matter of marriage and money. You ought not to walk down the aisle to declare marriage vows until both you and your partner confess to each other your financial situation and life goals. What is the extent of your debt, how many children would you like to have, and what is your ideal retirement age? Discussing these issues will help both of you to figure out the monetary implications of each other's financial condition and life goals. If you see major potential irreconcilable differences in your money aspirations, try to resolve these before you walk down the aisle. If you don't, you will likely be walking into a life of fiery money arguments, which could put a strain on your marriage. Therefore, before you tie the knot, please confess your money problems and aspirations to each other! Remember financial disagreement is one of the leading causes of divorce in the United States,[54] and no doubt in many other parts of the world.

In this chapter, I've highlighted the need for you to be aware of your dominant money personality and that money personalities are formed over a long period of time. I'm not asking you to change your dominant money personality—just be aware of the risks associated with it, and apply the relevant safeguards that will protect you from the downside of your money

---

54   Warren, "10 Most Common Reasons for Divorce."

personality. I also spoke about the importance of both parties in a relationship knowing each other's money personalities and aspirations. Failure to do so could put a heavy burden on your relationship.

In the next chapter we will talk about the importance of budgeting and saving. Budgeting is not just about crunching numbers. It is also about how you behave with your money.

Your Money Journal Assignment: Discovering My Dominant Money Personality

WORKING ADULTS: 18 YEARS & OLDER

- From the four money personalities described in this chapter and repeated below, pick the one that you believe is most dominant in you.

  o Investors (not afraid of losses or some risk)

  o Savers (like the feeling of security)

  o Moguls (big spenders; often grew up in poverty)

  o Ostriches (afraid to face financial reality)

- List one thing you should guard against, having now recognized your dominant money personality. Examples of things to guard against include the following:

  o Certain friends and places

  o Living to impress others

  o Keeping secret bank accounts

FULL-TIME STUDENTS: 14–24 YEARS

- High school and college students, look at the four dominant money personalities above and pick the one most dominant in you.

I am certain you already have some idea of your money personality. You may also think of the money personalities of your parents or guardians and see which money personality you think they may have, based on how you have seen them handle money; proceed to have a respectful discussion with them to confirm what you think.

chapter 7

STEP 4: BUDGET TO SAVE—LEARN FROM THE ANTS AND BE WISE

Learn from the Ants

Proverbs 6:6–9 (KJV) teaches that lazy persons should take a lesson from ants and be wise because, although the ants have no ruler or governor, they labor hard all summer, gathering food for the winter. The principle of saving is clear. It is wise to save.

The importance of saving money was also echoed by Arkad, the richest man in Babylon, when he explained to his colleagues that a big part of how he became rich was by saving 10 percent of his income first and then forcing himself to live off the other 90 percent.[55]

I call this chapter "Budget to Save," because without saving, as Arkad and the ants did, you will become stuck on the journey to financial freedom, like having a flat tire.

---

55   Clason, *The Richest Man in Babylon.*

Five Reasons Why You Need to Save Money

When you can save money, you will be able to do the following:

1. Attack your mountain of high-cost debt

2. Build your emergency fund

3. Make or increase your contributions toward your pension plan or retirement account

4. Invest for the future to protect your money from inflation, build wealth, and give you more resources to help those in need

5. Avoid a mountain of debt, especially for younger people who haven't yet made serious money mistakes and are not yet consumed by debt mountains

Let me say quickly that savings should be invested once you have taken care of items one to three above. It is not wise to have excess funds sitting in a savings account that offers extremely low interest rates, as this will result in your purchasing power being eroded by inflation. It is also unwise to start investing when (1) you have high-interest debt such as credit card debt or (2) you have no emergency fund. This is because (1) it will be difficult to find investments that consistently earn more than credit card interest rates, and (2) if you have an emergency, you may have to sell the investment, possibly at a loss, to deal with the emergency. More on investments in chapter 11.

Another reason I titled this chapter "Budget to Save" is that I strongly believe budgeting will enable you to save money. I can hear you saying, "Mr. Bruce, you introduced a fancy word here, *budgeting*. What is budgeting?"

What is budgeting?

The best way to explain budgeting is to use an illustration. Let's say a young man and a young lady decided to go on their first date at an upscale restaurant, and they decided to split the bill. They must first find out the average cost for a good meal for two people at this restaurant, transportation costs, how much they will likely tip the staff, and whether they will need to buy new clothes and scents. If the estimated cost of all the foregoing is, say, $300, and together, they only have $150 or are only willing to spend $150, then they will know ahead of time and can either find another restaurant or seek the additional funds. The budget (the estimated cost of $300) helped them to predict ahead of time, how much they were going to be spending. The budget allowed them to control "their expenditure" so that they didn't spend more than they had or wanted to.

A formal definition of budgeting, then, in my words, is a plan of how you wish to allocate your income between your needs, wants, and savings.

What do I mean by needs? These include the things you must have to live on each month—food, transportation, utilities, rent or mortgage, debt repayments (I believe debts must be honored!), and insurance premiums.

Wants include the "nice to haves," but you can live without them. For example, you don't have to eat out at a restaurant three times a week or at all.

Savings comes from the portion of your income you don't spend. It is cash that is left over after you allocate income to your needs and wants. In fact, some people advocate for taking out savings first and then forcing yourself to live off the rest. Whichever approach you choose, ensure that you allocate at least 10 percent of your income to savings, and it might be higher depending on the types of financial goals you have.

If more people performed this simple exercise, we would have more people saving money and more financially independent people. Do not ignore the simplicity and discipline of doing your budget. It will bring an abundance of blessings to you and your family. It is the simple things in life that often give us the most blessings, like watching a beautiful sunset or seeing the wonder of an orchid bloom.

Scripture also advises us to sit down and think about how we wish to spend our money before we start spending. The Gospel of Luke 14:28 states, "For which of you, intending to build a tower, sitteth not down first, and counteth the cost, whether he have *sufficient* to finish *it*?" (KJV). The passage continues, "What king, going to make war against another king, sitteth not down first, and consulteth whether he be able with ten thousand to meet him that cometh against him with twenty thousand?" (Luke 13:41, KJV). It should be the same with your money, which I am metaphorically calling foot soldiers. You must check how many soldiers you have before you engage in the war of spending, whether you are buying a house, car, clothes, or whatever else. If you don't have enough soldiers to accomplish a task, don't go to war, otherwise you could end up in unintended debt!

There are some people whose incomes are just too low to afford them a basic existence. This may be due to many life circumstances—for example, long-term illnesses may limit their ability to work for long periods. Alternatively, they may be working at a job that just does not provide the income needed to survive even if they reduced their expenses to the bare minimum.

For example, if John lives in Long Beach, California, where according to a 2022 GOBankingRates study the median income required to live comfortably is $86,276.27,[56] and he earns $29,000 a year, there is virtually little he can do to adjust his spending to save enough so he could live comfortably in Long Beach. His income is just too low.

The urgent solution here is for John to rapidly increase his income by changing jobs, seeking additional income streams to add to the low-paying job, or moving to another city or country that is more aligned with his earning potential.

I believe, however, that many people earn enough to not have to struggle as much as they may be struggling. A missing ingredient I believe is the absence of budgeting and saving. How do I know this? Because it was only when I started to live on a budget and stick to the budget that I was able to really start saving money and attack our debts. Before, I had an idea of how much I wanted to spend on different things, but I didn't have a set amount of money that I intended to spend each month.

---

56   Joel Anderson, "How Much You Need to Live Comfortable in 50 Major US Cities," GO-BankingRates, May 31, 2022, https://www.gobankingrates.com/money/economy/cost-to-live-comfortably-biggest-cities-us/.

According to a 2022 Debt.com survey, 80 percent of people say they do a budget. The survey also reported that almost 85 percent of budgeters said living on a budget got them or kept them out of debt.[57] These statistics support the argument that budgeting is a tool that can help to keep you from excessive debt and to help you save more.

You should also be asking the question "If such a high percentage (80 percent) of people do budgets, why is the savings rate in the United States (and other places) so low?" The answer can be found in a Bankrate.com survey that showed that 82 percent of those surveyed said they prepared a budget,[58] but when asked if they keep (or stick to) their budgets, the survey found that "about a third just scrawl it out on paper—and almost 20 percent say they budget just by keeping track in their heads."[59] The numbers suggest that 53.3 percent (one-third plus 20 percent) were not using effective means to track their budgets and, hence, would not have been able to effectively stick to their budgets. Other surveys, such as one conducted by Mint, also confirmed the struggles many people have in sticking to their budgets—a key finding was that three in five Americans didn't know what they spent last month.[60] I discuss strategies that you can use to help you stick to your budgets later on in this chapter.

Why is budgeting so important?

My arguments, so far, have clearly demonstrated that budgeting is a big deal because of the following:

1. It gives you control over what happens to your money. You can give a task or job to each dollar you earn. Many people see a budget as a cage to trap them and to take the fun out of living. It is quite the

57   "Americans Are Budgeting More Than Ever," Debt, accessed June 9, 2022, https://www. debt.com/research/best-way-to-budget/.

58   Claes Bell, "Budgets Can Crumble in Times of Trouble," Bankrate, January 7, 2015, https://www.bankrate.com/finance/smart-spending/money-pulse-0115.aspx.

59   Martha White, "The 1 Task Americans Just Can't Accomplish," *Time*, January 7, 2015, https://time.com/3657285/task-americans-cant-do/.

60   "Survey: 65% of Americans Have No Idea How Much They Spent Last Month," Intuit Mint Life, last modified December 11, 2020, https://mint.intuit.com/blog/budgeting/spending-knowledge-survey/.

opposite. The budget helps you to trap cash—save money today so you can live the life you dream about tomorrow.

2. It allows you to spend less than you earn so you can live within your means, save money, and avoid excessive debt.

3. It allows you to do "guilt-free spending." While living on a budget means discipline, it does not always mean no enjoyment. Although I budget to ensure there are savings, there is always some fun money, once the savings target has been set and basic needs are taken care of. Budgeting allows you to enjoy some of those wants without guilt.

Before getting into how to prepare a budget, I now briefly introduce a discussion on the importance of exhibiting the right behaviors that will help you to stick to your budget limits, with an illustration.

If, say, you have a limit of $100 for gifts this month, and on the 17th of the month you reach that limit, then there should be no more expenditures on gifts, even if your goddaughter—the daughter of your best friend since kindergarten—is having a party. Make her a nice handmade postcard, paste those memorable pictures of her life to date, and give her the biggest hug! There can be no more spending once the gift limit has been reached unless you plan to reduce spending elsewhere in the budget. What will help you to stick to the budget limits? It is the obsessive, Blind Bartimaeus, bulldog-like desire to see financial freedom. You must say no to exceeding spending limits and unnecessary spending, even if you become unpopular with friends and family. They will love you later! I will discuss later on the mechanics and options you can use to keep track of how much you are spending each month in relation to the budgeted limits.

How to Prepare a Budget

In summary, you can prepare a budget in three steps.

1. Track your spending.

Track your expenses for the last three months to see exactly how much money you have been spending, on average, each month. You do it by going back over your credit card statements, debit card statements, bills, and receipts over the last three months. You can also track your spending if you use free apps (e.g., Mint) that are linked to your online bank accounts and that will allow you to see how much you are spending each month. If for whatever reason, you can't access any financial records, you will need to use estimates based on memory. You may be in for some surprises when you see, for example, how much you are spending on food, clothes, dog food, or bank charges.

2. Analyze your spending patterns.

Look at each line item of spending and assign each a label of *need*, *want*, or *saving*. An example is shown below for the Goldsons.

TABLE 7.1: THE GOLDSONS' SPENDING PATTERNS

December	$
Income: Salary (After Taxes)[61]	4,133
Expenses:	
Mortgage (Need)	1,159
Food (Need)	620
Transportation (Need)	550
Clothing and other (Need)	248
Insurance: health, life, and disability (Need)	
Consumer debt[62] (Need)	1,873
Entertainment (Want)	150
Giving (Want)	233
Total Expenses Before Savings	4,833
Savings/(Shortfall)	(700)

The table above shows that the Goldsons spend 108 percent[63] of their after-tax income on needs, 9 percent on wants, and 0 percent on savings

---

61   Monthly gross household income before taxes is $5,417 or $65,000 gross annual household income.

62   Credit cards, line of credit

63   $4,450 (Needs) / $4,133 (After-Tax Income)

(actually, they have negative savings of –17 percent and are living above their means), which means they are borrowing each month to make ends meet. This is a tough situation to be in as they are unable to save money, and we already established that saving is the foundation to becoming financially independent. If you find that you are in the same position as the Goldsons, you may start to feel shame or guilt about how you have been handling your money. You may even feel a sense of shock as it could be that this budgeting exercise has revealed that your needs are not being fully covered by your income. More tragic is the fact that you had not even realized it, because the credit card just seamlessly covered the shortfall each month.

If your income is not covering your needs, the situation requires urgent action. As you will see later on, the bottom line is to create a plan to increase your income really fast and reduce spending on your needs and wants.

Whatever your emotional state may be at this stage of the budgeting exercise, I want you to be thankful that, at least, you now have more knowledge as to how much you are or are not saving and to see this knowledge as power. Why? Because you can use this knowledge to start figuring a way out of the problem. Prior to this realization, you were on the way to digging yourself into a deeper financial hole. So, let's keep on reading!

3. Establish spending limits and savings targets.

The third step in preparing your budget is to establish spending limits and savings targets. An important question that the Goldsons must be considering is how much should they now be spending on their needs and wants, in order to ensure that they are in a position to start saving money.

As discussed in chapter 4's table 4.3 that captures your 10 financial health indicators, the best practice is that you should aim to save at least 10 percent of your income each month. There is also what is known as the popular 50/30/20 rule that says you should aim to allocate your income to spend 50 percent on your needs, 30 percent on your wants, and 20 percent on savings.[64]

---

64   "The 50/30/20 Rule: How to Budget Your Money More Efficiently," N26, October 6, 2021, https://n26.com/en-eu/blog/50-30-20-rule.

The truth is that there is no one-size-fits-all rule. The 10 percent or 20 percent of savings mentioned above are simply guidelines, good starting points. Everybody must aim to achieve ratios that are best for them based on their personal situation at a point in time.

Ideally, the Goldsons need to be saving even more than 20 percent given the seriousness of their financial condition. Realistically, they may not be able to save more than 5 percent of their income for the first six months based on their current harsh realities. They currently spend 17 percent ($700) more than they earn. To improve their savings rate, they will need to have some tough discussions and to make some hard decisions around their current spending habits. Such discussions can be emotional and, if not managed, can take a toll on your relationship or marriage.

For example, I spoke to a couple recently who had a negative savings rate. They also went out to eat at their favorite restaurant every week. That habit was contributing significantly to the massive hole in their budget. The thought of removing the practice completely was so painful for the wife that instead of ripping it from the budget all at once, they initially decreased it to once per month and then eventually removed it completely. You may have similar challenges!

The main point here is that the Goldsons will need to establish new limits on their spending—i.e., their needs and wants—as well as try and increase their income in order to ensure that they put themselves in a position to start saving money. If your situation is like the Goldsons', you, too, must decide to make these adjustments.

Making adjustments is the third and hardest part of doing a budget. To help you make adjustments in a structured way, I introduce below my TTCI method.

The TTCI Method of Increasing Savings

Much of what you and the Goldsons need to do to get your needs and wants down and your savings up can be done from a practical and common sense basis. However, I still find having a structure for doing it to be very helpful in ensuring you find every last dollar that can be saved and every opportunity to increase your income! So here is the TTCI four-step approach.

1. *Track (Go Even Deeper)*

The first *T* stands for *track*. By this time, you would have already reviewed your expenses of the past three months to track your total monthly expenditure. I'm now asking you to go as far back as 12 months to find even more evidence of what you have been doing with your money. Going back for three months is like doing an x-ray. Going back 12 months is like doing an MRI. It will give you deeper insights into your spending patterns.

If you feel you have a good sense of where your money has been going after looking back at your expenses over the last three months, you can skip this step and go straight to "Trim."

2. *Trim*

This is where you go through all expenses, line by line, looking for opportunities to trim, to make tweaks and minor reductions. At this stage, you are looking for quick wins to see how much money you can save. Opportunities that exist (not an exhaustive list) for quick wins include looking carefully at what you are spending in the following areas:

1. Life insurance: Consider mixing your portfolio with term life insurance, which can be five to 15 times cheaper than traditional insurance policies (referred to, generally, as whole life policies) depending on the country in question.[65] Talk to your insurance adviser before you make any moves on this expense, and see chapter 10 on insurance for more.

2. Mortgage: Compare mortgage rates across mortgage companies and consider switching. Watch for costs associated with refinancing and also speak to your mortgage adviser.

3. Cell phone: Consider switching your post-paid phone for a pre-paid phone to get a better handle on your phone bill.

---

65   Daniel Kurt, "Term vs. Whole Life Insurance: What's the Difference?," Investopedia, last modified May 23, 2022, https://www.investopedia.com/term-life-vs-whole-life-5075430.

4. Food: Use a grocery list and stick to it. Also, purchase in bulk to achieve discounts, and buy produce from farmers' markets rather than supermarkets.

5. Entertainment: Cancel underutilized subscription services.

3. Chop

You have trimmed your expenses, but they still exceed your income. You must now take more radical strategies and move from trimming to chopping. This aspect is where you are really tested in terms of how serious you are about wanting to start saving money. These are painful, albeit worthwhile, steps, examples of which include moving from a bigger house to a smaller house to save on mortgage, rent, and utilities or switching from a new car to a used or pre-owned car to save on car loan payments. More on used cars to come in chapter 9, which deals with managing debt.

For certain countries like Jamaica, some people may need to abandon plans to send their children to expensive private colleges overseas in places like the U.S. or Canada and instead send their children to an accredited university in their country. The decision may be heart wrenching to some parents, but if you are already drowning in debt and expenses, that expenditure is an area you could chop. In his book *Outliers*, Malcolm Gladwell talks about research that argues success in life is not so much about the college or school you attend but more about things like emotional intelligence, being smart enough, and putting in hard work, which he describes as his 10,000-hour rule—to be an expert at anything you must put in at least 10,000 hours, he argues.[66] Parents, there are other ways to educate your child if you can't afford the expensive private college. If you can afford it, and that's your dream, then go ahead. If not, you should also consider sending your children to a community college, which is usually more affordable. According to *The Princeton Review*, community college tuition is usually thousands of dollars cheaper than tuition for private and public four-year universities. The article went on to make reference to the College Board, which stated that the average published yearly tuition for a public

---

66   Malcolm Gladwell, *Outliers* (New York: Little, Brown and Company, 2008).

two-year college (in the U.S.) was $3,440—and that this cost is a fraction of the cost of a private college and still thousands of dollars less than a four-year program at a state college.[67]

4. Increase Your Income

Maximize your earnings as an employee.

You can also get your savings up not just by reducing expenses but by increasing your income. There are several ways to do it. Robert Kiyosaki treats this topic very well in his book *Rich Dad's Cashflow Quadrant: Guide to Financial Freedom*.[68] He argues that people earn money from being an employee, being self-employed, being a business owner, and being an investor. Here I will give you my own perspective on how you can increase your income by using each of those four sources.

Most individuals start out as employees. To increase your earnings in this scenario, it means asking for a raise, which is easier said than done. You can, however, increase the chances of getting that increase by finding the right time and moment to ask. You would also have to justify the request by showing how you have been adding value to the company. A young lady told me how she approached her boss with a new idea of how to gain new customers. The idea was convincing, and it worked! She got a salary increase. Show, or bring, some extra value to your organization, and you might be rewarded.

Many people also increase their income by getting a second or third job. For example, they may deliver pizza, teach at night, or work as customer service representatives for call centers, among other jobs. Successfully taking on multiple jobs will require careful planning and stamina as well as managing the impact of not spending enough time with your family. If you work a side job, ensure that there is no conflict of interest with your main job and that you have received approval to do the side gig from your present employer. You don't want your side gig to cause you to possibly lose your main gig!

---

67   "4 Reasons to Consider Community College," *The Princeton Review*, accessed June 9, 2022, https://www.princetonreview.com/college-advice/community-college.

68   Robert Kiyosaki, *Rich Dad's Cashflow Quadrant: Guide to Financial Freedom* (New York: Business Plus, 2000).

Getting additional education is also another way to earn more. But don't think that it always has to be a three- or four-year degree program. It could be that a one-year, six-month, or three-month certificate in an area that you are already good in may be all you need to start earning more. If you are good at styling or cutting hair, in a relatively short time at HEART Trust NTA (a national training institution in Jamaica) you could get certified to become a barber or a cosmetologist![69] You can then use that credential to increase your earnings. When I completed my UK professional accounting exams (ACCA), my salary doubled. The raise was a significant demonstration of how much value PwC placed on professional education. Unfortunately, many persons are not fully recognized on the job for the full range of their qualifications. Don't let that fact discourage you. Use your knowledge to start a side gig or find a better job.

Yes, finding a better job is another way to increase your income. Too many people, however, are afraid to step out of their current jobs. They have become used to their current environment and their comfort zone, even though they may be miserable in their current job and can't make ends meet. It was Roy T. Bennett who said, "If you always do what is easy and choose the path of least resistance, you never step outside your comfort zone. Great things don't come from comfort zones."[70] Seek counsel, do some research, go for that interview, and step out of your comfort zone. That next job may be your strategic move to financial freedom.

The question, then, is "Can you achieve financial freedom by working for someone else all the days of your life?" The answer is yes, you can, but it will not necessarily be a walk in the park. There will be challenges along the way. One might be that your salary as an employee may not always keep up with inflation because salaries are not always adjusted in line with inflationary increases by some employers. By applying the money principles as outlined in this book, however, you can still achieve financial freedom.

69   "HEART College of Beauty Services," HEART-NTA, accessed June 9, 2022, https://hcbs. heart-nta.org/.

70   Roy T. Bennett, *The Light in the Heart: Inspirational Thoughts for Living Your Best Life* (self-published, 2021), 223.

Some people will always remain employees because they may not be cut out to be an entrepreneur, be their own boss or the boss of others. Becoming an entrepreneur requires additional skills, and believe it or not, in many cases may require longer working hours. Consequently, some people are likely to remain as employees all their working life.

You can achieve financial freedom as an employee all your life, especially if you start to save and invest early, like the school bus driver I spoke about earlier. Also, refer to chapter 2 in which I showed where an individual and a household that earned averaged incomes from their jobs were able to save and invest 15 percent of their income over 30 years and were able to amass enough money to live comfortably at the end of the 30 years.

If you spend a little less on clothes, food, brand-name shoes, and similar items you may be surprised how much you may be able to save and invest each month. Avoid the pressure from persuasive advertisements and the temptation of keeping up with your neighbor's latest "toys," and save and invest your way into financial freedom. If you are willing to make the sacrifice and remain disciplined it is that simple. You can do it!

YOUNG PEOPLE—YOUR INCOME AS A WEALTH-BUILDING TOOL

To college and high school students, let me emphasize at this point that the income you will earn in your first and subsequent jobs or entrepreneurial pursuits will be your best wealth-building tool. To maximize this income, be careful to choose the right subjects or majors that are in alignment with your natural abilities and passion, not in line with the desires and wishes of your parents or your friends!

I realized that I liked accounting in ninth grade, so I aligned my course choices with accounting and related subjects like economics and advanced mathematics. I went on to study professional accounting. I aligned my natural interest in accounting with a career that was built on what I liked—accounting!

Many young people, however, are not sure or don't know what career they will pursue after leaving high school or college. I believe there are three ways to help cure such uncertainty:

1. Choose subjects or majors in school that are in line with your natural gifts and talents. A lot of parents pressure their children to become a doctor or lawyer that they didn't become. Often, these children live empty, unfulfilled careers and switch to their real passions only after spending a lot of money and investing a lot of time. I heard a story of a young man who studied medicine because of his father's constant pressure. He went on to become a doctor and was, indeed, a good doctor because he was a person who took pride in his work when dealing with his patients. He even won the Doctor of the Year award. On the night he collected the award, dressed in his tuxedo and regalia, he used this opportunity to tell his medical colleagues that he would be quitting medicine to pursue his lifelong passion of music. There was a gasp and a deafening silence in the room. He thanked them and left the award with his dad as he headed out the hotel ballroom that night. He went on to become a world-class musician! How many people are suffering as this former doctor did?

2. Notwithstanding my argument about choosing subjects that line up with your natural gifts and talents, please also make sure that there is a balance, meaning that your course of study will allow you to make a decent living. It must not be that your passion is so strong for a certain career path through which you can't meet your basic expenses and allow you to save! If your current passion is leading toward such a career, try to find a related passion that will at least give you this minimum earning potential. Let's be real, everyone: Your career must be able to allow you, at the very least, to meet your basic needs and have money to save.

3. I strongly recommend that once you think you know what career path you want to take, you should try to get an internship in that particular field before you finish high school or college. I was blessed. Even though I didn't get an internship in accounting in the traditional sense, I got an experience that took me close enough to the real world of accounting before I actually left high school. I had a friend

who worked at an accounting firm, and he took me to the offices, showed me around, and pointed out different areas of the office. I was also able to learn more about the earning potential and challenges to be overcome in the accounting field, which included working late hours during the busy periods. To further drive this point of the importance of an internship, I share the following story.

I know this brilliant young lady who wanted to be a journalist. She had this dream while in high school. Her parents were able to get an internship for her at a media house, where she had the opportunity to go out with the news team—journalists and photographers—and she participated in how the stories were developed. Guess what? During the internship she found out that she absolutely hated being a journalist. That was her experience. She then switched to accounting and auditing, and she got an internship at an accounting firm and loves it. Such is the power of internships!

The discussion above focused on the income you make as an employee and ways in which you can increase that income as you seek to, ultimately, increase your ability to save money. We now turn to the income generated from being self-employed.

Becoming Your Own Boss

All employees are acutely aware of how things can change quickly in terms of job security at their job. COVID-19, the mortgage crisis of 2008, your company's losing a major customer or losing a major lawsuit all can change fortunes, and in a very short space of time, you could be out of a job.

Many people, therefore, find becoming their own boss, or being self-employed, very attractive as a way to improve job security as well as to increase their earnings. In many cases they can, in fact, earn more than they did as employees.

You can also have your own business while continuing to be an employee at another entity. I remember a man, let's call him John, telling me that the difference in what he earned from his first client after he became a sole accounting practitioner versus what he had made as an employee in his job was staggering. He never worked another day as an employee. Of course, it doesn't work out like that for everyone, but when it works, it can work really well.

Over 44 million, roughly 13 percent, of the U.S. population have side hustles, including small businesses.[71] I believe the rate is just as high in Jamaica and the Caribbean. This statistic speaks to the fact that many people have come to realize that to improve their living standards at the pace that they desire, they need additional income and that oftentimes that requires a small business either full time or on the side.

SPECIFIC BUSINESS IDEAS FOR THE SELF-EMPLOYED

There are some specific things you could consider doing to start your own business. Many of these are online opportunities and include the following ideas:

1. Sell your services on a platform like Upwork, which allows you to upload your résumé in order to match your skills with potential customers for which you may be able to provide a service at a reasonable rate. Not all services are available to every country. The possibilities are facilitated by the large listing of customers who are interested in various services and are already on the platform. Such assignments can last from one month to six months, and eventually, you could start working with these clients directly, outside of Upwork (subject, of course, to their policies). I've heard of individuals who make close to $1,000 on a monthly basis consistently. The great thing about this site is that the range of service offerings is almost endless. You can offer just about any service—for example, bookkeeping, virtual administrative assistance, legal services, customer support, sales, marketing, social media management, and the list goes on.

2. Start an online store. You can post pictures of your items online to your target customers and arrange for delivery to their addresses.

---

71   Anna Bahney, "More Than 44 Million Americans Have a Side Hustle," CNN, July 12, 2017, https://money.cnn.com/2017/07/12/pf/side-hustle/index.html.

If you have unique items valued by the market, you would have a business opportunity. You may also be able to strike a deal with Amazon to be one of their suppliers!

3. Become an online business consultant. COVID-19 and convenience have forced many businesses to go online. Many business owners don't necessarily have the skills, however, to move to an online platform, set up their social media accounts, and deliver good customer service. If you are good at both business planning and technology, you can mix those skills and help companies to make this transition successfully.

4. Sell your services on a platform like Fiverr. This is similar to Upwork with the main difference being that Fiverr offers one-day, one-off jobs, such as editing someone's video or article for a few dollars. Such activities quickly add up, over time.

5. Register at online platforms such as TutorMe.com, which allow you to teach, and they provide the technology you need to deliver the classes. If you are good at accounting, information technology, or any subject for which there is a market, then you can teach online and make money. If you have a course that you developed, you can sell that course to an online platform and get ongoing royalties each time someone uses the course.

6. Get recognition on YouTube. If you have the time and patience, you can become a YouTuber and make money from your videos even years after they have been uploaded. Success on YouTube will require long hours before you become well known. You will need 1,000 subscribers and 4,000 watch hours over 12 months to be monetized.[72] You can, however, earn a good income if you have great content and are willing to put in the work.

7. Enlist affiliation agreements. If you are well known or have some kind of influence over others, you can enter into affiliation agree-

---

72 "YouTube Partner Program Overview & Eligibility," YouTube Help, last modified March 10, 2022, https://support.google.com/youtube/answer/72851?hl=en.

ments with respected brands. If you include that brand on your website, for example, and refer to it with a unique code that persons use when they buy that brand, the supplier will credit you with a commission payment whenever someone buys that product.

This list is by no means exhaustive and is meant to give you specific ideas that you could consider.

Becoming a Big Business

The young accountant I referred to earlier chose to remain a sole practitioner, working full time in his accounting practice and never pivoted into being a big-business owner. *Big-business owner* refers to someone whose business has grown from their need to be present for day-to-day operations to a point where employees can run the business without the owner's daily presence. Some self-employed people, like this young accountant, are quite happy to remain the way they are. They often feel that it would take too much time and effort to grow the business to the big-business level. The downside is that they have to spend more time running the self-employed business than a big-business owner would.

There are other accountants, restaurant owners, teachers, doctors, and other entrepreneurs who have grown their one-person shows into businesses with staff of up to 300 and more. I think of Sonia's Homestyle Cooking & Natural Juices, an amazing Jamaican restaurant that started out with only Ms. Sonia Thomas. She started by selling potato pudding from a sky-juice cart on the side of the street. Some years later, in 1985, she had a fully established restaurant with a loyal band of dedicated followers, including me! Today, I'm always thrilled to see the long line of cars—many of them high-end vehicles, as her customers span all social classes—and the buzz, especially on a Sunday morning. Ms. Thomas was willing to push and pivot the business from just herself to the point where, from what I observe, she could choose not to be present. The last time I dined there, I asked the waiter for Ms. Sonia, and he said she was floating around the back, just overseeing and ensuring that all was going well. That description sounded more like her just loving cooking and wanting to make sure the quality is always present rather than her needing to be present for the day-to-day operations! Well done, Ms. Sonia!

Whether you choose to remain a solopreneur or grow into a big business will be based on your life goals and risk appetite. Whichever route you choose, you can still get to total financial freedom if you are saving and investing over long periods. That is the secret.

Becoming an Investor

To get to total financial freedom, where your money works for you and you don't work unless you want to, you need to save money earned either from being an employee, self-employed, or scaling up to become a large business or corporation. That money then needs to be invested (put to work) wisely over the years. It must work so hard that it is able to earn more than what you need to live on each month.

Investing in a good stock-based unit trust or mutual fund (I explain these terms in chapter 11)that averages 10–12 percent per year is generally the simplest way, in my view, to let your money work for you and to get you to total financial freedom. Of course, you could invest your money in other asset classes, such as real estate (stock-based unit trust or mutual fund is my personal preference), or even continue to invest in your big business and still achieve total financial freedom. The investment strategy is totally your choice, and you should seek financial counsel along the way before you invest your money!

If you choose to invest in real estate (rental properties and the like) or continue to invest in a big business, you must be prepared to spend some of your time dealing with practical matters relating to the business. There will be board meetings, shareholders meetings, and major staff issues, and in terms of your properties, there may be difficult tenants, plumbing problems, dealing with property managers, and so on. Investing in unit trusts or mutual funds are likely to give you the most passive form of income—the moneyis being made without much effort from the investor. Your money does all the work, and you earn even in your sleep! A lot more to come on investments in chapter 11.

We have come to the end of the discussion on the four ways to make money. Increasing your income is a critical piece of the puzzle in helping you to save more!

The Goldsons Have Reached the Land of Savings

The Goldsons decided, after seeing the poor results of their financial health check, that they were going to start living on a budget; they have since prepared their first budget (see table 7.2 below) using the three-step approach I described and using the TTCI principles. They have succeeded in adjusting their spending and their lifestyle, and they are now in a position to save money ($382 per month, a savings rate of 7 percent per month) after a lot of hard work, arguments, shouting, and sacrifice. These adjustments are shown in tables 7.2 and 7.3 below:

TABLE 7.2: THE GOLDSONS' SPENDING AND EARNINGS BEFORE AND AFTER THE USE OF THE TTCI PRINCIPLES

Items	Before Adjustments: Actual Spending ($)	After Adjustments: Budgeted Spending ($)	Adjustments[73]
Income: Salary (After Taxes)	4,133	4,133	Wage stagnation— no salary increase granted by employers
Income: Small business		914	Mr. Goldson started a small, successful online teaching business
Total Income	4,133	5,047	
Expenses			
Mortgage (Need)	1,159	1,043	Switched mortgage company and saved 10% in monthly payment based on better loan terms

---

73   Certain terms such as *term* life and refinanced mortgage may not be fully understood at this junction by all readers; however, the terms are further explained in later chapters dealing with life insurance and managing debt.

Items	Before Adjustments: Actual Spending ($)	After Adjustments: Budgeted Spending ($)	Adjustments[73]
Food (Need)	620	527	Smarter shopping and buying in bulk
Transportation (Need)	550	450	Carpooled with neighbors on certain days and switched to lower-cost car insurance company
Other (Need)	248	150	Better energy conservation re: utilities and reduced purchases of clothing
Insurance: health, life, and disability (Need)		1,012	Bought health and term life insurance for Mr. and Mrs. Goldson— these were not in place
Consumer debt (Need)	1,873	1,150	Converted half of the credit card debt to cheaper fixed-term loans and switched the card to another bank with a better rate
Entertainment (Want)	150	100	Canceled underutilized subscriptions
Giving (Want)	233	233	
Total Expense Before Savings	4,833	4,665	
Savings	(700)	382	Now able to save $382
Total Income	4,133	5,047	

TABLE 7.3: BUDGET ALLOCATIONS FOR THE GOLDSONS

Allocations	Before: Actual Spending	After: Budgeted Spending	% Change
Needs	4,450 (108%)	4,332 (86%)	–22%
Wants	383 (9%)	333 (7%)	–2%
Savings	–700 (–17%)	382 (7%)	+24%
Total Income	4,133 (100%)	5,047 (100%)	+22%

Secrets to the Goldsons' Success

They need to be congratulated for turning their financial health status around up to this point. This was a piece of work by the Goldsons—look again at table 7.2 to see what they did and how you could emulate some of these actions in turning around your financial situation! In addition to reducing their needs and wants, pay special attention to the fact that they increased their income dramatically, which was a major contributing factor to their success. They increased income by 22 percent. While there is only so much you can do to adjust your expenses, especially if you are already living on skin and bones, finding additional sources of income is likely going to be a part of your turnaround plan. Now may be a good time to look back at the discussion under the TTCI section that gives ideas for increasing your income.

What should I now do with my savings?

With their savings in hand, the Goldsons can now continue their journey along the road to financial freedom. They can now pursue goals (with different time horizons) around building an emergency fund (rainy day money), attacking their mountain of debt, starting contributions toward a retirement account, giving more, paying off their mortgage early, building a college fund for their children or grandchildren, and investing surplus funds to build their net worth. That list of what they can now do is the power of savings! You must learn to save money to "bruk out a brukness" (stop being broke).

At this point, however, the Goldsons still have a lot of work to do to complete their turnaround. So, what should their next immediate move be with their newfound monthly savings of $382? There are different schools of thought on what they should do given their situation. Remember, they have a mountain of debt (62 percent debt-to-income ratio), and they don't have any emergency fund. What should they do next? You will have to wait until chapter 8 on building your rainy day fund to hear my views. ("Bruce, you are so cruel," you must be saying right now.)

Monitor Your Spending

Earlier, I spoke about the importance of exhibiting the right behaviors in order to stick within the budget limits you have established. To assist in ensuring that that trajectory happens, you and the Goldsons must have a system or method of keeping track of what you are spending each month, which is what I will address in this section.

There are several ways to do this:

1. For the more traditional and perhaps more elderly persons who are not comfortable with technology, simply keep all your bills and receipts and put them in separate bundles, or files, by expense category.

2. If you live in a country where online banking is not available, go through your debit and credit card statements each month to see where your money is going.

3. Access your online banking platform (where you have it) to keep track of your spending. I actually review my accounts at least once per week.

4. Link a budgeting app (e.g., Mint) to your bank accounts, if possible, which allows real-time tracking of your expenses by category.

5. You can also use the method that I learned from Professor Michael S. Gutter, who teaches personal and family financial planning at the University of Florida in which you can work with a letter-size or A4 sheet of paper that you fold in half, then quarter until it has many squares. Each time you spend, write down the nature of the

item and the amount on a square. Carry this piece of paper with you throughout the week. It is a bit old fashioned, but older persons who are not really into apps and gadgets may find this simple and practical. Just don't lose the paper!

6. There is also the envelope system where you put cash in envelopes and label each envelope with the nature of the expense that it is supposed to cover. Limit the amount of cash you put in each envelop after receiving each month's paycheck to reduce the risk of being robbed. So, if you have $350 in an envelope that is labeled *grocery*, once that's finished, you know you spent $350 on groceries. Plus, it also helps you not to overspend, as it is actual cash, and there would simply not be any more cash to spend, unlike, say, if you were using a credit card. It may be difficult, however, to get a steady supply of cash, and the risks associated with walking with large amounts of cash has heightened in today's world. Again, if you can work with this system, then all power to you.

7. I also recommend weekly family meetings to discuss actual spending against budget. I especially recommend that practice for couples. We discuss money at our house after Sunday dinner. Somebody is responsible for tracking the actual spending, doing the budget, and having the information ready. You must figure out who is best suited for this task.

Adopt one or more of those methods of monitoring your actual spending against your established limits for your needs, wants, and savings, and you would be well on your way of taking control of where your money goes.

How much do I need to save for a specific goal?

In closing this chapter on budgeting, I show how to calculate how much you need to save each month in order to get to a specific financial goal or target.

It is important to note that if you're serious about saving and investing, then you must also understand how to use an investment calculator to help determine how much money you will need to save to achieve specific goals or targets. Many people, however, don't know how to calculate this amount, but the table below illustrates it.

Let's say I have a goal to save $6,000 toward a deposit on a car in three years' time, and I plan to put the amount being saved each month into an investment that yields 4 percent per year. How much do I need to set aside each month to get to $6,000?

TABLE 7.4: CALCULATING HOW TO ATTAIN YOUR SAVINGS GOAL

Scenario	Goal: Save $6K to deposit on a car
Return	4%
Timeline	3 years
Monthly savings required to reach the $6K target?	$156.62

The fastest way to get this figure is to use a financial calculator, like the one at Calculator.net. Go to the investment calculator section, and fill in the required amounts (i.e., the interest rate (4 percent), the target amount you want to accumulate ($6,000), and so on). The figure you want is the additional contribution amount, which is the equivalent of the monthly amount you need to save to hit your target. Once you have input all the variables, hit the Calculate button, and it will give the monthly figure you need to save each month to get to your goal of $6,000. The figure that you will need to save, based on my illustration above (table 7.4), is $156.62 per month. You must then ensure that there is room in your budget to accommodate this amount each month. Practice using such calculators. If you are still uncertain about how to do these calculations, watch an online video until you are comfortable using the calculator.

Hitting Your Financial Goals

If you have goals that you want to achieve in the short term, say within a year, then you should stay away from putting your savings in risky investments that are likely to go down by the time you need your funds. So, if you have six months to accumulate the closing costs for your house, it may not be wise for you to put the amount you're setting aside each month into a high-risk investment, such as the stock market, because the value of your money could fall by the time you need it in six months. Instead, it's better to place these funds in a high-yield savings account or a low-risk money market account. More on these types of options to come in chapter 11 that deals with investing.

For longer-term goals such as savings for college funds, retirement planning, and those over 10 years or more, you could go for something riskier like shares, in that over time, the volatility of the investment will likely smooth out.

We have come to the end of one of the longest chapters in this book, and perhaps the most important. The key message is that you must live on a budget as doing so will give you control over your money and help you to save. Living on a budget means allocating your income into your needs, wants, and savings. This allocation should be ruthless in ensuring that you have at least 10 percent of your income going toward savings. Some people argue that you should take out the amount you want to save first and then force yourself to live on the rest. The budget process is not only about reducing expenses but also about how you behave with money and also about how you go about increasing income either by asking for a raise, getting a better job, or working multiple jobs, including side hustles or starting a business.

It should now be crystal clear that you must learn to save money if you want to move further along the road to financial freedom.

In our illustration, the Goldsons were able to find some money to save after applying the principles I have taught in this chapter up to this point. We will now continue with the next steps for the Goldsons—what they should be doing with their newfound savings.

Your Money Journal Assignment: Budget to Save Like an Ant

WORKING ADULTS: 18 YEARS & OLDER

Classify your monthly expenses in the following manner:

Monthly Expenses (see tables 7.2 and 7.3 above for illustrations)

1. Living expenses; food, transport (car, taxis, bus), utilities, housing: **Need**

2. Insurance: life, health, disability, property: **Need**

3. Consumer debt repayment: credit card, personal loan, line of credit: **Need**

4. Entertainment: dining, subscriptions, golfing, vacation: **Want**

5. Giving: church, neighbors, charities, friends: **Want**

6. Savings: **Savings**

REQUIREMENTS

1. From the classifications above, quickly compute the percentage of your after-tax income that goes to needs, wants, and savings

2. Is the percentage (amount) you are able to save enough to get you to your financial goals? If not, see items 3 and 4 below.

3. Think of ways you can reduce your needs and wants (chop/trim).

4. Think of ways to increase your income.

5. Adjust your needs, wants, and savings after putting in the potential impact of items 3 and 4 (see tables 7.2 and 7.3 above).

FULL-TIME STUDENTS: 14–24 YEARS

- Is there something you would like to buy yourself, maybe a hot new smartphone or a laptop?

- To generate the savings to buy this item, look at what you have been doing with your lunch money and other moneys received (e.g., gifts from your grandparents and so on) over the last year.

- Examine which expenses you can chop or trim to save money. Determine if those expenses are needs or wants.

- Examine how you can earn some extra dollars. For example, could you walk your neighbor's dog each weekend?

chapter 8

STEP 5: BUILD YOUR RAINY DAY FUND— IT'S ONLY A MATTER OF TIME BEFORE IT RAINS

Emergency Fund Fundamentals

An emergency fund functions like an umbrella on a rainy day. If I were to put down a formal definition, I would describe it as funds set aside for unexpected expenses, which if you don't have in place could land you in debt. The idea, therefore, is that if you were to suddenly lose your job, have a big car-repair bill, or need to pay an unexpected medical expense, then your emergency fund would be used to deal with such eventualities. The general best practice is that you should strive to accumulate emergency funding to cover your expenses for three to six months. Why three to six months? One reason is that's the average time it takes for most people to find a new job in the event that they lose their current job.[74] This emergency money would be in place to deal with monthly expenses while a new job is being sought.

---

74   "How Long Does It Take to Find a Job?," Indeed, May 19, 2022, https://www.indeed.com/career-advice/finding-a-job/how-long-does-it-take-to-find-a-job.

Build an Emergency Fund First or Attack Debt Immediately?

In our scenario, the Goldsons now have savings in hand of $382 per month. But they don't have any emergency funds, and they have a mountain of expensive debt.

Should they attack the debt first, or should they build the emergency fund, which will earn little or no interest, or should they build the emergency fund and attack the debt at the same time?

There are varying schools of thoughts on what they could do first or next. However, I believe they should build a small emergency fund of one month's worth of expenses as their next move. Their revised monthly budgeted spend is $4,665 per month (and there is the assumption that they will stick to this budget), so that's how much they should target to save to build up a one-month fund. Given that they are now able to save $382 per month, it would take them approximately 12 months ($4,665 / $382) to build up their small emergency fund. Also, note that I suggest that they should be paying the minimum monthly amounts on all loans, each month, in order to keep them current while they are building their emergency fund.

Once they have this one-month fund in place, they could use the monthly savings of $382 to pay more than the minimum monthly amounts on their debts. When they have paid off their debts, at least the high-cost ones (credit cards and lines of credits), they can then build a more robust emergency fund at the recommended minimum of three months. More on managing debt in the next chapter.

Why am I suggesting a one-month emergency fund and not two months or another number? I believe a one-month fund should be enough to deal with most emergencies that would fall below their highest insurance deductible amount for the different types of insurance that they have. Deductibles represent the amount of money you need to pay before your insurance company is obligated to reimburse you for a loss. If you are claiming $1,333 from your property insurance company for property damage, and the deductible is $533, you will need to come up with the

$533 (40 percent deductible in this case), all other things remaining equal, and the insurance company will pay the $800. It is your emergency fund money that will give you that $533. If you did the math, and you found that it will take up to the equivalent of two months' expenses to pay your highest deductible (compare the deductible for all your insurance policies), then you can build a two-month emergency fund.

So why would they need to build a one-month emergency fund (or some level) before they start to mercilessly attack their mountain of debts? The advice is to prevent the Goldsons from going further into debt. Let's say that they had a $1,200 car problem while they were attacking their debts. They would simply take the $1,200 from their $4,665 emergency fund and would continue with their debt repayment strategy uninterrupted. If they hadn't spent the time to build the $4,665 emergency fund, and they had the $1,200 emergency need, they would have to stop their debt repayment and end up borrowing, more likely than not from their credit card to deal with the emergency. Reverting to using a credit card to cover expenses for which they don't have the cash to cover could be a huge psychological blow to the Goldsons. They are trying to get out of debt, and then suddenly they are racking up high-cost debt again due to an emergency. That situation could cause them to lose the drive to get out of debt. Money management is not just about the numbers; it is also about feelings, behavior, and psychology. Get the behavior right, and you will get the numbers right.

So far I have argued very strongly that you need an emergency fund before you start to aggressively attack your expensive debts. Whether you build a one-month, two-month, or whatever-number-of-months plan, this is really going to be up to the individual as there is no real hard-and-fast rule that says how much your emergency fund should have while you still have expensive debt. The key thing, though, is that you should have some kind of starter fund!

Another relevant question is "Bruce, what if I have the one-month emergency fund of $4,665, and then an emergency costing $12,000 happens? What do I do then?"

My answer is at least you have some of the money in cash. You would have been worse off without the fund. The question of finding the difference of $7,335, over and above the $4,665, still remains. An emergency need of that size is likely to be covered by one of your insurance policies—medical, house, or car. If that is the case, then your insurance company should pick up the difference. Remember, I insisted earlier that in building your budget, your needs must include insurance premiums for the various types of insurance that you should have. Having such insurance is exactly one of the reasons why these insurance premiums are so important.

Let's say for whatever reason, you did have an emergency that cost more than your small emergency fund and the balance was not covered by insurance. What should you do? I will answer by telling you a story.

I was coaching a couple who had a mountain of debt, and I shared with them that based on their situation they should consider keeping at least one of their credit cards (they had a number of credit cards) unavailable so that it is hard to access. If there were an emergency that exceeded their relatively small emergency fund, then they could use that credit card to cover the difference. They did not have strong insurance coverage. Let's keep it real, everyone. If a close or immediate family member needed a medical procedure to save their life, and you needed to fund the difference with your credit card, would you not do it? Yes, you would. But you must be disciplined in not using that card unless the expense falls into the category of a real emergency for which you don't have insurance coverage and your current emergency fund is not able to absorb it.

If you don't have a mountain of debt—you have paid off your high-cost debts, and your other low-cost debts (e.g., mortgage) are up-to-date and are under control—then you could go for it and develop at least a three-month emergency fund, which is what most personal finance experts view as the minimum.

When your debt is under control, you should now be thinking about whether you should have a three-, six- or 12-month emergency fund. The one you go for will depend on your life circumstances. For example, if only one family member works, it makes more sense to go for at least a six- to 12-month emergency fund because if the sole working member were to lose their job, then having a bigger fund would give them more time to find another job.

If your income is not predictable, and you are paid a commission, as with sales agents, then it would be smart to have at least a six-month emergency fund as there could be months where no sales come through, and you have to live off the savings.

The COVID-19 pandemic has taught us that maybe the ideal minimum for an emergency fund is 12–18 months. Many people who lost their jobs at the start of the pandemic still hadn't found a new job after 12 months. If you believe that COVID-like disruptions will become more prevalent in the future, you should consider at least a 12-month emergency fund.

Where should I keep my emergency fund?

Money you need on very short notice must be easily accessible. Consequently, this money should be placed in an easy-to-access savings account (yes, it pains me to say that because the interest rates are very low) or in a money market account from which, ideally you can obtain your money on the day you need it. For those who live in places like Jamaica, it may be good to convert at least 50 percent of this money into a "hard" currency like the U.S. dollar to hedge against adverse exchange rate movements, which erode the purchasing power of your money.

Put differently, do not put your emergency fund money in high-risk investments that can fluctuate in value or that might be hard to access when you need the money. Remember the stock market is typically volatile, so be aware that when you need your funds the market may be down. During the early to middle part of June 2020, the global and regional stock markets dipped due to COVID-19 uncertainties.[75]

This chapter dealt with the importance of building an emergency fund

75   Fred Imbert and Thomas Franck, "Dow Drops More than 700 Points in Worst Day Since June 11 as Virus Resurgence Concerns Grow," CNBC, June 23, 2020, https://www.cnbc.com/2020/06/23/stock-market-futures-open-to-close-news.html.

once you can save money each month. You need at least a small or starter emergency fund even if you have a mountain of expensive debt. A small amount will at least give you a cushion in the event of a small emergency while you continue repaying expensive debt, and it will prevent you from going deeper into debt. Once you have cleared your high-cost debt, build a robust emergency fund that covers at least three to 12 months of your expenses. The size of your fund will depend upon your life circumstances. Be careful where you put your emergency fund as you will need to be able to access it quickly and on short notice.

Your Money Journal Assignment: Building My Rainy Day Fund

Working Sdults: 18 Years & Older

- Quickly calculate how much three months of a rainy day fund would be for your family.

- Remember to multiply your monthly expenses by three.

- If you don't have such a fund in place, look at your budget and push to see how much you can save each month to go toward a three-month fund.

- Calculate how long it would take to build the three-month fund based on the amount you are able to save each month.

- Please note that you can run the numbers above for any number of months.

Full-Time Students: 14–24 Years

- How did your family manage during the COVID-19 pandemic or a recent family emergency?

- Did you have any money saved up that could have helped the family pay for food, utilities, or for a tablet or laptop for online classes?

- Having read this chapter and the one on budgeting to save, make it one of your goals to build an emergency fund over the next 12 months by saving money out of your lunch money and other allowances.

- A reasonable target for you as a high school or college student would be aiming to always have available between $300 and $700. (This could be far less depending on the country in which you live.) The amount of your rainy day fund should be enough to take care of practical things like replacing the screen of your smartphone or computer.

chapter 9

STEP 6: MANAGE DEBT—USE IT WISELY

The Book of Proverbs teaches that "the borrower is servant to the lend-er" (22:7, KJV). Unlike some people, I don't interpret this to mean that you should never, ever borrow money. The words are a caution but also a statement of fact. When you borrow, you should be prepared to subject yourself to the rules, terms, and conditions of the lender. Debt comes with mandatory obligations. You are required to repay your loan, and you are required to notify your mortgage company if you want to expand your home. Your sense of freedom diminishes when you borrow.

The Bank of Jamaica, in its *Financial Stability Report* in 2019, reported that 61.3 percent of household income in Jamaica goes toward debt payment, which is also known as the debt-to-income ratio discussed in chapter 4. This figure climbed to 71.5 percent in 2020, which represents a 10.2 percent increase over 2019 and confirms that Jamaican households were in more debt in 2020 than 2019.[76]

---

76   "Consolidate High Interest Loans to Reduce Debt in 2022," JN Bank, January 28, 2022, https://www.jnbank.com/consolidate-high-interest-loans-to-reduce-debt-in-2022/.

The typical American household carried an average debt of $145,000 in 2021, while the median debt was only $50,971 in 2000, representing an increase of 184 percent. Median household income was $79,900 in 2021, up from 35,000 in 2000,[77] representing an increase of 128 percent. These numbers show that American households are in more debt than they were 21 years ago and that household debt grew at a faster rate than household income.

Given the high debt burden on Americans and Jamaicans as suggested by these statistics, this chapter seeks to help you understand the steps you can take to reduce the debt burden in your household and how you can use debt wisely to acquire major items. For example, I will show how to use debt to buy a car or a house while minimizing the cost of the debt (interest).

Before we talk about these steps, let's reconfirm exactly what we mean by the word *debt*.

Debt Defined

What is debt? Its meaning may be obvious to the more schooled among us. The general definition of debt is, simply, money that you owe to a lender (an institution or a friend), which has a price (generally known as interest) that you pay to get the money.

My definition of debt is borrowing money today to do what your savings could do tomorrow, if you were willing and able to wait. Yes, wait. I spoke earlier about the culture of instant gratification and the culture of keeping up with the Joneses. Too many people want what they want right now!

There are two basic types of debt: secured debt and unsecured debt.

1. Secured Debt

Secured debt is when the lender demands something of value (that represents the amount of the loan) from you in case you don't pay back the loan. Popular forms of secured debts include the following:

- Mortgage debt: The house is used as security—the lender has the

---

77   "Demographics of Debt," Debt, last modified February 23, 2022, https://www.debt.org/faqs/americans-in-debt/demographics/.

right to sell the house and collect their outstanding debt if you can't pay back the loan.

- Car loans: They're similar to a mortgage in that the car is used as the security.

- Home equity loans: You use the excess of the market value of your home over and above the outstanding loan as security to borrow money.[78]

- Personal loans: They generally can be used to do anything the borrower decides e.g., to cover home repairs and debt consolidation. Loan disbursement is usually done within a few days.[79]

Typically, the repayment by the borrower is over a set period with a fixed amount paid each month until the loan is fully repaid. The interest rate on these loans is lower than that for unsecured loans because there is less risk that the lender will lose all their money if the borrower can't repay. (The lender could sell the security to recover the outstanding debt.)

2. Unsecured Debt

Unsecured debt is created when a loan is granted without the lender getting anything of value if the borrower is unable to repay.[80] In addition, sometimes the repayment amount is not fixed. Examples of that type of debt include personal loans, student loans obtained from government institutions, credit cards, and lines of credits. The last two are very similar in that they allow you to purchase goods and services within a set limit in which you can borrow. Each time you repay a portion of the debt, the limit resets. So, if you have a line of credit or credit card with a limit of $6,000, and you used up $2,500, you then only have $3,500 to use. Once you repay the $2,500, then the amount available for borrowing again resets to $6,000. The credit card is given that name because you literally get a

---

78   Christina Majaski, "Unsecured vs. Secured Debts: What's the Difference?," Investopedia, last modified February 17, 2021, https://www.investopedia.com/ask/answers/110614/what-difference-between-secured-and-unsecured-debts.asp.

79   Ben Luthi, "What is a Personal Loan", Experian, May 4, 2020, https://www.experian.com/blogs/ask-experian/what-is-a-personal-loan/

80   Majaski, "Unsecured vs. Secured Debts."

plastic card that you "swipe" or give to a merchant when buying goods and services. The interest rates tend to be much higher for unsecured loans than for secured loans as there is no security given to the lender if you default on the debt.

Types of Lenders
Traditional

The large commercial banks, investment houses, building societies, credit unions, and government-type bodies such as the National Housing Trust (NHT) in Jamaica[81] are traditional lenders of money. Banks, investment houses, and building societies offer both secured and unsecured loans, as do the credit unions. Bodies such as the NHT and building societies specialize in lending money for home purchases.

Micro Finance Institutions (MFIs)

MFIs extend two types of loans: 1) personal loans to individuals to cover emergencies such as car repairs and medical bills; and 2) business loans to purchase items such as inventory. Borrowers who choose MFIs are often those who find it difficult to qualify for loans from traditional financial institutions.[82] Many fail to qualify due to no or poor credit history and low income levels that don't meet the lending criteria of traditional lenders. MFIs therefore play an invaluable role in providing access to credit to millions of such underserved individuals, especially in developing countries.[83]

Generally, the interest rates offered by MFIs tend to be higher than those offered by traditional lenders[84] given the higher risk profile of their borrowers. MFIs also lend much smaller sums than traditional lenders, and they offer both secured and unsecured loans.

---

81   "Loans," National Housing Trust, accessed June 11, 2022, https://www.nht.gov.jm/loans.

82   Gordon Scott, "5 Biggest Microfinance Companies", Investopedia, December 29, 2001, https://www.investopedia.com/articles/insurance/090116/5-biggest-microfinance-companies-bbrijk.asp

83   Ibid.

84   Ibid

Borrowers must however be aware of predatory lending practices (use of unfair, deceptive, or abusive loan terms, aggressive sales tactics, and high loan fees)[85] of some MFIs, as well as some traditional lenders. Legislation such as the Consumer Credit Protection Act of 1968 (CCPA) and the Fair Debt Collection Act (FDCPA) in the US[86] and the Microcredit Act 2021[87] which was passed in January 2021 in Jamaica seek to protect borrowers from such practices.

Go to the websites of the regulators of financial institutions in your country to find the list of licensed MFIs and traditional lenders you may wish to consider.

Family and Friends

A class of lenders often overlooked includes family and friends who help when there is a medical or other type of emergency, someone starting a business, or a friend needing a loan to purchase a car or house. Generally, no interest is charged on these loans. Be very careful how you borrow from friends and family members, however. Some experts argue that it is better for friends or family members to give rather than lend money, if they can afford to. Why? Because when a loan is not repaid, it will put a strain on the relationship. Avoid borrowing from family and friends, then, if you can. Often, family and friends are forgotten or not even given updates on the status of their loans. The borrower's attitude is that "my friend or family member will understand." Never put your relationship at risk in this way. Keep in touch and develop a plan to pay back. People over money, always, please!

Guarantor

Many lenders often request that the borrower get other persons, known as guarantors, to agree that if the borrower can't pay, the lender can go after the guarantor. In other words, it is a kind of security arrangement

---

85   Adam Hayes, "Predatory Lending", Investopedia.com, July 3, 2022, https://www.investopedia.com/terms/p/predatory_lending.asp

86   Adam Hayes, "Consumer Credit Protection Act of 1968 (CCPA), Investopedia.com, June 30, 2022, https://www.investopedia.com/terms/c/consumer-credit-protection-act-of-1968.asp

87   Candice Stewart, "Microfinancing Institutions Urged To Prepare For Microcredit Act", Jamaica Information Service, https://jis.gov.jm/features/microfinancing-institutions-urged-to-prepare-for-microcredit-act/

that the lender has in place to get back their money if the borrower can't repay. "Nuh guarantee no loan fi nobaddy, unless yuh can afford it." (Don't guarantee a loan for anyone unless you can afford to pay it.)

Becoming a guarantor sounds like a noble thing, and you can feel as if you are doing an honorable act to help a friend get money for an education, a car, or some other expense. Remember, though, that if this person can't repay, then you as the guarantor will have to pay. There have been so many horror stories on guarantorship. Take Paul, for example, who signed as guarantor for his sister on a car loan. Two years later, his sister got married and moved to a different part of the country. Paul didn't even remember the loan. His sister ended up divorcing, and the settlement was expensive for her, so she stopped paying the car loan. You can guess what happened! The bank went after Paul who, at that time, was newly married and was just about to apply for a mortgage. He did not qualify for his mortgage loan because the debt obligations of the guaranteed loan for his sister pushed his debt-to-income ratio above the minimum that the bank offered. How did Paul feel? I don't have to answer that.

Is there ever a case where you should become a guarantor? I will leave you to answer that as it is a very personal matter. My view is to avoid guarantorship. If you feel that you want to be a guarantor, just make sure you work out whether you can afford to pay the monthly payments if the person can't repay. If the answer is yes, and it's someone you feel obligated to help or want to help, then you can consider going for it. If you can't afford to repay if they can't, then you can suggest to the person to either wait until they have cash to buy whatever it is that is wanted, use another lending entity that may have different security requirements, or some other advice. Again, it's your choice. I have outlined the dangers.

Debt carries risk, so be very careful.

I started the chapter by saying once you enter into debt, you will be in a kind of bondage. That statement, however, does not mean you should never borrow money. It means you must approach borrowing wisely.

If you can afford to wait and do everything debt-free, that choice is even better, but that alternative is not always possible as it would take too long for most people to save the money for purchases such as a house or car.

Here are three reasons why you should carefully manage your exposure to debt.

1. Economic downturn: If you lose your job, through no fault of yours, and you have, say, 30 percent or 50 percent of your income-going toward debt repayment, you would be at risk of falling behind with your debt payments and eventually losing the house or car on which you owed money. During the COVID-19 crisis, that reality happened to a lot of people who lost their jobs because their companies started doing badly. People who had little or no debt were able to manage better.

2. You could get sick or injured: The implications of being sick or injured are similar to an economic downturn. If you have disability income insurance, it will protect lost income, but in most cases, will not offer 100 percent protection.

3. Company reorganization: This situation is similar to the first item but involves losing your job due to the restructuring or downsizing of a company. The impact is the same: You are out of a job and stuck with your debt repayments.

Dealing with Large Purchases

I will now examine some good practices that you should consider when buying two of the most important high-cost items you are likely to acquire in your life and for which most persons are very likely going to use debt.

Buying a Car with Debt

In Jamaica, the Caribbean, and the world today, it is relatively easy to get a car loan. In many cases, you can get up to 100 percent financing for a car and up to 10 years to repay in Jamaica at interest rates of up to 8.95

percent.[88] With this combination you can access a loan with relatively low monthly repayments. The calculations will be demonstrated further.

Buying a car? Is it a brand-new car or a used car?

A new car will generally lose approximately 60 percent of its value in the first five years (12 percent per year).[89] Therefore, a new car bought for $41,000 generally loses $4,920 each year. The table below shows, in more detail, the financial implications of buying a new car versus a used car in with a loan.

TABLE 9.1: FINANCING A NEW CAR VERSUS A USED CAR

Loan Details	New Car: Model TX	Used Car (5 Years Old): Model TX	Comments
Loan amount	$41,000[90]	$16,400	
Age of car		5 years	
Loan period	5 years	5 years	
Interest rate[91]	9%	9%	
Monthly payment	$851	$340	$511 per month less for the used car

The table above shows that the same model car that is five years older is about 60 percent cheaper ($16,400) than the new model ($41,000), which means you would borrow less to purchase this used car. From the calculations above, you will see that the used car requires $340 per month versus $851 per month for the new car, saving $511 per month. Other financial realities to consider are a new car will cost you more upfront but is gener-

---

88   "Car Loans," Compare Jamaica, accessed June 10, 2022, https://comparejamaica.com/carloans.

89   Nicole Arata, "Managing the Hidden Costs of Car Depreciation," NerdWallet, July 17, 2017, https://www.nerdwallet.com/article/insurance/car-depreciation.

90   Adam Shapiro, "Average New Car Price Hits Record $41,000," Yahoo! Finance, July 28, 2021, https://finance.yahoo.com/news/average-new-car-price-hits-record-41000-130015214.html.

91   Rebecca Betterton, "Best Auto Loan Rates in June 2022," Bankrate, last modified June 15, 2022, https://www.bankrate.com/loans/auto-loans/rates/.

ally going to cost you less in terms of repairs in the early years, while a used car will cost you less upfront but is generally likely to incur higher ongoing maintenance[92]. You would therefore need to factor those costs along with the monthly car payments before you make a final decision on whether you buy a new or a used car[93].

There are some people who buy a brand-new car every four to five years as a way of ensuring that they are enjoying the latest features and gadgets in these cars, especially their favorite cars. That practice means they will always be giving up the potential savings in monthly car payments that I referred to above ($511 per month) over many years – all other things remaining constant. These individuals would however be enjoying the latest car features, lower maintenance in the early years and the prestige of driving their new cars.

Financial freedom is about being financially aware and being deliberate in our actions. Therefore, if you buy a new or used car just be aware of the financial and non financial implications articulated earlier. Remember my red Fiat Uno story where I drove this relatively ordinary car instead of a new fancy car because I was focusing on buying an apartment? That kind of sacrifice is what is required to get you to the land of financial freedom! Later, I went on to buy a brand-new luxury car when I was at a different stage of my financial journey -those were personal choices I made, and you must decide what's the best course of action for you.

Buying a house? Do you opt for a short or long repayment period?

Owning a home is the dream of just about everyone, regardless of where you are in the world. The average person will use a mortgage to help to complete the process. Again, just as with buying a car, there are some important things to think about to ensure that you buy the house in the most cost-effective way.

I believe the ideal mortgage loan period should be as short as possible but not too short to the point where you can't find the cash to make the

---

92   Lisa Smith, "Should I Buy a New or Used Car", Investopedia, 29 September, 2021, https://www.investopedia.com/articles/pf/07/neworusedcar.asp

93   Ibid

monthly payments. Recall that the longer you take to repay a loan, the smaller the monthly payments will be, and the opposite is true as well. A smaller monthly payment over a longer loan period will make the house appear to be more affordable. Before you sign the mortgage deed, stop and think about how much more interest you will pay over a longer loan period. It can be a staggering amount! You will pay more for the house with a smaller loan payment as you will be paying more interest!

The table below assumes a borrower in the U.S. got the loan, and the total interest paid for a 30-year loan is $211,296, versus $97,443 for a 15-year loan—that is a saving of $113,853, which you could use to bolster your retirement account or your children's college fund. How does that sound to you? Sounds like music to my ears!

"Is it that simple, Bruce? Can I just take a shorter loan period and save all of this money?"

Good question. Again, you will need to sacrifice to pay back the loan over 15 years. The shorter period will put the monthly payment to $2,175, or $771 more than the 30-year loan. You would have to cut back on some things or increase your income to pay that extra $771. The sacrifice is a kind of investment. You are investing in your house and the return on the investment is threefold:

1. You save thousands in interest: $113,853.

2. You get to enjoy a bigger equity or ownership in the house each year at a very fast rate.

3. You will enjoy the peace of owning your house earlier (15 years), using my example below.

Is it worthwhile to spend less on clothes, to eat out less, and to stop buying everyone expensive gifts at Christmas so you can find the extra monthly payment? I believe that it is worth the sacrifice for those three astounding reasons.

TABLE 9.2: 15-YEAR VERSUS 30-YEAR MORTGAGE IN THE U.S.

Loan Details	30-Year	15-Year	Comments
Loan amount	$294,000	$294,000	
Loan period	30 years	15 years	
Interest rate[94]	4%	4%	
Interest paid over the life of the mortgage	$211,296	$97,443	A savings of $113,853 is achieved on the 15-year mortgage
Monthly payment	$1,404	$2,175	An additional $771 is paid on the 15-year mortgage per month

Getting My Starter House

"Can I start with a thirty-year mortgage and then switch it to a shorter period later on?"

Yes, this is possible. I fully accept and understand that some persons will only be able to afford a mortgage by starting at the lower monthly payments over a longer period of time. For example, when I was teaching a course on financial freedom to some teachers, one of them raised a real issue.

She related that she had been renting a place and had become so exhausted and tired of the disrespectful treatment that was being dished out by the landlord to her and her family. She said, "Bruce, I had to leave that place." She pushed to get a 30-year loan (with the relatively smaller monthly payments) just to be able to afford a place of her own, and she moved out with lightning speed!

I fully understand. When I bought my first apartment in my 20s, I chose a long mortgage period (25 years) and therefore a smaller monthly payment, as that was the only way I was able to afford the apartment at that time of my life. I have been there—I fully understand! I'm just saying be aware of the implications of borrowing for longer periods.

---

94 Jeff Ostrowski, "Compare Current Mortgage Rates Today," Bankrate, last modified 25 June 2022, https://www.bankrate.com/mortgages/mortgage-rates.

Later in this chapter, I discuss whether it is really always better to use your extra cash to pay off your mortgage early (i.e., going for shorter repayment periods) or if you should invest it (i.e., the extra cash) elsewhere and try and earn a better return than the interest on your mortgage. In conclusion, there is no prescribed law with what you do with your extra cash—it is a matter of personal preferences and your tolerance for risk!

Are you really ready to buy a house?

Ideally, before you buy your house, you should have your emergency fund in place, proper health insurance, and of course, your closing costs and deposit. But don't forget to shop around for the best interest rate. I want to focus on having the emergency fund in place. If you earn $3,500 per month ($42,000 per year), then you should aim to have $10,500 in your emergency fund as a minimum (three months). The emergency fund would be in addition to your closing costs and deposit. In other words, if you want to buy a house for $300,000 with closing costs of $18,000 (6 percent) and a deposit of $30,000 (10 percent), then you should have $48,000 available. So, ideally, you need to have $58,500 ($48,500 plus $10,500) on hand before you start talking about buying a house. It is hard for a lot of people to accumulate that amount or meet these criteria before they buy a house, especially for young college graduates who are trying to clear large student loans and trying to meet basic expenses.

"Are you saying that unless I have $58,500 and proper health insurance, I should not buy the house? Suppose I only have the $48,000 but no emergency fund and no health insurance."

Ideally, that's what I am saying—perhaps you're not ready to buy that house. But it is a decision that you will have to make in the end. I am saying that you should be aware of the risks involved in buying a house without having the emergency fund and proper health insurance in place. If you have a major health crisis after buying the house, a major emergency with termites in the house, or major plumbing or roofing issues, then you could be forced to spend what should be your monthly mortgage payments to deal with the health crisis or the house emergencies. You are likely, thereafter, to fall behind on your mortgage payments, and before you know it, your house could be taken over by the lending institution. This is real talk!

I was coaching someone who had bought a house but had no emergency fund and no proper health insurance. Shortly after purchasing the house, he had major medical challenges that required expensive surgery. His tight financial situation (no emergency fund or health insurance), now compounded by the medical crisis, caused major stress. The mortgage payments fell into arrears. This house was hanging in the balance, requiring major negotiations with the lender and cries for mercy.

What is the reality on the ground?

I am fully aware that many people struggle to meet all of these requirements—emergency fund, health insurance, house deposit, and closing costs—especially early in their career. Also, it is a cultural norm for people to want to own their homes. Lenders have compelling ads, and some landlords are very difficult. The aforementioned forces have caused many people to go ahead and purchase without meeting all these ideal conditions that I am recommending. When I bought my first apartment, I pushed to get the deposit funds, and I can safely say I had no emergency fund after buying the apartment, but at least health insurance was covered through my office.

The point is to just be aware that if you buy a house without having health insurance and an emergency fund, you are at risk of falling behind with your mortgage if you have a major house-related or other emergency, including a health crisis. Even if you go ahead with the purchase, just have in the back of your mind some idea of how you would manage. Also, you should plan to quickly try to build an emergency fund and address your health insurance situation as soon as possible after the house deal closes.

Should I buy or rent?

Many people struggle with this question. They have the deposit and everything else in place to be able to buy a house or apartment, but they are not sure if they should buy or rent. Generally, I believe you should buy. A portion of your mortgage payment each month will be paying down on the loan balance and will increase your percentage of ownership in the house. The value of the house will generally experience average annual increases in the long run, which will increase your net worth as your ownership share in the house will go up as well. These are powerful incentives to buying rather than renting.

Please be aware that owning a house has related expenses such as property taxes, maintenance, and other costs, so be prepared to deal with these additional expenses before you buy, and factor them into your budget. Notwithstanding such expenses, you should be better off overall buying than renting.

Renting can be a good short-term option until you save the deposit and meet the required conditions to buy a house. One of the good aspects about renting is that you don't have to worry about maintenance, property taxes, and similar expenses. Please speak to your real estate and or financial advisers before making a housing decision.

Some young people can live with their parents to save money in order to build their house deposit at a faster rate. Different views prevail on that subject. Some people believe parents should require their children to pay even a small portion of the household expenses to help them develop a sense of responsibility and an understanding of what it means to be an adult. Becoming accustomed to paying expenses would build a level of independence that will set their children in good stead when they get married or go out on their own. The reality is that in the U.S., a general expectation is that young adults will move out of their parents' home at 18 and therefore start to assume financial responsibilities such as paying rent, owning a car, and so on. Recent statistics, however, have shown that due to the ever-higher cost of living, more young adults (up to 52 percent) are living longer at their parents' homes than did previous generations.[95]

95   Richard Fry, Jeffrey Passel, and D'Vera Cohen, "A Majority of Young Adults in the U.S. Live with Their Parents for the First Time Since the Great Depression," Pew Research Center, September 4, 2020, https://www.pewresearch.org/fact-tank/2020/09/04/a-majority-of-young-adults-in-the-u-s-live-with-their-parents-for-the-first-time-since-the-great-depression/.

Finally, when you do decide to buy a house, it is very likely that you could be approved for a really large mortgage amount toward a much bigger house than you actually need. Avoid this temptation. Don't buy more house than you need, especially if the monthly payment is stretched over a very long period like 30 or 35 years. (I already explained that longer mortgages will cause you to pay more interest.) It may make you feel rich and successful if you have a house that will impress your friends and neighbors, but why spend money on extra space that you will hardly use or need? Why not go for a smaller house with a smaller mortgage that you can pay off more quickly and enjoy the amazing feeling of not having mortgage payments sooner? When you pay off your mortgage, you can take the money you were paying and dump it on some form of investment each month that is aligned with your other goals! Don't fall into the trap of buying more house than you really need.

A Special Word on Credit Cards

Earlier we looked at credit cards under the category of unsecured loans. The Bank of Jamaica indicated in May 2017 that credit card debt in Jamaica was valued at $314 million (JA$40.2 billion). That amount is no small change for a country with a small population of just under three million people with only a relatively small percentage of individuals (11.89 percent in 2021)[96] owning a credit card. A credit card offers many conveniences such as not having to walk with cash and risk losing the cash or being robbed, and some cards offer benefits such as cash back, airline miles, and the ability to earn appliances and other physical goods. There are some dangers, however, that you need to safeguard against if you plan to use a credit card.

First, always pay off your credit card statement balances in full. Failure to pay off the balance in full will mean that you will be charged interest at the high credit card interest rate. (The averages are 40.37 percent in

---

96   "Share of Individuals with Credit Cards in 161 Different Countries and Territories Worldwide up until 2021," Statista, accessed July 31, https://www.statista.com/statistics/675371/ownership-of-credit-cards-globally-by-country/.

Jamaica[97] and 16.3 percent in the U.S.[98]) If you live in the U.S., and you owe $6,000, but you pay less than the $6,000, you will be charged interest at 16.3 percent for the portion of the balance that you didn't pay. If you didn't pay any of the total, you would pay $81.50 of interest computed on the full $6,000 owed for the month! Imagine not paying off the balance in full each month for a one-year period! Such a tragedy would rack up fast into a lot of interest being owed. The interest would also be computed on a compound interest basis, as interest owed from the previous month would become a part of the balance for the following month, which explains part of the reason credit card balances that fall in arrears can rapidly balloon into very large sums being owed.

Second, credit card companies allow you to pay what is called the minimum balance. Don't fall into the trap of paying only the minimum balance. It differs for each financial institution and can range from 1 to 5 percent.[99] So, if your statement balance is $7,000, your minimum payment could be $70 to $350. If you find yourself, for whatever reason, unable to pay the balance in full (which ideally you should be able to, but life happens) then, at the very least, pay the minimum. At least, paying the minimum will avoid late charges and not adversely affect your credit score, which is computed by credit bureaus, if you have them in your country. Just to repeat, credit bureaus are entities that look at all your credit history with lenders and give you a score—your credit rating—as to how cred-it-worthy you are. More on credit reports later in this chapter.

While it is better to pay the minimum than to pay less than the minimum or miss paying the minimum payment altogether, the ideal is for you to manage your spending so that you pay off the card balance in full each month.

Another word on minimum payments. I know a teacher who was quite comfortable paying only the minimum balance as he felt he was honoring

97   Gillyj, "What Is the Credit Card Market Like in Jamaica?," Financial Centsibility, January 1, 2020, https://financialcentsibility.com/credit-cards-in-jamaica.

98   Ivana Pino, "Average Credit Card APR," Bankrate, January 20, 2022, https://www.bankrate.com/finance/credit-cards/average-credit-card-apr/.

99   Adam McCann, "Credit Card Minimum Payments," WalletHub, December 17, 2021, https://wallethub.com/edu/cc/credit-card-minimum-payments/97692.

his credit obligation. Paying the minimum balance is very costly. If the minimum is the amount you pay each month, then you will be paying off that remaining balance for many years—sometimes as much as 30 years,[100] depending on the minimum balance percentage for that particular financial institution and the amount owed. Be aware that most of the minimum balance payment goes toward interest and only a very small portion toward paying off the charges (what you spent)—hence, the reason paying the minimum payments only could cause you to take so many years to pay off the entire balance! Therefore, always try to pay something above the minimum balance, if you find that you can't pay off the credit card balance in full.

There are those who believe that you should never use a credit card. A recent study showed that people tend to spend more on goods and services than they really need to when they use a credit card versus using cash.[101] The argument is that people spend more simply because it is easier to charge items to a card than if they had to pay hard cash. Interestingly, a part of the brain actually feels the pain of separating with cash more than when you pay with the card. The choice is dependent on the individual, as I am careful to spend on only what I need while enjoying the benefits that come with using a credit card. However, each person must understand and know their money personalities and tendencies. Big spenders could switch to using debit cards rather than credit cards.

In fact, I have two credit cards. My reason is because at some point something is going to go wrong with one of the cards. There might be a suspicious transaction that requires the card to be replaced, and you might have to wait for the replacement. The card might expire before you get the new one. Another situation might be that the bank's systems are having technical issues while you are at the front of a line with 50 hungry people

---

100 Latoya Irby, "The Cost of Paying Off Debt with Minimum Payments," The Balance, last modified October 25, 2021, https://www.thebalance.com/how-long-to-pay-off-balance-with-minimum-payments-961120.

101 Drazen Prelec and Sachin Banker, "How Credit Cards Activate the Reward Center of Our Brains and Drive Spending," MIT Management: Sloan School, June 9, 2021, https://mitsloan.mit.edu/experts/how-credit-cards-activate-reward-center-our-brains-and-drive-spending.

waiting to pay, and your card just won't go through! In these cases, a second card is useful. Again, "know thyself[102]," said Socrates. Having two credit cards may be too much for some people. Instead, you can go for two debit cards if you tend to overspend!

Should you be investing while you also have debts?

Earlier, we had to deal with the matter of whether you should build an emergency fund while you are in debt. The idea was tricky because emergency funds earn basically nothing in savings accounts or only a little more in a money market account, but your credit card debt could be exploding at 40.37 percent in Jamaica or 16.3 percent in the U.S. We concluded that it still made sense to establish some kind of emergency fund before really going after paying down high-cost debt.

A similar but different concept exists for investments. Should I invest extra cash that I have that is over and above my emergency-fund needs while I am in debt? The easiest way to answer this question is to use an illustration. Let's say that you live in the U.S., and you owe credit card debt of $10,000 at 16.3 percent interest, and you find yourself with $5,500 in extra cash. (This is over and above what you allocate to your emergency fund.) To even think about investing that extra cash would only be practical if you could earn interest or a return greater than the 16.3 percent that you are paying on the credit card, right? I think you would agree with me. If you were even able to find an investment that you could earn, say, 20 percent per year, should you invest the extra cash in that investment? First, you have to check if the promised return would be taxed because if you have to pay, say, 25 percent tax on it, then your real return is now 15 percent (20 percent less 25 percent), which is less than the 16.3 percent.

You should also note that it will be extremely difficult to find investments that produce average returns of 15–50 percent per year consistently every year in Jamaica or anywhere else in the world. In one year, one of the top-performing unit trusts (a type of investment) in Jamaica grew by 44

---

102   Xenophon, *Memorabilia*, trans. Amy L. Bonnette (Ithaca: Cornell University Press, 1994).

percent[103]—that is ridiculous growth, and it is still below the credit card interest rate of some financial institutions in Jamaica[104]. Note that the unit trust does not perform at this rate every year. In light of all this, it might be prudent to pay down the credit card debt with any extra cash you have rather than trying to invest that cash.

What if you have an unsecured line of credit that costs less than your credit card interest rate but is still relatively expensive and, at the time of writing, ranged from 14 to 24 percent interest per year in Jamaica?[105] In the U.S. it ranges from 5 to 36 percent, depending on your credit score.[106] The same mathematical principles should be applied and checked as was done for the analysis with credit cards. Again, in reality, finding investments that consistently beat 14–24 percent in Jamaica is difficult. In fact, the best-performing long-term investments in Jamaica tend to average 10–15 percent per year (but in exceptional years can go higher). The best-performing mutual funds or even index funds—funds that mirror the performance of a selection or group of stock on a stock exchange—in the U.S. tend to average 8–12 percent per year.

For relatively lower-cost debt, such as the mortgage on your home (which in Jamaica averaged 6.95–8.5 percent in 2022[107]), one could make the mathematical argument that putting the extra cash toward a long-term investment that could yield 12 percent per annum is desirable if your mortgage interest rate is, say, 7 percent per year. The net would be 5 percent (12–7 percent) higher than what you would have saved if you had paid the extra cash toward the principal on your mortgage debt. As stated before,

---

103   "A Top Performing Fund," Barita, accessed 31 July 2022, https://www.barita.com/top-fund/.

104   "Credit Cards," Compare Jamaica, accessed August 23, 2002, https://comparejamaica.com/creditcards.

105   "Personal Loans," Compare Jamaica, accessed June 11, 2022, https://comparejamaica.com/personalloans.

106   Justin Song, "Average Personal Loan Interest Rates," ValuePenguin: The Lending Tree, last modified September 15, 2021, https://www.valuepenguin.com/personal-loans/average-personal-loan-interest-rates.

107   "First-Time Mortgages," Compare Jamaica, accessed June 25, 2002, https://comparejamaica.com/mortgages/calculator/repayments.

you must check if taxes and other deductions will need to come out of the 12 percent return to see the real rate of return and how it would compare to the mortgage rate of 7 percent.

For some people, they would rather have the peace and contentment of putting that extra cash toward paying off their primary residence early even if they could make more money investing the extra cash somewhere else. Yes, there is a special feeling that comes when you don't have a mortgage on your primary residence. Some people are terrified of the thought of losing their jobs and still having a mortgage. They get peace from not having a mortgage on their home. If you fall in that group, then you should pay off your home mortgage debt as well as high-cost debt before you start to invest.

Note that in addition to the feeling of security, the full capital appreciation in the house would be an additional benefit to you much sooner, as you would have paid off the loan on the house in a much shorter time frame. The answer to the question then, about whether or not you should invest extra cash while you are in debt, is a function of your ability to get a net investment return (after transaction costs and taxes) that is higher than the interest you are paying on your existing debt. The answer is also dependent on your risk appetite and how much you value nonfinancial benefits of carrying little or no debt (e.g., peace of mind) in comparison to the prospect of making a net investment return while carrying debt.

There you have it—and I could have said more. Buying large items such as a house or a car requires careful thought. You must consider all the aforementioned factors before spending your hard-earned money on large purchases.

I am drowning in a sea of debt. Is there hope for me?

If you are in a sea of debt, what can you do to get out?

You would be considered to be in a sea of debt if your debt-to-income ratio is much higher than the acceptable DTI in your country. Therefore, if you live in the U.S. like the Goldsons and have a DTI of 62 percent, which is much more than the acceptable 43 percent, then you would be in a sea of debt!

There are basically two ways to be rescued from a sea of debt.

Debt Consolidation

This act finds one lender to take over the debts that you owe to multiple lenders, with the outcome being that what you pay the single lender is smaller than the total of what you were paying to all your current lenders. After all, what would be the point of going through all that consolidation if you are no better off in the end?

The monthly payment to the single lender will be smaller for two basic reasons: (1) the interest rate of the single lender is expected to be lower than the average rates offered by the multiple lenders, and (2) you may be able to stretch the repayment period to the single lender over a relatively long period of time to help to reduce the monthly payment. In this case, stretching the monthly period to help establish a smaller monthly payment is a survival technique to give the borrower some breathing space in terms of the monthly cash payout. The focus is on survival, not so much on the fact of paying more interest.

The question, then, is "Where on earth could you find a single lender that could structure a consolidated loan as I have described above?"

Most banks, credit unions, and other lending institutions offer debt consolidation products, so you don't have to look too far. Note, however, that you would still need to go through the formal process of applying for a loan with the usual amount of paperwork. The secret sauce for the debt consolidation to really work at its best is if you have an asset that the lender can use as security to offer a more attractive interest rate on the consolidated loan. The greater the value and quality of the security, the lower the interest rate you would be offered on the consolidated loan. Real estate security is likely to get you a single-digit loan in Jamaica and in the U.S. as of the time of writing. For a car as security, the rate could be 9–11 percent in Jamaica and around 2.5–12.5 percent in the U.S., depending on your credit score.[108]

---

108   Betterton, "Best Auto Loan Rates in June 2022."

If you don't have any security, then the lender can only offer an unsecured consolidated loan with a higher interest rate (14–24 percent range in Jamaica and 5–36 percent in the U.S.). While those interest rates are higher, it is still possible to have a successful debt consolidation if you are consolidating high-interest debts, such as credit cards that have interest rates as much as 48 percent in Jamaica or 16.3 percent in the U.S.

Let's bring all of these concepts to life with an actual example. In table 9.3, you see where Ms. Burrowes is paying a total of $3,511 per month to three lenders. In contrast, table 9.4 reveals where she was able to consolidate the debts (using real estate as security) to pay $622 over 10 years at 6 percent. Notice how much lower this rate is compared to the range of 6.5–16.3 percent she was paying on the multiple loans she had before.

Did this debt consolidation work? Yes, it did. Instead of paying $3,511 per month, she is now paying $622, a saving of $2,889. The main driver of the saving is the 6 percent interest as opposed to the high rates she had before. Another driver is the period of the loan, 10 years, which is a longer period than any of the other three loans. Notice that she was able to use real estate (land) as security, which was one of the main reasons for the 6 percent interest rate.

TABLE 9.3: MONTHLY PAYMENTS BEFORE DEBT CONSOLIDATION FOR A U.S. BORROWER

#	Loan	Amount Owed	Monthly Payment	Interest Rate per Year
1	Credit card	$30,000	$1,500[109]	16.3%
2	Car loan (5 years)	$21,000	$411	6.5%
3	Personal loan (unsecured)	$5,000	$1,600	15%
	Total	$56,000	$3,511	

---

109 Minimum balance at 5 percent

TABLE 9.4: MONTHLY PAYMENT AFTER DEBT CONSOLIDATION

#	Loan	Amount Owed	Monthly Payment	Interest Rate
1	Consolidated loan secured with land (10 years to repay)	$56,000	$622	6%

I have done debt consolidation twice on my financial journey and used both real estate and a vehicle as security. Debt consolidations that are done well, using the principles that I'm outlining in this section, can really help you to save a ton of money. However, for you to benefit in the long run, you must also do at least the following three things:

1. Quit Bad Money Habits

You must first be brutally honest with yourself and cut out all the bad habits that caused you to end up in so much debt. Whatever those root causes are, you must find them and root them out. Whether it's excessive shopping, dining, vacationing, etc., you must cut these out. Otherwise, you will quickly build another mountain of debt.

2. Live on a Budget

It is very likely that you weren't living on a budget before you ended up with so much debt. Start living on a budget as of now. Identify your needs, wants, and amounts you want to save, and stick to these limits. Living on a budget will help you to spend less than you earn, and, hence, avoid the debt trap. Again, if you don't live on a budget, you're very likely to land right back in debt.

3. Establish an Emergency Fund

Make it a priority to build an emergency fund of at least three months' expenses, using some of the savings from your debt consolidation. That money will provide a cushion against future emergencies and, therefore, should prevent you from going back into debt.

A Word of Caution

As far as possible, do not use the house in which you are living as security for the debt consolidation loan. If you were unable to pay back the consolidated debt, your residence would be at risk! It would also mean that you would be extending the length of time it would take you to pay off your mortgage. Let's say you had seven years left to pay off your mortgage. Taking out a 10-year consolidated loan on the house would add another three years until you owned your house outright and enjoyed all the benefits that come with it. I am aware that some people use their primary residence to take out home equity loans not just to repay debt but to make down payments toward purchasing investment properties. I would also caution against this move where you use your primary residence for the same reasons mentioned above. But if you have the risk appetite to put your primary residence at risk in this manner (although many make big returns from their investment property purchases), then go for it!

You still have another option that doesn't require you to borrow money to get your debt under control.

The Lean Machine: Debt Snowball

I call this method the lean machine. The approach was popularized by personal finance expert Dave Ramsey.[110]

The basic idea is that you stop all borrowing and, instead, do everything possible to find money that can be used to attack your debts. This extra money will come from a combination of radically cutting expenses, increasing your income, and living on a budget, if you weren't doing so before.

You don't stop making adjustments to your life until you are able to generate enough cash to pay the minimum monthly payments on all debts plus generate extra cash over and above the total of these minimum payments. You must, however, want to get out of your debts really bad—it must become an obsession. This obsession will lead to a bulldog-like, Blind Barti-

---

110   "How the Debt Snowball Method Works," Ramsey Solutions, April 13, 2022, https://www.ramseysolutions.com/debt/how-the-debt-snowball-method-works.

maeus persistence that will give you the drive to find the extra cash to attack your debt mountain. The next step is to compile a list of all your debts with every person or institution you owe, starting with the smallest to the largest amount. (See the table below.) Each month, you pay the minimum debt payment on all debts and then use the extra cash referred to above to attack the smallest debt first regardless of the interest rate on that debt.

You may be asking, "Bruce, how does this make any sense at all? What if the smallest debt has the smallest interest rate? Wouldn't it be better to pay the extra cash toward the debt with the highest interest rate and save some interest?"

Yes, mathematically it would be smarter to pay the debt with the highest interest rate first, but Moty Amar, in his study on the psychology of debt, argues that people are more motivated to keep making sacrifices to attack their debts when the number of debts is falling.[111] So if you had five debts, and two of them were less than, say, $1,000, and you were able to knock these out quickly, say over two months, you move from five to three debts in a short space of time. The reduction is a huge psychological boost for most people. It will make them feel motivated to stay the course of paying off their other debts.

The concept reminds me of the situation of a young married couple in Florida I was helping through their financial challenges. They had about nine credit cards with some small balances and some large ones. They had cash in a savings account earning virtually nothing. But it made them feel a sense of security amid the mountain of debt they had. We agreed that they could use a chunk of the cash to immediately knock out about four of the smaller credit cards in one night. That knowledge created an amazing boost for them to continue to attack the other five cards.

Once you pay off the smallest balance, you will use the monthly payment plus the extra cash that you were using to pay the smallest debt toward attacking the next smallest debt. You repeat that cycle. Each time,

111   Moty Amar et al., "Winning the Battle but Losing the War: The Psychology of Debt Management," *Journal of Marketing Research* 48, Special Issue (2011): S38–S50, https://www.jstor.org/stable/23033464.

the debt repayments for the next debt becomes larger and larger, like a snowball! An example would be helpful here, so let's look at how Mr. Snow, from Miami, uses this strategy.

TABLE 9.5: DEBT SNOWBALL STRATEGY

Loan Type	Amount Owed	Minimum Monthly Payment	Interest Rate
Personal loan	$5,000	$1,600	15%
Car loan	$21,000	$411	6.5%
Credit card	$30,000	$1,500	16.3%
Total	$56,000	$3,511	

Mr. Snow found extra cash of $350 per month through a ruthless process of cutting expenses and increasing income over and above the total minimum monthly payment for all his debts of $3,511. He diligently pays off the $5,000 by paying the $1,600 each month plus the extra of $350 (total of $1,950) while continuing to pay the minimum on all the other balances. Upon repaying the entire personal loan, he now pays $2,361 per month toward the car loan by adding the $1,950 to the $411 mini-mum. He pays that amount until the car loan is paid off, and then he adds the $2,361 to the $1,500 on the credit card and pays $3,861 per month until the credit card is wiped out. So, just like a snowball that starts out very small, the repayment gets bigger and bigger as it rolls. It started with $1,950 on the personal loan until it snowballed into paying $3,861 per month toward the credit card debt!

You will end up paying relatively more in interest using the strategy of the debt snowball, but you are more likely to keep fighting and to win your battle with debt.

If you find it more attractive to attack the loan with the highest interest rate first in order to save on interest costs, then use the extra cash to pay down the highest interest debt first. It's up to you and what you think is best for you. That strategy is called the avalanche method of debt repayment.[112]

Whether you use the debt consolidation, snowball, or avalanche strategy, you must decide to change the bad behavior and practices that landed you in a sea of debt!

If you are not able to develop a plan to eliminate your debts, especially high-interest credit card and line(s) of credit debt, it will be very difficult for you to grow your wealth (net worth) and become financially free. Those expensive debts will cause you to pay out a lot of money each month. Once you stop this debt bleeding, however, you can take what used to be debt payments and start to save and invest!

Imagine Mr. Snow saving and investing $3,861 per month and how that could boost his retirement account! Many times, people's debts on credit cards and lines of credit were spent on purchases that have no lasting positive income or value, such as overly expensive clothes, shoes, dining, and vacations.

Nothing is wrong with nice things. Buy them when you can afford to do so, rather than spending to impress others, especially on places like Instagram.

Restructuring Individual Debts

Let's now examine how you can focus on restructuring your debt using specific techniques for specific types of debt. Remember, the objective of debt restructuring is to reduce your monthly payments so you can save money. I will restrict the discussion to the four most popular types of loans.

1. Mortgage Loan

The first scenario is that while you can afford to pay your mortgage each month, you are looking for a way to reduce your monthly mortgage payments.

---

112   Ashley Eneriz, "Debt Avalanche vs. Debt Snowball: What's the Difference?," Investopedia, last modified April 13, 2022, https://www.investopedia.com/articles/personal-finance/080716/debt-avalanche-vs-debt-snowball-which-best-you.asp.

You may simply call other lending institutions to get an idea of what their interest rates are for a mortgage similar to the one you have. If you find a company that offers a better interest rate, then discuss the option of switching. That entity may then send you an offer of the terms and conditions under which you could switch your loan. Oftentimes, in order to get your business, they will waive the transaction costs (e.g., loan processing fees, certain legal fees, and so on) associated with switching the mortgage as well as offer you a lower rate of interest. If you have such an offer in writing, you can then call your current mortgage company and let them know the offer that you have received and ask if they are willing to match it. Most companies will seriously consider a match as they don't want to lose your business. If they say they can't match what you are being offered, you will then have to consider whether the reduction in the interest rate plus other factors, such as switching costs, will result only in a relatively small overall monthly savings. If the overall savings make sense, then you should switch; if not, then it would be better to remain with your current mortgage provider. The idea is to recognize that you can possibly get your mortgage payments down by calling around.

The second scenario is that you have fallen behind with your mortgage payments (you may have experienced a pay reduction due to something like COVID-19), and there is the possibility of losing your house.

I suggest that you call your mortgage company and explain your situation. Most companies will try and work with you to prevent you from losing your house. The strategies could include the following:

- They might offer to increase the number of years on the mortgage, which would result in you paying a smaller monthly payment that may be more manageable. In this situation you are really trying to survive, and you will not be too interested in the fact that a longer repayment period means more interest cost in the long run. You just want to get your loan current and keep the roof over your head.

- They could also give you some time to try to fix your problem and to get your income back up by allowing you not to pay your monthly mortgage for a period of, say, six months. The six months of nonpayment would not be viewed as your being delinquent. Many lenders did the foregoing during COVID-19 to help their borrowers whose income was reduced due to the pandemic. If you fail to reach out to the lender and discuss your situation, however, then you will be considered delinquent and could end up losing your house! You will still owe the six months' worth of mortgage that you had not paid. Usually, the lender will add that amount to your overall loan balance and let you pay it over the life of the mortgage. For example, if the six months of outstanding mortgage payments was a total of $9,950, and your principal owed was $300,000, the lender will oftentimes add the $9,950 to the $300,000. So, you will be paying back $309,950 over say 15 or 20 years.

The key message is go talk to your lender. The worst thing is to do nothing. You would be inviting debt collectors and lawyers to come after you and, ultimately, lose your home and ruin your credit score.

2. Student Loans

Student loans are generally unsecured loans from a government body such as the Students' Loan Bureau in Jamaica. I will restrict the discussion here to student loans from government-type bodies only, as student loans issued by private financial institutions tend to be similar to their other loan products. Government entities tend to be very flexible with their terms and conditions. For example, students generally are allowed the option to start repaying their student loans within six months after their graduation, the loans are often unsecured, and the interest rates are usually lower than loans from a private sector entity. Remember, the government is trying to assist as many people as possible to achieve their educational goals, hence the favorable terms. The government knows that a more educated population will result in a stronger economy and country.

Please, please, if you are not able to find a job within the six months after graduation (or the equivalent grace period that is given for your student loan lender), reach out to your student loan organization and explain.

They are generally very willing to work out a plan for you not to be viewed as delinquent. If you got a job and are working but are struggling to repay your loans because the starting salary is low, the remedy is the same. Please call the student loan organization, have a discussion, and get your loans restructured. If you fail to call and negotiate new loan terms, the student loan entity will eventually be forced to take actions that they would prefer not to take, such as handing over your loan to debt collectors and lawyers. Those actions will affect your credit score.

3. Credit Cards

If you find that you are unable to pay off your credit card balance each month, then it means that you will be paying interest at an average of 16.3 percent in the U.S., or 40.37 percent in Jamaica per annum. I already discussed the topic of credit cards and concluded that credit card interest is classified as high-cost debt and should be avoided like the plague. I don't mean avoid credit cards. I mean avoid finding yourself paying the high-cost interest.

You have at least two options to stop paying this high interest rate.

1. Look into converting the credit card debt to a regular fixed-term unsecured loan that has a lower rate of interest. (There are entities in Jamaica at the time of writing that are willing to lend and provide unsecured fixed-term loans with interest rates of between 14 and 24 percent, which is clearly much lower than the 40.37 percent average on a credit card.)

2. You also have the option of trying to lengthen the repayment period of the fixed-term loan to reduce your monthly payments. Again, that strategy is not about trying to save interest but giving you some breathing room to stabilize your monthly payments. If you convert your credit card in that way, then you will not have access to the revolving credit that comes with the credit card. You will also lose any other features such as future airline miles, cash back rewards, and so on. These losses, however, will pale in comparison to your gaining control of your finances and becoming current with your credit card.

3. Another option is for you to switch your card to another bank. Some banks will allow you to switch from your existing credit card to theirs, and for the first, say, three to six months, you pay 0 percent interest (or benefit from a big discount on the interest rate that they would normally charge on the card). For example, switching from bank A to bank B, where bank B's usual credit card interest rate is, say, 48 percent (in Jamaica), but it offers you 0 percent interest for the first six months on the transferred balance or a reduced interest rate of, say, 24 percent, which would be a 50 percent reduction. You should consider the switch if you can use the six months for which you now have either no interest cost or a reduced interest rate to try and pay off the credit card debt that you brought to the new bank. That strategy will give you a fresh start on your debt. Be very careful, however, to make sure you understand the fine print governing the terms of the credit card switch. Different banks have different conditions. The key thing to watch for is if you don't pay off the total credit debt that you transferred before the grace period, you could end up paying interest at the bank's usual rate on that amount dating back to when you first made the transfer or the portion that is still owed at the end of the period. Also, watch out for processing and transfer fees and include them in your analysis to see if the overall deal makes sense. Sometimes there is no transaction processing fee for the transfer, or at times there is a relatively small fee that can go up to 2 percent on the amount transferred—these are incentives used by financial institutions to make the deal more attractive to you.

4. Car Loans

If you are struggling with your car payments, you may consider the following.

Try to sell the car and buy a cheaper one. Ensure that the cheaper car is going to result in a much lower payment that you can afford.

Here comes the principle again: Managing your money is not only about the numbers and the math; it is also about psychology and human behavior.

I explained those factors earlier. The question then is, would you be willing to sell your existing car, for a cheaper less luxurious one and not worry about what others may have to say? Only you can answer that question. Becoming financially free is about making sacrifices today for a better tomorrow.

If you were leasing[113] a car and are struggling to pay the monthly lease payments, it may suit you to take in the car before the lease term is up, pay the penalty for the early termination, and buy a cheaper car that will have a lower monthly payment even when you factor in the penalty. Leasing a car is usually more expensive than buying one, given that you will own the car when you buy it as opposed to leasing it. At the end of the lease term, you generally don't own the car. Additionally, the leasing company usually sets the monthly charges to include all the costs associated with the running of the car over the lease period— namely, the annual reduction in the value of the car each year (i.e., depreciation), taxes, and related charges. You, the lessee, are therefore basically paying for all the cost of ownership of the car without actually owning the car at the end!

Credit Reports

In wrapping up this chapter, we will take a look at the important subject of credit bureaus, credit reports, and credit scores. You must understand those three things and their implications for your ability to get access credit in the first instance.

In Jamaica, there are three credit bureaus at the time of this writing: Creditinfo Jamaica, CRIF Information Bureau Jamaica, and Credit Information Services.[114] Credit bureaus were established in Jamaica within the last 10 years. A number of other Caribbean territories and developing countries haven't yet established credit bureaus. In the U.S., Canada, and many other countries, credit bureaus are well established.

---

113   This is where you pay a monthly rental fee to a car leasing company to use a car for a set period of time, but the car is still owned by the leasing company at the end of the lease period. This is similar to how you pay rent to live in a house, but the house still belongs to the landlord when you are ready to move out.

114   "Credit Reporting," Bank of Jamaica, accessed June 10, 2022, https://boj.org.jm/ core-functions/financial-system/credit-reporting/.

Credit bureaus in Jamaica are authorized under the Credit Reporting Act 2010 to collect credit information on individuals from financial and other institutions.[115] The credit bureaus use this information to produce a credit report that includes details on your credit history (e.g., list of amounts you owe to different entities, your payment history). The bureaus take this credit history and produce a credit score. Imagine the credit score to be similar to a grade such as an A, B, or C on a test in school. The better your credit history, the better your credit score. The credit score terms that are used by Experian in the U.S. are as follows:

- Very Poor: 300–579

- Fair: 580–669

- Good: 670–739

- Very Good: 740–749

- Exceptional: 800–850[116]

Those ranges should give you an idea of how the credit-scoring system works.

My aim here is not to exhaust you on the inner workings of credit bureaus but to make you aware that these entities exist, that all of your credit history is being tracked, and that you have a credit report and a credit score.

Financial institutions check your credit reports and your credit scores with one or more of the credit bureaus, and if your results are poor, you may be denied credit, or you will have to pay a higher rate of interest. Those two factors—denial of credit or getting more expensive credit—could actually prevent you from being able to buy a house or car! It's serious business. So, let this reality challenge you to do your very best to pay your bills on time and to avoid excessive debt that you can't manage.

---

115   "Credit Reporting."

116   "580 Credit Score: Is It Good or Bad?," Experian, accessed June 11, 2022, https://www.experian.com/blogs/ask-experian/credit-education/score-basics/580-credit-score/.

The credit score and history are basic indicators of how trustworthy you are with money. Given that these indicators are a reflection of your trustworthiness, employers and some landlords may also want to see them.

If you don't know what your credit score is or what your credit report looks like, now would be a good time for you to call one of the bureaus (if you have credit bureaus) in your country to find out. Usually, you can get at least one free copy of your credit report from most bureaus; however, you usually have to pay the bureau a fee to get your credit score. Remember, your credit report is different from your credit score. Nowadays in the U.S., many financial institutions are providing credit scores directly to their customers free of cost.[117]

Should young college and high school students have credit cards?

If you are a young—less than 24 years old—college or high school student, you are unlikely to have a big credit history, given your stage in life. You should, therefore, pay keen attention to the matters relating to credit reports and scores and make a personal commitment to repay your debts on time and not to get into excessive debt when you start to earn. Some financial professionals argue that credit cards are good for young college and high school students to pay for basic items in order to feel the responsibility of managing a card early in life and to start building a credit history. While that can be debated, beware of the opposite effect where students get carried away and rack up huge charges by living the high life with their friends. Also, keep in mind that financial institutions bombard and target students, especially college students, with unsolicited cards, and having access to all that credit can prove to be deadly.

My opinion is if a college or high school student reads and understands the concepts in books like this one, then having a card with a small credit limit to give them exposure is not a bad idea. If the student does not

---

117   Anya Kartashova, "8 Credit Card Issuers That Offer a Free Credit Score," *Forbes*, May 31, 2022, https://www.forbes.com/advisor/credit-score/credit-card-issuers-that-offer-a-free-credit-score/.

have basic personal financial literacy, though, they should stay away from credit cards and wait until they become more financially mature.

Does a good credit score mean you are good with money?

In closing, I will caution by saying that there are people with good credit scores who still live hand to mouth. A good credit score does not necessarily mean that you are financially strong.

Many people know how important a good credit score is, so they find ways to keep their credit payments current by paying only the minimum amount. If you can't pay off your credit card statement balance each month, then you are not doing well financially. It means you are (1) spending more than you earn and (2) paying out high-interest costs, which drain your net worth. The credit score is, therefore, not necessarily a full picture of your financial stability. So don't get too caught up by saying, "Oh, my credit score is exceptional," when your overall financial health is poor. Many people boast about how good their credit is but fail overall in their financial health.

Focus on your overall financial health using the 10 financial indicators discussed in chapter 4 and apply the 14 grow, protect, and sow (GPS) your-money principles in this book as a better measure of how you are doing financially.

Options for the Goldsons

We have been tracking the Goldsons throughout this book. Recall that before they made changes to their lifestyle, they were spending more than they were earning and were in a quicksand of debt with a debt-to-income ratio of 62 percent. The changes they implemented were successful in generating monthly savings of $382 per month, and they could therefore use the debt snowball method to attack their debt. It may take them some time to repay all their debts, given how much they owe, but at least that effort would represent a start.

Alternatively, they could think about debt consolidation to attack their mountain of debt. As I recommended, if they chose debt consolidation, they should avoid putting up their house as security, start living on a budget, and quit bad money habits to stay debt-free!

If you are not like the Goldsons with a mountain of debt, or if you are not yet working, keep this book close at hand to remind you to avoid excessive debt or to show you how to get out of a mountain of debt, if by some unfortunate means you end up there. Now that you understand how to better manage debt and to break out of your debt bondage, your next step along the road to financial freedom is to ensure that your retirement money is going to be enough for you to live with dignity in your golden years!

Your Money Journal Assignment: Defeating Debt Giants

WORKING ADULTS: 18 YEARS & OLDER

If you have a mountain of debt, consider whether you are ready for the following:

- Consolidate debt, or implement the debt snowball to get out of debt.

- Look at the two options below, and decide which one suits you better.

DEBT CONSOLIDATION (SEE TABLES 9.3 AND 9.4 FOR ILLUSTRATIONS)

- Action items

  ○ Call different financial institutions and check if they do debt consolidation.

  ○ Compare the interest rates and loan terms they offer to the rates and terms on your existing debts.

  ○ Do the math to ensure their offers would save you money.

  ○ Seek advice before making a decision.

- Pay attention to the following:

  ○ Caution: try not to use your primary residence as security, if at all possible.

- ○ You will need to live on a budget.

- ○ Leave behind all bad money habits.

Debt Snowball (see table 9.5 for an illustration)

- • Action items

  - ○ List debts from the smallest to the largest.

  - ○ Do not borrow any more and live a bare-bones lifestyle.

  - ○ Find extra cash to throw at your loans from this lifestyle:

    - ◻ Cut expenses drastically.

    - ◻ Sell stuff to get cash to pay down debts.

  - ○ Pay the minimum balance on all loans.

  - ○ Use extra cash found to help pay off the smallest loan first.

  - ○ Add the monthly cash no longer needed to repay the smallest loan to the monthly payment for the next smallest loan until it has been paid off.

  - ○ Repeat the cycle until all loans are paid off.

FULL-TIME STUDENTS: 14–24 YEARS

The best way to defeat your debt giants is to avoid creating them in the first place. But given that you are unlikely to have debt giants at this stage of your life, decide today to practice the following to avoid creating them and the mental and financial distress they bring. Make the following promises to yourself.

- • I will always live on a budget (within my means) so that I don't have to borrow to pay for basic needs.

- • I will avoid people, places, and things that cause me to want to overspend and go into debt.

- I will only borrow money where, depending on my circumstances, it may not be practical to wait until I can save the amount I need (buying a house or car)—even then, I will only acquire debt that will help me to generate income (student loans for a good education) or increase my productivity (a car loan to buy a used car).

chapter 10

STEP 7: PLAN FOR YOUR GOLDEN YEARS
IN RETIREMENT

In Proverbs 22:3 (NLT), Solomon says, "A prudent person foresees danger and takes precautions." We all will grow old one day, and it would be dangerous if you get to normal retirement age without being prepared financially. It is dangerous to be old and broke. According to the June 2021 Financial Services Commission (FSC) *Private Pensions Industry Statistics Report*, only 11.56 percent (139,419) of the employed labor force in Jamaica (1,206,000 as of April 30, 2021) were part of a private pension plan. The vast majority of Jamaicans (outside of the public sector) are not part of a pension plan, which does not augur well for their retirement years.[118]

For the U.S., recall in chapter 1 where I discussed the low savings rate that exists in America. Those statistics are further corroborated by a 2016 GOBankingRates survey, which says 35 percent of all adults in the U.S. have only several hundred dollars in their savings account, 34 percent have

---

118   Oran Hall, "Trends in the Private Pension Industry," *The Gleaner*, November 14, 2021, https://jamaica-gleaner.com/article/business/20211114/oran-hall-trends-private-pension-industry.

zero savings, and only 15 percent have $10,000 stashed away.[119] According to a 2019 GOBankingRates survey, 46 percent of men and women had $0 in retirement savings.[120]

Those statistics suggest that many Jamaicans and Americans are not well positioned to face their golden years with dignity.

I believe the major contributing factors for that lack of readiness in both Jamaica (a developing nation) and the U.S. (a developed nation) include the high cost of living (which makes it difficult for some people to save), ignorance on the importance of making retirement planning a priority, and the adverse impact of the four cultural influences that rob people of the ability to save.

All the money principles outlined in this book so far have been designed to take the reader through a series of steps that will ultimately lead to savings. Notice that I keep saying you must learn to save money if you are going to be financially independent. I am saying it again because it is your savings that will give you the fuel to plan for retirement.

How much money do I need during retirement?

According to Business Insider, the average person will need approximately 70–80 percent of their income earned just before entering retirement to live a relatively comfortable life during retirement.[121] People with chronic health issues may need to budget more due to higher medical bills. Therefore, if your pre retirement income was $3,000 per month, your ideal retirement income is estimated at $2,400 ($3,000 × 0.80). Given that inflation will take its toll each year, you may want to increase your preretirement

---

119   Ester Bloom, "Here's How Many Americans Have Nothing at All in Savings," CNBC, June 19, 2017, https://www.cnbc.com/2017/06/19/heres-how-many-americans-have-nothing-at-all-in-savings.html.

120   Sean Dennison, "64% of Americans Aren't Prepared for Retirement—and 48% Don't Care," GOBankingRates, September 23, 2019, https://www.gobankingrates.com/retirement/planning/why-americans-will-retire-broke/.

121   Stephanie Colestock, "4 Steps You Can Take to Get Your Retirement Savings on the Right Track," Business Insider, December 16, 2021, https://www.businessinsider.com/personal-finance/how-much-do-i-need-to-retire.

income each year by the expected inflation rate. Assuming an inflation rate of 5 percent using my prior example, retirement income in the following year should be $2,520 ($2,400 × 1.05) per month.

The next obvious question then is "If I am not working anymore, where am I to get the money that I need to help me live with dignity during retirement?" Generally, there are three ways to fund your retirement: (1) employer-sponsored pension plans or retirement accounts, (2) government pensions, and (3) personal investments. I address each of these items below.

1. Employer-Sponsored Pension Plan or Retirement Account
Pension and Retirement Plans: U.S. and Jamaica

Many employers set up plans into which both the employer and the employees put money for the purpose of the employees having money to live off during retirement. In Jamaica, where employers choose to set up such a plan, they will typically contribute a certain percentage (many choose 5 percent) of the employees' gross salary, and the employees are required to contribute a certain percent (5 percent is often the minimum required).[122] The combined contributions of the employee and the employer, which cannot exceed 20 percent of the employee's gross salary, is invested by a pension fund manager or a brokerage firm.

In the U.S., many employers set up 401(k) retirement accounts to which their employees contribute, and oftentimes employers would partially or fully match their employees' contributions up to a certain limit. The employers decide on the investment securities available to the employees as well as the company or broker that manages the underlying investments.[123] Let me pause to emphasize that if you are given the opportunity to participate in an employer-sponsored pension plan or 401(k) retirement account, and your employer is willing to match (contribute) the same percentage, or even if it's less than your portion, do not hesitate to participate

---

122   Latoya Mayhew-Kerr, "Back to Basics—What You Need to Know About Pensions," August 2, 2021, https://www.jamaicaobserver.com/all-woman/back-to-basics-what-you-need-to-know-about-pensions/.

123   Dayana Yochim, "What Is a 401(k) Plan?," NerdWallet, December 21, 2021, https://www.nerdwallet.com/article/investing/what-is-a-401k.

in this plan. Sign up fast! In Jamaica, most employers will seek to match up to 5 percent of the employee's contribution. The total of your retirement contributions and that of your employer along with the investment returns will all go to you (with certain vesting requirements as described below). Are you starting to see why I am saying sign up fast?

Let me illustrate further. If you decide to participate and you contribute, say, 5 percent of your salary, which is $150 per month, and your employer matches your $150 each month, this means you would get a 100 percent return on your money each month. Such an arrangement must be one of the best returns you could make on your money anywhere. The employer's contribution is what some people call "free" money. Note, however, that employer-sponsored plans usually require that you stay with the employer for a period of time before the employer's contribution becomes totally or partially yours, which is known as becoming vested. So, please check out the vesting period before you decide to resign from your job. Most employers in Jamaica require five years before you become vested. Many employers use vesting periods as a way of attracting and keeping talent. The shorter the vesting period, the more attractive a prospective employee will find an employment offer.

Defined Benefit Plans

A pension fund can be established as a defined contribution plan or as a defined benefit plan. Defined benefit plans, which were very popular in the 1980s and early 1990s, outline the benefit that the employees will get upon retirement. Put differently, the employees know from the start the specific formula that is used to determine how much money they will receive on retirement. The pension benefit is defined, as the name of the plan suggests. Many defined benefit plans can provide up to 70 percent of the employees' income in the years leading up to their retirement.[124] In other words, if you were earning $3,000 per month in the year you retired, once you stopped working you would receive approximately $2,100 ($3,000 × 0.70) per month. Isn't that amazing?

---

124   "Understanding Defined Benefit Plans," Equitable, accessed June 15, 2022, https://equitable.com/retirement/articles/understanding-defined-benefit-plans.

It is amazing because, as stated above, the average pensioner will need between 70 to 80 percent of what they were earning in the last year of their working life to survive in their retirement years. Recipients under these defined benefit plans would therefore be able to cover a substantial portion of their monthly pension requirements (subject to inflation, of course, over the years).

Many corporations and governments started to feel the huge burden of the cost of defined benefit plans, however, as their retired employees started living longer. Consequently, since the 1980s to the early 1990s, a significant portion of corporations and some governments have switched their pension plans from defined benefit plans to defined contribution plans, which are much cheaper for employers to operate. [125]

The shift toward defined contribution plans has definitely been observed in Jamaica. According to the FSC's *Private Pensions Industry Statistics Report*, as of June 30, 2021, only 14 percent of members in an active pension plan were in a defined benefit scheme—the other 86 percent were in a defined contribution plan.[126] The shift has also been seen in the U.S. where, according to the U.S. Bureau of Labor Statistics in 2018, only 17 percent of private sector workers participated in defined benefit plans.[127]

Defined Contribution Plans

Unlike a defined benefit plan, a defined contribution plan does not guarantee the employee a set amount of money when they retire. Such plans simply pay to the employee whatever both the employee and the employer contributed to the plan along with any investment returns to the employee, and that's it! This makes them much cheaper for employ-

---

125   Nathaniel Lee, "How 401(k) Accounts Killed Pensions to Become One of the Most Popular Retirement Plans for U.S. Workers," CNBC, March 24, 2021, https://www.cnbc.com/2021/03/24/how-401k-brought-about-the-death-of-pensions.html.

126   Hall, "Trends in the Private Pension Industry."

127   "Retirement Benefits: Access, Participation, and Take-up Rates," U.S. Bureau of Labor Statistics, accessed June 10, 2022, https://www.bls.gov/ncs/ebs/benefits/2018/ownership/private/table02a.htm.

ers to operate than defined benefit plans.[128] Given that cost factor, most retirement plans (401(k)s, IRAs) in the U.S. and pension plans in Jamaica are established by employers as defined contribution plans. The huge challenge, then, that employees face in this scenario, given that there are no guaranteed amounts to be received when they retire, is whether what will have been accumulated at the time of retirement will be enough to live off. It also means that millions of people around the world are at risk of not having enough money to survive during their retirement years.[129]

Will I have enough money during my retirement?

How, then, can individuals better prepare to reduce the risk of not having enough money during their retirement years?

Remember that we established earlier that the average person will need 70–80 percent of their preretirement income to live comfortably during retirement, which means that we can estimate how much money you will need per year during retirement. (For the sake of simplicity, we will ignore the effects of inflation.) Therefore, if before retirement you make (or are expected to make) $3,750 per month, you would need $3,000 per month (using the 80 percent end of the range) during retirement.

The next step is to establish how much you will receive from government sources, such as your country's national pension scheme (this would be the National Insurance Scheme (NIS) in Jamaica). The current maximum monthly NIS pension benefit[130] is $98 (JA$14,733) per month, which would leave you to find the remainder of $2,902 per month ($3,000 less $98) to live on. This would come from your pension or retirement account and or your personal investments. We will assume for the rest of the analysis that your next move is to try to find this amount from your retirement or pension account.

---

128   "Defined-Benefit vs. Defined-Contribution Plan: What's the Difference?," Investopedia, last modified March 27, 2022, https://www.investopedia.com/ask/answers/032415/how-does-defined-benefit-pension-plan-differ-defined-contribution-plan.asp.

129   "Five Million People Approaching Retirement at Risk of Not Having 'Adequate' Pension Income," Centre for Aging Better, accessed July 2, 2022, https://ageing-better.org.uk/news/five-million-people-approaching-retirement-risk-not-adequate-pension-income

130   "National Insurance Scheme" Ministry of Labour and Social Security, https://mlss.gov.jm/departments/national-insurance-scheme/.

In order to ensure you are in a position to generate the shortfall of $2,902 per month from your retirement or pension account by the time you retire, you should have accumulated enough money that, when invested, can generate that amount ($2,902) on a monthly basis. So how much would you need to have accumulated at retirement to generate that amount of $2,902? If you have a retirement account like a traditional 401(k) in the U.S., you can use the 4 percent rule to do the estimate. Using the 4 percent rule assumes you will be allowed to withdraw all the amounts you've accumulated at your time of retirement and invest them so they can generate enough income to meet your retirement needs. Some 401(k) plans allow you to do that.[131] Alternatively, you can estimate the amount of money you will need to purchase an annuity that will generate the shortfall each month ($2,902). Some 401(k) plans allow you to use the funds accumulated at retirement to purchase this annuity. In Jamaica, however, the only option for the funds accumulated at the time of retirement is to purchase an annuity (although you can take a lump sum of 25 percent as a tax-free distribution, the other 75 percent would have to be used to purchase an annuity).[132] I will explain annuities further later.

The 4 Percent Rule

To apply this rule, multiply the annual income you need during your retirement ($34,824 ($2,902 × 12) in my example above) by 25 (100/4), which is $870,600. Wow, I can hear you saying, "Bruce Scott, that is a whole heap of money!" Before I address how we deal with this large sum, let me finish the analysis.

The next step is for you to withdraw 4 percent of the $870,600 per year as your retirement income. Guess how much 4 percent of $870,600 per year is? It is $34,824, which is the amount of your required annual retirement income.

---

131   Claire Boyte-White, "How Does a 401(k) Work When You Retire?," Investopedia, January 25, 2022, https://www.investopedia.com/articles/personal-finance/111615/how-401k-works-after-retirement.asp#:~:text=How%20a%20401%20%28k%29%20plan%20works%20after%20you,until%20you%20are%20required%20to%20begin%20taking%20distributions.

132   Mayhew-Kerr, "Back to Basics."

William Bengen developed this 4 percent rule in 1994 in an attempt to figure out how much a retiree could draw off their investments without eating into the base amount or running out of money. He calculated that a withdrawal of 4 percent each year is a safe amount given that, on average, each year your investments should be earning upward of 4 percent. The rule assumes that your investment portfolio is at least 50 percent stocks and 50 percent bonds.[133]

Depending on the average inflation rate and average investment return in your country or on your portfolio of investments, you may find that you are able to draw a little more or less than the 4 percent because the rule is not cast in stone. If your average investment returns are, say, 12 percent each year, then you could draw up to 5 percent or even 6 percent per year without worrying about eating into the underlying investment. This is because there would be a big enough cushion of between 6 and 7 percent left to deal with inflation (this will depend on your country's inflation rate) and to protect against the years when the actual investment return will be lower than the average (12 percent in my example). I should point out that if you plan to withdraw 5 percent off your invested sum each year, then instead of multiplying the annual required retirement income by 25 (100/4), you multiply this sum by 20 (100/5). In my example above, the sum you would need to have at retirement if you plan to withdraw 5 percent per year would be $696,480 (20 × $34,824) instead of $870,600. The same logic would apply if you believe 6 percent is a reasonable withdrawal rate for you.

The whole point of this discussion is that you should do a computation, like the one above, to figure out how much money you need to accumulate by normal retirement age to generate your expected annual retirement income. Your next move is to call your human resource department or your pension fund company or check online (if that facility exists at your pension fund company) to find out how much money you have accumulated to date in your pension account. Compare that amount to your target, $870,600, using my example. You will then see if you are on or off

---

133   Julie Kagan, "The 4% Rule," Investopedia, last modified January 20, 2022, https://www.investopedia.com/terms/f/four-percent-rule.asp.

track. If you are off track, it means you will need to be saving and investing more than you are currently doing to close the gap by the time you retire (all other things remaining equal). Below, I have outlined specific ideas and actions you can consider to close any gaps you may foresee.

Purchasing an Annuity

I introduced the topic of annuities earlier. An annuity is a product sold by a life insurance company that guarantees the pensioner a set amount of pension income for the rest of their life or a particular period. The amount that is used to purchase the annuity is the amount you would have accumulated or are expected to accumulate in your retirement account at the date of your retirement.

This is the formula to estimate the amount you need to purchase an annuity: *annual pension required × annuity factor*. The annuity factor is used by the insurance company to determine the cost or the amount they should charge you for purchasing an annuity.[134] It is based on a person's age, mortality rates, gender (women have longer life expectancy than men) and other factors. Don't worry too much about how it is computed or derived. It is based on complex mathematics done by actuaries. The key thing is that the insurance company will multiply the annuity factor by the annual pension required to get the amount you need to pay for your annuity.

At the time of writing, the annuity factor for a 60-year-old Jamaican male is 12, and using my example above, he would need to have $417,888 ($34,824 × 12) to purchase an annuity that would pay $2,902 per month or $34,824 per year.

As was done with the 4 percent rule, you should compare the amount you have accumulated to date and compare it to the amount you will need ($417,888 in my example) to purchase your annuity. If the amount you have accumulated to date is way behind, and you have a very short time to close the gap, then you will need to consider some radical actions to get to the amount you will need to purchase your annuity.

---

134   Julia Kagan, "Annuity Factor Method," Investopedia, last modified December 19, 2021, https://www.investopedia.com/terms/a/annuity-factor-method.asp.

Hitting My Retirement Fund Target

I will now address the question "How on earth can I accumulate so much money ($417,888 to purchase an annuity or the 4 percent rule's $870,600) using the examples above by the time I retire?" The secret is to start saving and investing early and let the law of compound interest do the work for you. It is that simple. You will learn more about compound interest in chapter 11.

So, for those of you in your 20s and 30s, if you start saving and investing now, you won't need to worry about getting the base of money you need to live during retirement. If you are starting later, in your 40s and 50s, then you will need to save and invest a lot more each month to make up ground.

How much should you contribute to your pension plan during your working life?

As I discussed in chapter 4, if you invest 15 percent of your income over your career (30 to 40 years), and if you start in your 20s or early 30s, then the growth in this investment should lead to a comfortable retirement.

The reality is that most people may need to start off with a small percentage (less than 15 percent) due to budget constraints, such as student loan repayment obligations, and the need to focus on their immediate needs, such as housing and transportation.

Earlier, I stated that in Jamaica, the general minimum pension contribution required by an employee to participate in an employer-sponsored pension scheme in Jamaica is 5 percent. The maximum combined contribution of employee and employer is 20 percent of the employee's gross salary. Similar rules around contribution limits apply in the U.S. for the traditional and Roth 401(k) retirement accounts. Retirement fund contributions attract varying levels of tax savings to employees in Jamaica and the U.S. The more you contribute toward your pension plan, the higher the tax savings and therefore the faster your retirement or pension account will grow![135] Governments used these tax savings as a means of encourag-

---

135   Yochim, "What Is a 401(k) Plan?"

ing persons to save toward their retirement years. See chapter 12 on tax planning, where I discuss and illustrate these tax-planning concepts further with the use of computations.

What happens when you reach retirement age?

In Jamaica, upon attaining retirement age, you are presented with a retirement option form to elect the benefit option of your choice. These options are as follows:

1. Pension for your lifetime only (pension payments stop when you die)

2. Pension for your lifetime with a guaranteed period of five, 10, or 15 years[136]

What is a guaranteed period you may ask? A guaranteed period ensures that upon your death, your beneficiaries receive the same pension payments you were getting while you were alive for the remaining number of years in the guaranteed period. Not so clear? Let's use an example. At retirement, John chose the lifetime pension with a guaranteed period of 10 years, which paid him $2,900 per month. He, unfortunately, died two years after accessing the pension payments. As his beneficiary, his wife, Marva, continued to receive $2,900 for the next eight years of the guaranteed period. If he had only picked the pension for life option, Marva would have received nothing! You should seriously consider taking the pension for life with a guaranteed period of 10 or 15 years, if you have dependents. That option will provide the type of benefit that accrued to Marva above. You will receive a lower monthly figure for the option with the guaranteed period; however, don't let that be the only factor that sways your decision. Talk to your pension adviser before finalizing your choice.

Each of the two pension options described earlier is further subdivided into two suboptions. The first offers a pension amount using the pensioner's full balance, and the other presents, as mentioned before, a one-time 25 percent tax-free lump sum paid at the onset of retirement and a reduced

---

136   Oran Hall, "Annuity Plans for Retirees," *The Gleaner*, July 24, 2011, https://jamaica-gleaner.com/gleaner/20110724/business/business5.html.

monthly pension payment.[137] If, say, you had amassed $500,000 in your pension account on reaching retirement age, and you opted for the one-time lump sum option, you would receive $125,000 (25 percent) tax-free, and the other $375,000 (75 percent) would be used to secure an annuity. Be careful to manage the lump sum payment if you choose to take it, and don't fall into the trap of splurging. If, for whatever reason, you have expensive credit cards and similar debt at retirement, taking the lump sum or a portion thereof may be a wise choice to clear expensive debts!

In the U.S., the general rule is that once you reach normal retirement age, you can (1) withdraw the funds periodically in lump sum amounts, (2) as stated before, you can withdraw all the moneys accumulated at once, and (3) you can use the sum accumulated to purchase an annuity.[138] Speak to your financial adviser here on your best course of action based on your life expectancy, your risk appetite, and the type of lifestyle you want to enjoy during your retirement.

What if I decide to change jobs?

In Jamaica, if you should resign from your job instead of retiring from your job, you are generally entitled to (1) get a refund of the personal contributions that you made plus interest earned, (2) move all of your personal contributions to the pension plan of your next employer or an individual retirement account, or (3) purchase a deferred annuity with your personal contributions. A deferred annuity is a pension purchased now but is only accessible at normal retirement age.

In Jamaica, if you were vested, that portion of the pension due to you from your employer can be (1) left in the pension fund of your former employer to accumulate with interest until retirement, (2) transferred to the pension plan of your new employer or a new individual retirement account, or (3) used to purchase a deferred annuity. Unlike your personal contributions, employers' contributions are nonrefundable and must be used toward retirement.

---

137   Hall, "Annuity Plans for Retirees."

138   Boyte-White, "How Does a 401 (k) Work."

Similar rules to the ones in Jamaica apply to the U.S. when you change jobs—generally you can (1) take the moneys accumulated to the plan of your new employer or invest it in an individual retirement account, (2) leave it with the former employer, or (3) cash it out altogether.[139]

Whether you live in the U.S., Jamaica, or any other part of the world, it is wise to either take the pension amounts to your next employer's plan, leave it in your former employer's plan, or put it in an individual retirement account rather than taking it into your hands and running the risk of blowing it! Spending this money would mean you giving up many years of investment returns and the attendant benefits of compound interest as well as the tax savings.[140] The average person will change jobs multiple times during their careers, and if you take your retirement money and spend it on anything other than retirement, you will be giving away those investment returns and tax savings.[141] Nearly half of all workers in the U.S. take their money out of their retirement plans and spend it on things other than their retirement when they change jobs.[142] In Jamaica, my informal research through discussions with a pension administration manager for a leading financial services entity revealed that at least 90 percent of workers request their personal contributions when they change jobs rather than rolling it into another pension plan. Those heavy withdrawal rates of personal contributions, will likely serve to put the future financial security of these individuals at risk.

Please therefore speak to your HR department or your pension adviser before you make any decisions about your pension choices when you are changing jobs. In the end, whatever you do, try your best to avoid taking that money and spending it on anything other than your retirement!

What if I am self-employed, or my employer does not offer a plan?

---

139   Boyte-White, "How Does a 401 (k) Work."

140   Lisa Smith, "Changing Jobs? Reinvest Your Retirement Funds," Investopedia, November 15, 2021, https://www.investopedia.com/articles/retirement/06/transfersavings.asp.

141   Smith, "Changing Jobs?"

142   Smith, "Changing Jobs?"

In Jamaica, if you are self-employed, or your employer does not have a pension plan, you can open an individual retirement account at a pension management company. With this, you can enjoy similar types of pension benefits as those enjoyed by persons who have employer-sponsored pension plans.[143] If you fall into one of those categories, you should seriously consider opening one of these accounts at your earliest opportunity to help secure your retirement funds and the related tax benefits! In the U.S., similar opportunities to those just described for Jamaica also exist for self-employed people[144] and employees [145] whose employers don't offer an employer-sponsored plan.

2. Government Pension

The second source available to fund your retirement or pension is your country's social security program or national pension scheme to which I alluded earlier. Most countries of the world, including Jamaica, other Caribbean countries, the UK, the U.S., and Canada have some form of national pension or social security program. In Jamaica, each person in the labor force is required by law to contribute a portion of their salary to the national pension plan (NIS). At the time of writing, employees in Jamaica are required to contribute 3 percent on a maximum of $20,000 per year.[146] Employers contribute at the same rate. The Jamaican government manages these contributions and pays individuals an amount each month when they get to retirement age. The amount is relatively small, and the current maximum monthly amount receivable, as previously mentioned, is $98 (JA$14,733) per month. In the U.S. the government pension system is known as Social Security and is similarly funded through payroll taxes.

143   Camille Steer, "Retirement Planning for Self-Employed Individuals: 21 Years vs 55 Years," *Jamaica Observer*, March 27, 2022, https://www.jamaicaobserver.com/business/retirement-planning-for-self-employed-individuals-21-years-vs-55-years/.

144   Arielle O'Shea, "Retirement Plan Options for the Self Employed," NerdWallet, March 16, 2022, https://www.nerdwallet.com/article/investing/retirement-plans-self-employed.

145   Carmen Reinicke, "What to Do if You Aren't Offered an Employer-Sponsored Retirement Plan at Work," CNBC, https://www.google.com/amp/s/www.cnbc.com/amp/2022/04/07/what-to-do-if-you-dont-have-a-401k-retirement-plan-at-work.html.

146   "Jamaica: Individual—Other Taxes," PricewaterhouseCoopers, last modified February 18, 2022, https://taxsummaries.pwc.com/jamaica/individual/other-taxes.

I would not encourage anyone to look to their government's pension plan as the main source of their pension income. First, the amount is relatively small and is unlikely to be enough, on its own, to meet your total expenses. Second, many nationally funded schemes may not be able to afford their pension obligations at some point in the future due to persons living longer, meaning that the annual pension payments are growing at a rate that is higher than expected.

Even though the government pension amounts tend to be insufficient for you to depend on totally for your retirement, you still need to be aware of it and claim it when you get to retirement (assuming the plan is still able to afford to make payments). Why leave money on the table?

3. Personal Investments

Your personal investments (i.e., money that you invest outside of a pension plan or a retirement account) can serve as a way to supplement shortfalls in your income from your pension plan or retirement account. In fact, if you check on your pension account, and you see where the total accumulated to date is unlikely to grow to a sum that will generate the money you will need to live during retirement, your personal investment (or some other source of income) will need to be strong enough to help close the gap. You can use your personal investments to purchase an annuity to supplement the income you expect to receive from your pension plan. Also, if you choose not to go with annuities, you can continue to manage your personal investments—for example, by investing in a mutual fund or unit trust in such a manner that it will generate the extra income you need to supplement the income from your pension or retirement plan. You will need to be careful to ensure that you manage your personal investment in a manner that you don't run out of money during your retirement years. As discussed earlier, a way to solve this problem is to use the 4 percent rule to guide your withdrawal rate.

There are pros and cons of purchasing an annuity versus investing your money in something like a mutual fund. For example, you are guaranteed your monthly pension payments with an annuity regardless of any turmoil in the financial markets. However, monthly payment amounts are generally fixed and therefore do not protect you against inflation, although you can negotiate for an escalating annuity that protects against inflation.[147] Investing your money in a mutual fund or unit trust does not guarantee a set monthly or yearly return, but the potential also exists for you to out-perform the market. Do your research, and speak to your financial adviser on the options that may be best for you. I must acknowledge that the reality on the ground for many people that I coach is that the amount of money they have accumulated in their retirement accounts and personal investments is just not enough for them to generate the income they need during their retirement years. There are a number of reasons for this, some of which I alluded to earlier. They include the following:

1. Many people don't realize the importance of starting to save and invest early in their careers so their money can grow over a longer period.

2. The rising cost of living reduces the amount of goods and services the income earned from retirement investments can purchase.

3. Many people's income during their working years was just not enough in the first place for them to save and invest the amount required for them to live comfortably during retirement.

4. Inherent risk exists with the most popular form of pension arrange-ment chosen by employers in the last 20 plus years—the defined contribution plan.

This plan, as discussed, does not guarantee a set amount of money when you retire that is close to what you need during your retirement. As a consequence, those people who simply don't have enough money to live comfortably during retirement often have to continue working after reach-ing retirement age or depend on their children, other family members, their church, or other support groups.

---

147   "Buying An Annuity: Annuity Options and Shopping Around," Money Helper, accessed July 7, 2022, https://www.moneyhelper.org.uk/en/pensions-and-retirement/taking-your-pen-sion/annuity-options-and-shopping-around#:~:text=One%20way%20to%20use%20your,the%20best%20deal%20you%20can.

You should also note that the discussion here has been about those persons who are part of a pension plan and who need to supplement that income from personal investments. Imagine, therefore, the additional hardship being experienced by those who are not even part of a pension plan or have a retirement account. Recall that I indicated how only 11.56 percent (139,419) of the Jamaican labor force (outside the public sector) are part of a pension plan. I also indicated earlier that according to a 2019 GOBankingRates survey that 46 percent of men and women in the U.S. had $0 in retirement savings. Those statistics shout that life is not pretty for many older people entering or who are in retirement. It is therefore imperative for people, especially those in their 20s and 30s, to continue to educate themselves about retirement planning and to make saving and investing a top priority!

We have now completed the discussion on the three sources of income that typically make up the average person's pension income (i.e., employer-sponsored or individual retirement plans, government pension plans, and personal investments). I will now move to the concept of doing your retirement budget before you actually retire.

Do your retirement budget before you retire.

It is very important that you budget your monthly expenses and income starting at least 10 years before your actual retirement date. It is a very powerful exercise that, depending on your situation, you could find to be joyful (if you are on track) or painful (if you are way behind). You should roll or update this budget each year as your actual retirement age comes closer in order to identify any shortfall between your expected retirement income and expenses. Below I have listed the key expenses (this is not an exhaustive list) and items of income you need to consider in doing your retirement budget.

Estimating Your Monthly Expenses

Mortgage expense: You should aim to be mortgage-free by the time you hit retirement, which will reduce the pressure on your monthly expenses in that housing costs are generally at least 25 percent of a typical household's monthly expenses. I implore you to aim to pay off your mortgage by the time you retire. Don't yield to the temptation, as so many people do (especially in the U.S.), to enter retirement with large home equity loans (loans taken out against their primary residence), which they use to go on expensive vacations or buy expensive cars without apparently fully assessing the impact on their retirement years. (See an interesting article at Urban.org on this subject.[148])

Health insurance: Ensure your budget for health insurance is in order to avoid being financially wiped out due to a major medical issue. Health insurance typically is going to be one of those costs that go up as you age. Check if you can extend health insurance coverage that you enjoyed on the job into your retirement, as it may be cheaper. If not, you should start the negotiation process early with your health insurance provider to secure the best health insurance premiums possible.

Consumer debts: As with your mortgage, aim to be free of all consumer debts and lines of credit during retirement, which will reduce your monthly obligations and your stress levels.

Transportation expenses: Public transportation or having a car without a loan will definitely reduce your expenses in this area.

Property taxes: You must include those costs in your budget, which only tend to increase with time and do not cease to exist once you own your home.

Leisure expenses: Such costs come down to the type of lifestyle you envision during your retirement years. If you had always dreamed of traveling the world or spending more time playing golf, those are expenses you will need to project and include in your budget.

Gifts to grandchildren: It can be heartbreaking if as a grandparent you are not able to treat your cute little grandchildren on special occasions (e.g., birthdays, graduations, Christmas) during your retirement years. Think through just how much you would like to give on these special oc-

---

148   Karan Kaul and Linna Zhu, "More Older Americans Are Drawing Wealth from Their Home Equity, but Racial Gaps Persist," Urban Wire, October 15, 2021, https://www.urban.org/urban-wire/more-older-americans-are-drawing-wealth-their-home-equity-racial-gaps-persist.

casions, and compare that figure to how much you can afford to give based on the reality of your budget.

Gifts to churches and charities: A key part of financial freedom is helping those in need—giving is one of the most liberating and fulfilling activities any one can do. What better time to continue to give than in your golden years when our mortality becomes more apparent, your sense of purpose is heightened, and you even have more of your personal time to give in addition to your money. Budget to see how much you can give to worthy causes, and donating will certainly add to the quality of your life during retirement.

Miscellaneous: In addition to all the above, plan to grab all senior citizen discounts, allowances, and benefits offered at all pharmacies, financial institutions, and other outlets in order to reduce expenses and fees.

Estimating Your Monthly Retirement Income

The three sources of income that the typical retiree will have, which I covered earlier are pensions, government social security programs, and personal investments. You should estimate how much income you will get from each.

Closing the Gap in Your Retirement Budget

I started to address this matter of closing the gap earlier at a high level; here, I will address it in more detail. If your budget reveals that you are likely to have a shortfall in your retirement income, the steps below should be considered in helping to close this gap. Doing this budget at least 10 years before your actual retirement and updating it each year as you approach retirement will allow you some time to close any shortfall in your budget.

- Consider working past retirement age. (Up to 46 percent of Americans in a survey conducted by AAG say they plan to work part time after they retire.[149]) Working after retirement will mean ensuring that

---

149   Palash Ghosh, "A Third of Seniors Seek to Work Well Past Retirement Age, or Won't Retire at All, Poll Finds," *Forbes,* May 6, 2021, https://www.forbes.com/sites/palashghosh/2021/05/06/a-third-of-seniors-seek-to-work-well-past-retirement-age-or-wont-retire-at-all-poll-finds/amp/.

you have a good personal brand with skills that others are willing to pay for and that you are in good or reasonable health. You may want to consider learning a new skill or skills to supplement your income before you actually retire; you may actually become quite proficient at this new skill by the time you reach retirement age.

- Start saving "hard", which could mean you downsizing your house (to save money), downsizing your car (to save money), and selling stuff around the house to generate cash that can be invested. These radical strategies are usually for persons who are really close to retirement (less than five years) and are for various reasons way behind with the amounts they need to have in their retirement accounts to live comfortably in retirement.

- Revisit your investment strategy by talking to your financial adviser. This discussion should be around any adjustments you need to make in your personal investment portfolio that will help to grow your money as well as any additional monthly contributions you may need to make to your pension plan or retirement account.

As I close this chapter on retirement or pension planning, I want to capture some final thoughts to reinforce some of what I said earlier about planning for retirement:

Start investing as a young person: You are not too young to start putting aside money for your pension years. The examples of Marcia and Tom in chapter 11 will make this point come to life. The earlier you start, the more time your money will have to work for you!

Maximize your pension contributions: As soon as your high-cost debt is under control, consider increasing your pension contribution to the legal maximum to optimize tax savings (e.g., income tax).[150] These savings will put a turbo engine on the rate of growth of your pension account. More to come on tax benefits.

---

150   Amy Bell, "401(k) Tax Benefits and Advantages," Investopedia, last modified May 20, 2022, https://www.investopedia.com/articles/investing/102216/understanding-401ks-and-all-their-benefits.asp.

Monitor your pension account: Call your HR department or the pension fund manager or use the pension plan's online service (if available) to see how your pension investment is performing. I log on at least twice per year to see how my pension investment is performing and whether it will be enough to generate the income that I will need to live during my retirement.

Refrain from taking a refund when you resign from a company: Transfer your pension contributions to your next employer's plan (or leave it behind if it is prudent to do so). However, the main point I want to make is for you to avoid the temptation of taking that money into your hands and run the risk of blowing it!

You may need a bigger emergency fund: Some personal finance experts argue that you may want to have up to a two-year emergency fund during retirement. Wow! That is steep! Why such a big fund? Some people argue that if you had a major slump in your investment portfolio that is generating your pension income (due to something like the 2008 recession or the COVID-19 pandemic), then it may not be wise to be pulling out money while the portfolio has fallen so sharply as it could take up to two years to recover. (Two years is the average time it has taken markets to recover based on prior economic downturns.) Hence, the reason for the two-year emergency fund, which would be used by the pensioner while the markets recover. If you had bought an annuity, you would not need to worry about market movements, given that the annuity contract guarantees the payment of your monthly pension income.

Accumulating such a large emergency fund will not be easy or possible for most persons (many of whom are already struggling to even have basic retirement income). I believe that if people follow the 4 percent rule discussed above it should provide a suitable cushion to deal with fluctuations in the market. The 4 percent withdrawal was seen to be the safe withdrawal amount regardless of what is going on in the market. You will still need an emergency fund but maybe not a two-year fund. If you can afford the two-year fund, go ahead.

Exercise your mind, not just your body: Too many people believe that retirement is about sitting on a beach all day. Talk to people who have retired, and they will tell you that if not planned carefully, boredom can become your archenemy. The story was told of a man who didn't plan well for retirement and ended up going to the pharmacy to fill his prescriptions in increments instead of all at once because each trip to the pharmacy gave him something to do! Wow! That is boredom galore! Use your mind, and exercise your body too—teach, mentor, work part time at your own pace—but do something productive and purpose driven. You could learn to play the piano or another instrument. Studies have shown that those types of activities help to fight off Parkinson's and similar diseases!

I have demonstrated the importance of saving and investing for your retirement years in this chapter. The next chapter goes into greater detail with investments outside of your pension contributions—i.e., personal investments.

The Goldsons

Let's now turn our attention back to the Goldsons and their progress:

- They have been able to build a one-month emergency fund of $4,665, using their $382 savings per month. It took them 12 months ($4,665/$382) to build the fund.

- They decided to use the debt snowball method to attack their debts after they had built their one-month emergency fund. They started paying back family and friends first as those debts were the smallest ($6,667), and they took 17 months to pay it off ($6,667/$382).

- They are currently attacking the loan shark debt ($14,000), the next smallest debt.

- They accept that becoming financially free will be long and hard given the size of their debt (now at $53,999, excluding mortgage and friends) versus what they are able to save at the moment ($382 per month).

- Mr. Goldson indicated that he will be stepping out of his comfort zone to find a better job so that they can save even more and attack their debts faster.

Congratulations to the Goldsons, who are a source of inspiration to all of us. I trust all readers will take similar actions.

Your Money Journal Assignment: I Don't Want to Be Old & Broke

WORKING ADULTS: 18 YEARS & OLDER

- If you are in a pension plan or an employer-sponsored retirement fund, do you know how much money you have accumulated to date?

- If not, call your HR department or the pension company or check online (if the facility exists) to find out the balance.

- Request a projected retirement quote from your pension administrator to fully quantify and assess how much you would be receiving per month when you retire.

- If the balance is relatively small and wouldn't give you enough income in retirement, and you are a few years from retirement, you should consider doing the following while consulting with your financial adviser:

  ○ Target saving and investing as much as 25 percent or more of your income by taking the following actions:

    ◻ Downsize your house to save money if it makes sense.

    ◻ Downsize your car if it makes sense.

    ◻ Sell stuff around the house to generate cash.

    ◻ Find additional income sources urgently to help you save and invest more.

    ◻ Consider learning a new skill.

FULL-TIME STUDENTS: 14–24 YEARS

- I just want to remind you that you must not believe that retirement planning should start when you are older. Don't say, "I am young; I can't worry about that now," because the longer you take to start to save and invest, the greater the amount of work you and your money will need to put in to generate your retirement income. Time is literally money!

- Reflect on the power of starting to save and invest early by thinking of the huge difference in wealth that Marcia, in chapter 11, accumulated ($1,103,286.26) compared to Tom ($592,643.15). She accumulated much more, simply because she invested for a much longer period (40 years, compared to Tom's 20 years) even though she invested a much smaller amount ($24,880, compared to Tom's $105,200). Such is the power of starting to invest early!

- Decide to be like Marcia and put those money foot soldiers to work immediately upon getting your first job by signing up for your company's retirement plan if one is offered. Contribute as much as you can afford. Alternatively, open your own individual retirement account with a financial institution, if your company does not have an employer-sponsored plan.

chapter 11

STEP 8: INVEST TO BUILD WEALTH— DON'T PANIC DURING MARKET DOWNTURNS

My simple definition of investing is putting your money to work so that it will grow over time. That statement is best illustrated by the parable of the talents (*talent* was an actual reference to a certain amount of money) in Matthew's Gospel, where an estate owner gave talents to his three servants. Two of them went out and increased their talents through hard work and wise investing. Those servants were commended by their boss when he returned to the estate. The third servant buried his money and was rebuked for not increasing it through some form of investment (Matthew 24:14–30).

The message here is that we need to be good stewards of all we have, including our money! The message here is that making more wealth is not an evil or bad thing. I was talking to a man we'll call Tyrone (not his real name) who said he'd been raised to believe having large sums of money was evil and that it was virtuous to be financially poor. This mentality affected even how he negotiated business deals, saved and invested, and lived his life in general. Later on, during his retirement, he realized the missed invest-ment opportunities and just how much more prepared he could have been for retirement if he had a more accurate view of money. A proper interpre-tation of scripture teaches that money itself is not the problem—rather it is the love of money that is a root of all kinds of evil.

My definition of investment above also shows that there is no shortcut or magic formula to investing and growing your money. Investing requires time, much like waiting for a seed to shoot out of the ground before it bears fruit.

The Time Value of Money
What is the time value of money?

It is "how the value or worth of your money changes over time." It is an extremely important concept to grasp and one of the main reasons why investing your money is so important. Many people, having learned how to save money, simply stop there. They leave their money in a savings account that earns practically nothing in interest, or they leave it under their mattress. When you save in that way, you may feel a sense of security. But you will end up losing big-time because the value of your money will dwindle over time because of the archenemy called inflation. Money has at least one friend and at least one enemy. Inflation is, in my view, the enemy. Return on investment is a friend. Make friends with investment returns, and safeguard against the enemy of inflation.

Inflation is the general increase in prices, over time, that reduces how many goods and services your money can buy. Remember when you used to pay $1 on the bus one-way? Today, your children have to pay $5 for the same bus ride. This is inflation. So, if you had $2 under your mattress when the bus fare was $1 until the time bus fare moved to $5, your $2 would not even be able to take a bus today. It would now take two and a half times your $2 to take a one-way bus ride. That is the monster of inflation. That is what happens when money lies idle under your mattress or in a savings account that pays virtually nothing. Inflation reduces the value of your money over time, hence the importance of understanding the time value of money.

The good news is that investment—money's good friend—does the opposite. When you put the money to work by investing it, it earns more money. There are several ways to invest your money, and I cover them later on in this chapter.

For now, let's just continue the discussion on the battle between inflation and investment returns. According to the Statistical Institute of Jamaica (STATIN) in 2019, the inflation rate was 3.9 percent compared to the savings account interest rate of less than 1 percent. You can see that your money, if left in a savings account, would have lost at least 2 percent (3–1 percent) of its value, all other things remaining equal.[151]

If, however, you had invested your money in Jamaican bonds (a form of investment where you lend money to others, such as governments or corporations, and charge a fee called interest) you would have earned in general between 4 and 7 percent. Even the 4 percent rate would put you ahead of inflation, thereby protecting the value of your money. The same principle would hold if you invested in other types of assets that generally beat the inflation rate.

So, in the words of Arkad in the book *The Richest Man in Babylon*, in order to become wealthy, you must "make thy gold multiply."[152] Put your money to work so it can earn more money.

The Law of Compound Interest

To fully grasp the concept of the time value of money, you must also understand the law of compound interest.

Compound interest, a concept that I introduced earlier, is essentially interest earned on interest over a period of time, which results in the growth of your investment.

The best way to illustrate the power of compound interest is to provide a more detailed illustration. In the scenario below, both Keisha and Bob

---

151   "Jamaica: Inflation Rate from 1987 to 2017," Statista, April 2022, https://www.statista.com/statistics/527084/inflation-rate-in-jamaica.

152   George S. Cason, *The Richest Man in Babylon* (New York: Penguin, 1926).

separately contributed $140 per month over 40 years to different invest-
ments. Keisha's money grew to $1,040,693.18 over 40 years, while Bob's
grew to $82,653.63 over the same period, even though each of them in-
vested the same total ($67,200) over the 40 years (see table below). What
could have caused Keisha's savings to do so much better than Bob's? The
answer is the power of compound interest working harder for Keisha than
for Bob. Compound interest worked for both Keisha and Bob, but it works
even better when you are getting a higher rate of return, as Keisha did.

TABLE 11.1: THE POWER OF COMPOUND INTEREST

Scenario	Keisha, the Investor	Bob, the Saver
Timeline	40 years	40 years
Total invested	U.S.$67,200	U.S.$67,200
Investment return (from an index fund: a type of investment)	10.5% per annum	
Savings account		1% per annum
Total accumulation after 40 years	U.S.$1,040,693.18	U.S.$82,653.63

Because Keisha was getting an annual return of 10.5 percent per year
while Bob was getting 1 percent per year, Keisha's money grew each year,
while Bob's money was virtually stagnant. The consistent addition of
money plus compound interest at a higher rate over the 40 years resulted in Keisha's savings skyrocketing to over $1 million, compared to Bob's
$82,653.63.

Then, you may ask, "Bruce, how can I get a 10.5 percent investment
return? Is it even possible?"

It is possible because one of the most widely tracked investment in-
dices (S&P 500) actually returned an average annual growth rate of 10.5
percent over the 64-year period from 1957 to 2021.[153] Many investment

---

153   J.B. Maverick, "What Is the Average Annual Return for the S&P 500?," Investopedia,
last modified January 13, 2022, https://www.investopedia.com/ask/answers/042415/what-aver-
age-annual-return-sp-500.asp.

managers invest their clients' money to track the S&P 500 Index and can generate returns similar to the 10.5 percent per year for their clients. More to come on the S&P 500 Index later in this chapter.

The real message behind all of this number crunching and talk about compound interest and rates of return is that when you save money each month, it must really go to work for you. You have to take some risk (not recklessly) over the long term (10 years and beyond) as Keisha did. It can't be left in the safe harbor of a savings account as Bob had done with his money.

Adjusting for the Effects of Inflation

To preserve the spending power of the money being amassed over a period of time, it makes sense to increase your monthly contributions to keep pace with the inflation rate per year, a concept I discussed in chapter 2.

Compound Interest: The Miracle of Starting to Invest Early

I want to now show another critical variable that will affect the growth of your money. Let me illustrate. Marcia got a job right out of college at age 22 and invested $207 per month for 10 years in a shares-based index fund—just like the one Keisha invested in above. She stopped contributing to the fund after 10 years, by which time she had contributed $24,840 ($207 per month over 10 years), and her money had grown to $44,020.50. She didn't make any further monthly contribution for the next 30 years— she simply allowed the $44,020.50 to grow in the fund.

Tom also left college at age 22. Upon landing his first job, he started living the "good life." He took out a big loan and bought a nice sports Benz and a fancy condo with a view. He lived lavishly for the next 18 years like the prodigal son in the Gospel of Luke 15:20–24. After those 18 years, he realized he had nothing to show as assets, and so he started to save with zeal and passion. He got really serious about his personal finances, albeit at age 40. He amassed $50,000 over the next two years. After picking up a copy of this book, *14 Steps to Financial Freedom*, he learned that it is not wise to have money lying idly in a savings account, and so he started to invest his money. He invested the $50,000 as a lump sum contribution in the same mutual fund (stock-based fund) that Marcia invested in. He also invested another $230 per month over the next 20 years.

Within 40 years after leaving college, both Marcia and Tom were now 62 years old and had retired. Marcia had contributed $24,840 ($207 per month for 10 years) toward her investment, while Tom put in $105,200 ($50,000 plus $230 per month over 20 years). Who was better off financially? The answer is Marcia. She had accumulated $1,013,286.26, while Tom had accumulated $592,643.15. Marcia had $420,643.11 (42 percent) more money than Tom! See table 11.2, which summarizes their individual performances.

TABLE 11.2: THE MIRACLE OF STARTING TO INVEST EARLY IN LIFE

Scenario	Marcia	Tom
Investment period	40 years	20 years
Total invested	$24,840	$105,200
Investment return (index fund)	10.5%	10.5%
Total accumulated	$1,013,286.26	$592,643.15

Some of you may be surprised that Marcia accumulated more, given that Tom invested so much more than Marcia. Marcia's much smaller sum grew to a larger amount simply because she invested her money for a longer period—she invested for 40 years, while Tom did so for over 20 years. Marcia outperformed Tom even after she stopped her monthly contributions after year 10. Mind blowing! Right? Yes, it is!

The implications are very simple: Start investing money as soon as possible regardless of how small it is. Young people, that command is especially important for you because you have so much more time to let your money work for you!

It is investing money, not only saving money, that will jump-start your ability to build personal wealth. Later on, I will talk about people like Jeff Bezos who were able to build tremendous personal wealth by virtue of the shares they held. Bezos held many shares in Amazon, and the value of these shares grew to astronomical amounts, making him one of the richest persons in the world. You may not get to Jeff Bezos's level, but you can certainly learn to be an investor and grow your personal wealth as well.

Having this wealth will put you closer to total financial freedom and give you the ability to let your money work for you while you are free to use your time as you choose and your wealth to influence your communities and your legacy. The biggest community influences I have found come from donating to educational projects, which include but are not limited to monthly financial contributions to low-income high school students to cover lunch and transportation costs, summer camps that teach etiquette and conflict-resolution skills, and college tuition financial support to young people from low-income homes. In effect and in the long term, such projects position young people "to fish"—that is, how to earn money—which is what I was able to accomplish as an inner-city youth through my accounting education. In my view, projects like those, therefore, represent the single most important strategy to break intergenerational poverty.

I believe you are now convinced as to why you should be investing your money. Let's dig deeper into the subject of investing.

Are you really ready to start investing?

I believe you should have the following fundamentals in place before you start investing surplus funds outside of your retirement account or pension plan. I also refer to this as personal investing. I will only summarize them briefly as the concepts have already been discussed or introduced:

1. Have an emergency fund in place. If you don't, then you may be forced to sell your investments at a loss if an emergency were to happen.

2. Pay off high-cost debt (e.g., credit card debt).

3. Purchase your primary residence (using a mortgage or cash). You can simultaneously have a low-cost residential mortgage while investing in other assets that make a higher return than the interest

on your mortgage—although there are some people like me who would prefer to pay off the mortgage on their primary residence first because of nonfinancial benefits, such as the peace of mind this brings.

4. Contribute the maximum amount allowed to a retirement account or pension plan to take advantage of any matching employers' contributions and tax savings.

Investment Timelines

You can invest your money for the short- (up to one year), medium- (one to 10 years), or long term. It is generally agreed that "long term" is usually 10 years and beyond. The discussion on investment timelines makes for a good pivot into one of the most important things having to do with investments—the type of investor that you are.

Three Types of Investors

The three types of investors are aggressive, moderate, and conservative.[154] If you are an aggressive investor, it means that you are not averse to risk and that you won't worry if your investment goes down by large amounts (drops greater than 10 percent). You have a stomach of steel, and these wild swings don't affect you. In fact, you will sleep very soundly in the midst of shocks such as the mortgage crisis in 2008 or the COVID-19 pandemic when many investment classes saw significant declines in their values.

If, at the other end of the spectrum, you cannot afford to see or lose even one cent of your money, you are conservative. You will clutch your wallet so tightly that not even air can pass through. You can't stand the roller-coaster movements of investment markets.

If you are willing to take some losses but up to a limit of 10 percent of your money, then you would be considered a moderate investor. The moderate investor falls between the aggressive and conservative investor.

154   The Wincom Team, "3 Basic (Risk) Investor Profiles," Good Audience, February 5, 2019, https://blog.goodaudience.com/3-basic-risk-investor-profiles-73e796bebb2f.

The type of investor you are will influence the type of investments that you are willing to make. Different types of investments carry different types of risks.

The Link Between Investor Profile and Investment Returns

The aggressive investor is likely to make more money but also could lose more money than the moderate or the conservative investor because of the age-old principle of "the greater the risk, the greater the potential reward," and its counterpart of "the greater the risk, the greater the potential loss." Aggressive investors tend to invest for the long term, though, and they don't worry about the day-to-day market movements. Over time, they usually will see their money grow and oftentimes in double digits. One investment class, for example, for aggressive investors is owning shares or stocks (where you own a portion of a company, which will be addressed in more detail later on). Although the price for each share can swing wildly from year to year, most stock markets on which shares are traded, in the long run, tend to produce double-digit returns. Earlier, I gave the example of the S&P 500 Index, which represents the share price performance of the 500 largest companies in the U.S., noting its average return of 10.5 percent over the 64-year period to 2021.[155] In 2015 and 2018, the Jamaica Stock Exchange (JSE) was cited by Bloomberg as being the number one performing stock exchange in the world. In 2018, the main index rose by 29 percent![156] Of course, such exceptional performance does not happen every year, but it shows the power and potential of investing in shares.

Moderate investors typically get better returns than the conservative investor but less than the aggressive investor. The asset class of bonds (where you make money by lending others your money) is a good example of an investment that fits the moderate investor. Bonds tend to pay less than the returns on shares and in general can range between 4 and 7 percent in most countries.

---

155   Maverick, "What Is the Average Annual Return."

156   "Jamaica Stock Exchange Ranked Best Performing in 2018," Business Television, May 15, 2019, https://b-tv.com/jamaica-stock-exchange-ian-mcnaughton-ceo-clip/.

Typically, conservative investors make the lowest return in low-risk government investment securities, earning up to 2 percent in most countries.

What's your tolerance to deal with roller-coaster markets?

People who are in their early 20s and 30s are usually encouraged to invest in riskier investments like shares because time is on their side. Older people, however, are generally encouraged to buy less risky investments (bonds and government securities) as a proportion of their overall investment portfolio, because they would not have enough time on their side to wait for massive declines in the market prices of risky investments such as shares to recover. Recall that even though, on average, share prices do well in the long run, there can be some rocky times where they decline for sustained periods. On average, these periods of decline can be as long as two or three years with the exception of the period between 1999 and 2009, where the S&P 500 Index did not return double digits. In fact, it experienced a 2.72 percent decline, hence the reason older investors are encouraged to be more conservative in their investment portfolios.[157]

Even though aggressive investors have time on their side to help them overcome market fluctuations, that is just one element of being an aggressive investor. There is also the psychological element. Some people simply can't stand to see the wild market fluctuations, despite knowing the benefits of investing for the long term. This is an important element too. You have to know yourself. Why put money down on a risky investment and then experience sleepless nights due to wild market fluctuations? Age will influence the type of investor you are, but your mental state in dealing with roller-coaster market movements is also a factor.

Finally, if you also understand that winning with high-risk investments such as shares is not about timing the market but more about the time you let your money stay in the market, you will not worry about the

---

157   Kevin Mahn, "It's Not Really a Lost Decade," *Forbes*, September 13, 2010, https://www.forbes.com/sites/advisor/2010/09/13/its-not-really-a-lost-decade/?sh=268e87d27cf8.

roller-coaster movements that stock markets tend to go through.[158] Why? Because successfully timing the market, which day traders[159] are required to do consistently, is very hard when you consider the number of variables you have to analyze before you buy or sell a share and how hard it is to assess the implications of those variables. Variables include but are not limited to things like wars, pandemics, change of governments, inflation, and the actions of competitors on a company's shares. Investing for the long term (buy and hold), however, reduces the effects of market volatility, with the added assurance that in the long run you are very likely to earn an average of around 10–11 percent per year. If you plan to become wealthy by day trading as a side hustle, especially if you are a novice, you should seriously bear the above factors in mind and manage your expectations about the level of success you are likely to achieve. There is some debate about how much money novice day traders make or lose[160]—I'm not for either side of the debate; I'm simply highlighting important factors that must be considered before you embark on your day-trading activities.

Types of Investments

Let's now turn to the different types of investments, a few of which I briefly introduced already, for which I will list the fundamental concepts that you can build on. Your financial education never ends—remember, financial intelligence leads to financial independence.

A range of investments are available for us to talk about, but we will restrict the discussion to the most common forms that the average person is likely to consider. They are shares or stocks, bonds, money market instruments, real estate, unit trusts, mutual funds, index funds, and private business ventures. Other forms of investments such as cryptocurrency, art, gold, and other similar commodities are beyond the scope of this book. This book targets persons who

---

158   Ryan Downie, "Trying to Time the Stock Market Is a Bad Idea—Here's Why," The Motley Fool, July 4, 2021, https://www.fool.com/investing/2021/07/04/trying-to-time-the-stock-market-is-a-bad-idea/.

159   People who trade for short-term gains in securities such as shares or foreign exchange using online trading platforms.

160   Douglas Jordan & J. David Diltz, "The Profitability of Day Traders," *Financial Analysts Journal* 59, no. 6 (2003): 85–94, https://doi.org/10.2469/faj.v59.n6.2578.

need to know the fundamentals about growing, protecting, and sowing their money, which are the three master keys to financial freedom.

Shares or Stocks
Definitions

Investing in shares, also known as stocks, makes you a part owner of a company, and you become known as a shareholder. The opportunity to purchase shares generally comes when a privately owned company decides to sell some of its shares to the public, which is known as an initial public offering (IPO). Recent IPOs in Jamaica include those of Wigton Wind Farms (2019)[161] and Transjamaican Highway (2020).[162] They gave the general public an opportunity to become shareholders in these two companies. Famous IPOs in the U.S. include Facebook (2012)[163] and Uber (2019).[164]

Trading Shares on a Stock Market or Exchange

You can also purchase shares when an existing shareholder decides to sell their shares to someone else. Such transactions usually take place on a stock exchange or market. In Jamaica, it's the Jamaica Stock Exchange; in the UK, the London Stock Exchange; in the U.S., the New York Stock Exchange (among others); in Trinidad, the Trinidad & Tobago Stock Exchange; in Canada, the Toronto Stock Exchange;[165] and in the eastern Caribbean, the Eastern Caribbean Securities and Exchange, and so on.

To buy or sell shares on a stock exchange, you typically have to go through a stockbroker who will assist you in making the transaction. Stock

---

161   Chris Patterson, "Wigton Windfarm Now on Jamaica Stock Exchange," Jamaica Information Service, May 22, 2019, https://jis.gov.jm/wigton-windfarm-now-on-jamaica-stock-exchange/.

162   "Transjamaican Highway Biggest IPO on the JSE, Raising JA $14.1 Billion," Jamaica Stock Exchange, March 24, 2020, https://www.jamstockex.com/transjamaican-highway-biggest-ipo-on-the-jse-raising-ja14-1-billion/.

163   Julianne Pepitone, "Facebook Trading Sets Record IPO Volume," CNN Money, May 18, 2012, https://money.cnn.com/2012/05/18/technology/facebook-ipo-trading/index.htm.

164   Dan Blystone, "The Story of Uber," Investopedia, last modified September 19, 2021, https://www.investopedia.com/articles/personal-finance/111015/story-uber.asp.

165   "List of Stock Markets," TradingHours.com, accessed June 10, 2022, https://www.tradinghours.com/markets.

exchanges and stockbrokers have invested in technology that makes the ordering and selling process of shares a lot easier for the investing public. You can put in an order to buy or sell shares in your pajamas! It is that accessible. There are a number of stockbrokers in Jamaica. Their details can be found on the Jamaica Stock Exchange's website. A similar listing should be easily accessible via the website of your country's stock exchange.

When buying shares, you must first open an investment account with a broker, which is usually a straightforward process of showing a recognized form of identification, giving personal details, and providing the amount for which you would like to start the account.

Why invest in shares?

You stand to benefit in three ways when you invest in shares.

Dividend Yield

The first benefit is that many companies pay dividends. When companies make profits, they give the shareholders some of the profit in the form of a dividend, which is paid out on a periodic basis over the course of a year. There are some companies that are well known for paying high dividends. If you are interested in shares that provide a steady stream of cash coming in, then you may want to consider purchasing shares in one of these companies. Coca-Cola, for example, is well known for paying high dividends relative to many other companies.

To illustrate dividend yield, if you spent $10,000 (10,000 shares at $1 each) purchasing shares in a company, and in year one they paid out $300 in dividends, then you would have made a 3 percent return based on the initial price ($10,000) you paid for the shares. You can then compare this 3 percent return with other forms of investments such as bonds to see how they compare.

Capital Gains

Another reason investors put their money in shares is because of the potential increase in the share price, also known as capital gains. Going back to my example above, if the share price moved from $1 to $1.20 per share, that would be a 20 percent increase. That is the capital gain or appreciation, which is another benefit to the shareholder. These types of potential capital gains help to explain how persons can increase their wealth (net worth) over time when they invest in shares. You should start to see a big part of the reason why some of the richest people in the world—Jeff Bezos, Bill Gates, Jamaican Canadian billionaire Michael Lee-Chin,[166] and others—have amassed great wealth. They own shares in these highly profitable companies, and the share prices continue to grow in value. Let's take Jeff Bezos (ranked among the top three richest persons in the world in February 2022[167] with a net worth of $188 billion), who is a major shareholder in Amazon. The closing price of Amazon's share on December 31, 1999, was $3.81[168] and on December 31, 2021, it was $166.72,[169] a wild increase in his wealth—a 4,275 percent increase in the per unit price of his shares. Imagine how his net worth skyrocketed!

You should now be asking, "How do I calculate my total investment returns in shares given that I can make money in at least two ways: (1) dividend payments and (2) capital gains?" In our example above, a share price movement from $1 to $1.20 delivered a 20 percent capital gain, and the dividend received ($300) represented a 3 percent return on the original investment of $10,000, so in total, the return on this investment in shares is therefore 23 percent!

Insulation Against Inflation

The third reason people invest in shares is because it helps to fight the monster of inflation. Once the return you make on your investments is higher than the inflation rate, then you are being protected from inflation.

---

166   "Michael Lee-Chin," *Forbes,* accessed June 10, 2022, https://www.forbes.com/profile/michael-lee-chin/?sh=4695b1e93416.

167   Dan Moskowitz, "The 10 Richest People in the World," Investopedia, last modified June 1, 2022, https://www.investopedia.com/articles/investing/012715/5-richest-people-world.asp.

168   "Amazon Stock Price in 1999," Statmuse, accessed June 10, 2022, https://www.statmuse.com/money/ask/amazon+stock+price+in+1999.

169   "Amazon Stock Price in 2021," Statmuse, accessed June 10, 2022, https://www.statmuse.com/money/ask/amazon+stock+price+in+2021.

In fact, you could argue that the real rate of return on your investment is what is left after taking out the inflation rate. So, if the inflation rate was 5 percent for the year and, using my example above, the shares returned 23 percent over the same year, then the real rate of return would be 18 percent.

So, should I now be investing heavily in shares?

Before you start thinking that you want to buy up all the shares in the world because of amazing potential returns, remember that the price of the shares can go both up and down, and by down, I mean plummet.

Why do share prices fall?

There are a number of reasons the price of a share may fall. The main reason is a fall in a company's profits, and people conclude it will continue to fall in the foreseeable future. When Enron filed for bankruptcy in 2001, for example, its share price dropped from $90.75 per share in mid-2000 to less than $1 by the end of November 2001.[170] The shareholders in Enron lost it all. Imagine that you had 10,000 shares in Enron, which prior to the bankruptcy had been worth $907,500, and then in November 2001, they were worth less than $10,000. The example shows that shareholders can lose money and that there are risks associated with owning shares. Enron collapsed because it fraudulently overstated its financial performance (and therefore it wasn't as strong as it appeared to investors). When the investors discovered the accounting fraud, they lost confidence in the company, started selling their shares, and the share price dropped significantly.[171] So, speak to your financial adviser for advice before you invest in shares or make any other form of investment.

How do I pick the right company's share or stock to buy?

The following represent at least three things to consider about a company before investing your hard-earned money in its shares.

---

170   Troy Segal, "Enron Scandal: The Fall of a Wall Street Darling," Investopedia, last modified November 26, 2021, https://www.investopedia.com/updates/enron-scandal-summary/.

171   Segal, "Enron Scandal."

1. Leadership and Management

Leadership guru John Maxwell argues that "everything rises and falls on leadership."[172] That statement underscores and confirms the fact that a company's performance is heavily influenced by its leaders and managers. Certainly, leaders are not perfect, but their influence and strategic vision can seriously influence the success of a company. Just think of great corporate leaders such as Jack Welch and his influence on General Electric, Steve Jobs and his influence on Apple, Bill Gates's impact on Microsoft, and Jeff Bezos's impact on Amazon. Leaders and managers with the right vision, experience, and skills are more likely to lead their companies in achieving sustainable growth, while simultaneously practicing good environmental, social, and governance practices. You should, therefore, review the background and track record of the core leadership team before investing in a particular company. To dig deeper into understanding what good corporate leadership looks like, books such as *The Effective Executive* by Peter Drucker[173] as well as *Winning* by Jack Welch should prove to be very helpful.[174]

2. Deep Understanding of the Company's Business Model

To understand a company's business model, you must develop a deep understanding of the company's unique competitive advantage in delivering its products and services in the marketplace. Companies with a clear competitive advantage will attract and retain more loyal customers and, hence, make more profits. Just think of the phenomenal levels of profits and brand loyalty that exist for Apple products by millions of persons across the globe. On December 23, 2021, Apple remained the world's most valuable company with a market value or capitalization of $2.9 trillion (no, that was not a typo), up from $2.2 trillion as of December 31, 2020. Microsoft remained second

---

172   John C. Maxwell, *The 21 Irrefutable Laws of Leadership* (New York: Harper Collins Leadership, 2007), 267.

173   Peter F. Drucker, *The Effective Executive: The Definitive Guide to Getting the Right Things Done* (New York: Harper Business, 2017).

174   Jack Welch, *Winning* (New York: HarperCollins, 2005).

with $2.5 trillion up from $1.7 trillion.[175]

Such staggering valuations don't happen by chance! They happened because, among other things, Apple was able to establish a business model and create a unique place in the market for its innovative and highly functional products. Those factors have helped Apple to weather all sorts of economic and competitive storms and stand today as one of the most durable and profitable brands. Therefore, make sure you spend time understanding each company's operating model and what gives them their competitive advantage in the marketplace. *Blue Ocean Strategy* by W. Chan Kim and Renée Mauborgne,[176] and *Good to Great* by Jim Collins[177] will prove to be good reads on the matter of business and corporate strategy.

3. History of Profitable Growth

Anything that is not growing will eventually die, which also applies to companies. Companies that demonstrate a track record of profitable growth should be attractive as their success signals their long-term survival and the ability to pay dividends to shareholders. You should look at the historical performance of each company's profitability that you are considering. A strong and unique operating model, great management, and leadership set the foundation for a highly profitable company. The opposite is true. Listed companies (their shares can be traded on a stock exchange or market) are required to publish the financial statements to the public along with management's discussion and analysis of the company's performance; it is very easy to access the historical information you need directly via the company's website or through the stock exchanges.

---

175   Nicolas Vega, "Microsoft's Market Cap Grew More than $800 Billion in 2021—Here's How It Compares to the Most Valuable Companies in the World," CNBC, December 27, 2021, https://www.cnbc.com/2021/12/27/how-much-the-biggest-companies-grew-in-2021.html.

176   W. Chan Kim and Renée Mauborgne, *Blue Ocean Strategy: How to Create Uncontested Market Space and Make the Competition Irrelevant* (Boston: Harvard Business School Publishing Corporation, 2015).

177   Jim Collins, *Good to Great: Why Some Companies Make the Leap ... Others Don't* (New York: HarperBusiness, 2001).

Do you have the time and skill?

I've given you at least three factors to consider when picking stocks, but the analysis required is no easy walk in the park. You must have the time and skills to do this. You must comb through many years' worth of financial and nonfinancial information for multiple companies in different industries. I believe the average investor would not have the time or the skill to do the required deep research and analysis. It is therefore prudent for the average person to reach out to a trained investment professional for help in navigating the world of investing in shares. In today's world it is as easy as one, two, three for anyone to set up an online trading account with online brokers such as Robin Hood and start trading stocks right from the comfort of their homes or a streetside café! If you have the time and skill, certainly you can go ahead and trade stocks on your own, but be prepared for the necessary time and risks, and ensure you have the skill required.

A lot more could be said about shares, but this book is not seeking to make you into an investing expert.

Bonds

A bond is a loan that an investor makes to a borrower (usually a company or a government) for a period of time and for which the investor is compensated with fixed interest payments. Investors in bonds are basically lenders—investors in shares are owners.[178]

To illustrate, a company that wishes to raise funds via a bond issue would typically do so by a bond circular, the essence of which reads:

> Company A hereby invites purchasers of bond series ABC with a total issue amount of $10 million paying a coupon (interest) rate of 6 percent per annum. The bond will mature in five years. The bonds can be purchased in denominations of $1,000 (face amount) for each unit of the bond.

If you saw this circular and decided to invest $15,000, you would get 15

---

178   Tim Parker, "The Basics of Bonds," Investopedia, last modified March 31, 2021, https://www.investopedia.com/financial-edge/0312/the-basics-of-bonds.aspx.

bond units at $1,000 per unit, paying a coupon of 6 percent per year. If you hold the bond units until the end of the five years (until it matures), you will get back the face amount of $15,000 plus the interest earned at 6 percent.

The main issuers of bonds are governments and companies. Governments issue bonds to raise funds to help run their countries—for example, to build roads, schools, hospitals, police stations, and similar infrastructure. The entity issuing the bond is the bond issuer, and the entity or person buying the bond (the investor) is the bondholder. Companies also issue bonds and use the funds to expand their businesses, develop new products, enter new markets, and do large capital projects. The bond issuers typically issue the bonds in tranches or denominations at the interest rate that the bondholders would be compensated, which is called the coupon rate.

The process by which bonds are acquired is similar to that described under the section above on shares. It starts with opening an investment account with an investment management company or broker.

Why invest in bonds?

The reasons to invest in bonds are similar to those for investing in shares—to get a better return than that on a savings account, to be protected from the ravages of inflation, to grow your money, and to increase your net worth. People also invest in bonds if they are interested in getting a predictable amount of cash flow in the form of interest payments each month or quarter, unlike shares where dividend payments are not guaranteed. Persons approaching retirement age typically find bonds attractive because of the predictable flow of cash.

How do I make money on bonds?

The return you make on a bond is two-fold. First, you receive interest payments per year, and second, if you sell the bond (or hold it to maturity), you may make a gain or loss compared to the price at which you acquired the bond. You don't have to hold the bond until the maturity date. You can sell it before then on what is known as the bond market, similar to buying and selling shares on a stock market. The combination of the coupon (interest) payments and the gain or loss on the bond sale (or if you hold it to maturity) would give the effective rate of return on the bond. You can then compare this rate of return to other types of investments to see how they perform.

The sale price of your bond is dependent on whether current interest rates in the market are higher or lower than the coupon rate on your bond that you bought some time ago. If current interest rates are higher, then people would want to buy your bond at a lower price (at a discount) to compensate for the fact that they would be getting a lower interest rate than what they could get in the market today. If current rates are lower, then you would want to sell your bond at a higher price (a premium) to compensate for the fact that you would be giving up a higher rate of interest on your bond than what you could get in the market today.

You may be saying, "Bruce, my head is spinning with all of this premium and discount stuff."

Sorry, I tried to keep it as straightforward as I could. The key thing to note is that you can make money on bonds from the interest payments received plus or minus the gain or loss you make when you sell a bond or hold it to maturity. If you get this point, then you have understood.

How to Pick Bonds

The most critical factor to consider is the bondholder's ability to repay the principal that was borrowed and the periodic interest payments that are due over the life of the bond. Bondholders are said to default on their payments if they are not able to honor those obligations. A default would, therefore, put the bond investors at risk of losing all or part of their investment. Argentina, for example, has defaulted nine times in its history on its debt payments, the last time being December 2021.[179] Therefore, anyone considering investing in bonds from any government or corporation should definitely take default history into consideration before investing.

---

179   Agustino Fontevecchia, "2001 to 2021: Argentina, A Ticking Time Bomb," *Forbes*, December 24, 2021, https://www.forbes.com/sites/afontevecchia/2021/12/24/2001-to-2021-argentina-a-ticking-time-bomb/?sh=3d349aac3310.

International ratings agencies such as Moody's Investor Services, Fitch Group, and Standard & Poor's provide the independent bond ratings that can guide investors as to which bonds are safe and which ones are high risk.[180] Caribbean Information & Credit Rating Services Limited (CariCRIS) provides bond ratings for bonds issued by governments and companies in the Caribbean.[181]

You should speak to your financial adviser before you invest in bonds as there is no need for you to try to do all these financial analyses on your own as an everyday, ordinary investor unless, of course, as mentioned above, you have the time and skill to do the required analyses.

Who should buy bonds?

Bonds are targeted at investors with a moderate risk profile, given that the bond prices generally don't swing as wildly as share prices. Typically, bonds are issued for one year or more, so depending on your investment horizon, you can pick a bond that matches your investment goals. The key is to purchase from a financially sound entity that has a low risk of default.

Your financial adviser will recommend bonds in keeping with your investment horizon, risk profile, and goals. The general idea is that, if you can take some risk but not as much as an aggressive investor, bonds may be an option for you. Bonds will generally pay higher than what you earn in a savings account and can range from 4 to 9 percent in Jamaica and are influenced by a number of factors including but not limited to the prevailing inflation rate and the financial strength of the bond issuer.

Money Market Instruments

These are short-term investments that have maturity dates of one year or less. These instruments can also be readily converted to cash before the maturity date in the event the funds are needed, and they represent a form of borrowing, similar to bonds, where the investor lends money in ex-

---

180   "S&P, Moody's, Fitch Ratings Compared," Moneyland.ch, accessed June 14, 2022, https://www.moneyland.ch/en/rating-agencies.

181   "About CariCRIS," Caribbean Information & Credit Rating Services Limited (CariCRIS), accessed June 14, 2022, https://www.caricris.com/index.php/about.

change for one of these instruments. The interest rates are lower than on bonds due to the low risk involved, but the rates are higher than what you would earn on a savings account. Risk is low because the money invested is virtually guaranteed to be repaid in full (unlike bonds and shares) and because the issuers are usually financially sound, such as companies and governments with sound financial metrics.

Types of Money Market Instruments

These include treasury bills, repurchase agreements, and commercial paper. Investors will purchase money market instruments when the investors have excess cash but know that the excess cash will be needed in a short period of time.

These instruments are, therefore, good if you know that you will be, say, paying the closing costs on your house in three months' time. Purchasing a money market instrument is a good middle ground instead of putting that money in the stock market—risking losing a portion of your principal—or putting it in a savings account at extremely low rates.

Another great use of money market instruments is to stash some of your emergency fund instead of leaving all of it in a regular savings account. To buy money market securities, you typically will go through your investment management company and follow a similar process to that of opening an investment account as you would for a bond.

Treasury bills are considered to be risk-free given that they are usually issued by government entities such as a central bank. Interest rates are low, and the maturity periods are one year or less.[182]

Repurchase agreements are issued by both companies and governments and create an arrangement in which the borrower sells a security to the lender and agrees to purchase it back at an agreed date and price. The original sum received (the principal) is returned on the maturity date while the interest is paid over the period of time leading up to the

---

182   Adam Hayes, "Treasury Bills (T-Bills)," Investopedia, last modified June 2, 2022, https://www.investopedia.com/terms/t/treasurybill.asp.

maturity date.[183]

Commercial paper is a form of short-term lending by companies without any form of security or collateral (it is basically an unsecured loan) that pays back the principal at the end of the maturity period and interest up to the time that the commercial paper matures.[184]

Real Estate

Real estate is another investment option for investors.

Real estate spans commercial and residential properties. Residential properties include apartments, condominiums, townhouses, and single-family homes. Commercial properties include warehouses, office spaces, parking lots, plazas, and malls. Both types of properties represent investment opportunities, given that the investor is able to make a return through rental income and capital appreciation on the value of the properties. More on rental income and capital appreciation to come later.

Six Challenges to Understand Before Investing in Real Estate
1. Up-front Costs of Real Estate Investing

It usually takes a lot more money to buy a piece of real estate than it takes to invest in shares or other types of investments. Typically, the minimum cash required for an investor to participate in a real estate transaction that is being financed with a mortgage loan is 5–10 percent of the price of the property plus transaction cost, with the remaining 90–95 percent coming from the mortgage company. Therefore, a one-bedroom apartment costing $150,000, requiring a 10 percent deposit and $3,000 of closing costs, would require $18,000 up front from the investor compared to $1 or less to buy a single share or stock. The higher up-front cash requirement for real estate often creates a barrier for some investors and may take several years to accumulate the minimum up-front cash required.

---

183   Nathan Reiff, "Repurchase Agreement (Repo)," Investopedia, last modified March 5, 2022, https://www.investopedia.com/terms/r/repurchaseagreement.asp.

184   Adam Hayes, "Commercial Paper," Investopedia, last modified March 31, 2021, https://www.investopedia.com/terms/c/commercialpaper.asp.

2. Time to Complete a Real Estate Deal

It also usually takes a longer time to complete a real estate transaction than it does to purchase stocks or bonds. In Jamaica, a property sale can take between three and six months compared to buying bonds or shares, which can take two or three days for the transaction to close. Again, investors must take note of these timelines before pursuing real estate investment opportunities.

3. Time to Find the Right Property

According to real estate experts, perhaps the single most important factor that should drive a real estate investment decision is the location of the property. The right location is usually influenced by how close the property is to schools, employment opportunities, shopping malls, golf courses, parks, and other conveniences. You may need to look at a hundred properties before you find one that you are really interested in, even with the help of a real estate broker.

4. Transaction Costs

Real estate transactions usually have relatively higher transaction costs than other investment options such as stocks or bonds. Transaction costs include legal fees paid to attorneys (e.g., reviewing sale agreements), real estate agents' commissions, and government taxes. In Jamaica, transaction costs can range between 5 and 10 percent of the selling price of a piece of real estate. Transaction costs relating to stocks, on the other hand, usually range between 0.05 and 3 percent of the amount being invested and typically are paid to a brokerage firm that facilitates the transaction. Again, investors must estimate transaction costs when buying real estate, to determine the true cost of their purchases.

5. Cost to Maintain Real Estate

Another factor that you will need to consider is the cost to maintain real estate. Failure to consider all costs could result in a lower return on your real estate investment than you expected. Maintenance costs include property taxes, gardening, repairs, and property insurance, among others.

6. Time Commitment

Real estate also requires major time commitments, which must be factored into your decision before you choose to own investment property. Time will be needed to deal with tenants, plumbers, strata meetings, and similar items. Alternatively, you could pay a property manager to attend to all these items, but of course, that cost must be factored into your overall return on investment calculation. That degree of time commitment does not exist with stocks, bonds, mutual funds, or unit trusts (discussed in detail later on) as the fund managers are paid to do all the work.

Notwithstanding those six challenges, real estate still represents a popular and attractive investment class for those who are willing to face the challenges head on and reap the following rewards:

1. The ability to earn monthly cash flow from rental income, unlike dividend income from shares, which are not guaranteed.

2. The potential average annual increase in the value of your property, as landlords tend to increase the rentals charged to tenants in line with the inflation rate — this then drives up the amount of the rental income, which then drives up the value of the property itself.

3. The ability to leverage a relatively small amount of cash on an investment property by putting down a deposit of 5–10 percent of the value of the property and then using a low-cost mortgage to complete the purchase of the property. This property could then go on to generate significant rental income and capital appreciation for the investor. For example, Beverly could put down only 10 percent ($29,500) on a property being sold for $295,000 and then obtain a low-cost mortgage for the remaining $265,500 (90 percent) to purchase this property. Within 10 years, this property, which she was able to access with only $29,500 of her money, went on to value $430,700, which represents a 46 percent increase. That potential is not impossible, as according to RenoFi,[185] house prices in the U.S. increased by

---

185   Jasmin Suknanan, "This Is How Much It Could Cost to Buy a House in the U.S. by 2030—and Tips on How to Start Saving Now," CNBC, January 26, 2022, https://www.cnbc.com/select/how-much-will-a-home-in-the-us-cost-by-2030.

48.55 percent in the last 10 years. Recall also that Beverly would be collecting rental income from her tenant, which adds to the overall return on her investment. Beware of the risks involved though—if, say, Beverly lost her tenant for six months or a year, she would have to continue paying the mortgage to prevent the property from being foreclosed. Would Beverly be able to do that? Would you be able to do that? You must therefore think of all the risks and have your safeguards before you take the plunge into leveraging debt to purchase investment properties. Read chapter 9 again where I talk about some of the risks and rewards of borrowing. I also recommend Michael Dominguez's book, *Armchair Real Estate Millionaire*,[186] in which he gives important truths about building wealth through real estate investing while leveraging debt.

4. The ability to buy a fixer-upper property (say you got a deal for $100,000), spend a relatively small amount (say $20,000) to repair and remodel the property, and then be able to sell (flip) that property for, say, $180,000 after a 12-month period and earn $60,000 ($180,000 less $120,000) all other things remaining constant. That's a 50 percent return on investment ($60,000/$120,000) and shows the magnitude of the potential gain as well as the time commitment required for flipping houses. Again, another caution, assess the risks involved in flipping houses, and then make your moves after establishing your safeguards. For example, in 2021 in the U.S., two key risks that property investors had to grapple with were lower profitability due to rising inflation and mortgage rates.[187]

Real estate, (principal residences and investment properties) form a key part of the net worth of 90 percent of millionaires.[188] It is, therefore,

186   Michael Dominguez, *Armchair Real Estate Millionaire: If You're Sitting There Anyway, You Might as Well Build Your Wealth* (Bazinga Publishing, 2020).

187   Diana Olick, "Home Flipping Is Getting More Competitive—and Less Profitable," CNBC, last modified December 20, 2021, https://www.cnbc.com/2021/12/20/home-flipping-more-competitive-less-profitable.html.

188   Jonathan Yates, "90% of the World's Millionaires Do This to Create Wealth," The College Investor, October 24, 2011, https://thecollegeinvestor.com/11300/90-percent-worlds-millionaires-do-this.

an investment class that you should seriously consider as part of your investment portfolio.

Calculating Investment Returns on Investment Properties

You must also know how to compute the rate of return on your real estate investments so that you can see how it compares to other types of investments. The return is the combination of rental income (what you charge tenants for using the property for a period of time) net of expenses associated with earning the rental income plus capital appreciation (or depreciation) in the value of the property over time.

For example, if you bought a property for $300,000 on January 1, 2021, and you earned rental income of $33,600 ($2,800 per month) for the 12-month period to December 31, 2021, how would you go about computing the return on investment? As indicated above, first, you must deduct any expenses incurred in earning the rental income (mortgage interest expense, repairs and maintenance, property taxes, etc.). Let's say these expenses amounted to $2,000 per month. The net rental income would be $800 per month ($9,600 for the year), which gives a 3.2 percent return ($9,600 / $300,000). But wait! That's not the total return on the investment. There is another component.

Let's say that if, as of December 31, the value of the apartment increased to $315,000, the increase would represent a capital appreciation or gain of $15,000. The total return on the initial $300,000 investment on January 1, 2021, would, therefore, be the $9,600 of net rental income plus $15,000 of capital gain, which gives a total gain of $24,600 for the year, or an 8.2 percent return ($24,600/$300,000).

Unit Trusts and Mutual Funds

Unit trusts and mutual funds are referred to as collective investment schemes in which many individual investors agree to pool their money to create greater returns and benefits that an individual investor would not necessarily be able to enjoy.

Unit trusts and mutual funds are the same for all practical purposes except for the legal structures that give rise to them. The unit trust has a trustee who owns the underlying securities in the unit trust on behalf of the unit holders, and there is a trust deed that specifies how the unit trust is to invest and operate. The presence of the trustee means that the investors' (unit holders) funds are 100 percent segregated from those of the fund manager (see definition below), which provides protection to the unit holders in the event of any financial difficulty with the fund manager. A mutual fund does not have a trustee—however, there is an independent custodian (usually a company) that holds the securities or assets of the fund on behalf of the fund. Note that the custodian holds the underlying securities, as opposed to having beneficial interest in the securities, on behalf of the mutual fund investors. As of March 31, 2019, in Jamaica, there were 19 local unit trusts, one local mutual fund, and 10 overseas mutual funds registered by the Financial Services Commission (FSC) for sale.[189] There are thousands of mutual funds in the U.S.[190]

For the discussion that follows, and given that unit trusts and mutual funds are substantially the same, I will be referring to unit trusts only, except where otherwise noted or the context suggests otherwise.

In a unit trust, each investor is allocated units (shares in the case of mutual funds) based on the amount of money they invested in the pool of funds. This pooling introduces one of the big advantages of investing in a unit trust: A smaller investor would now have the ability to invest in certain types of securities that they perhaps wouldn't otherwise be able to invest in on their own. For example, investing in certain bonds normally requires at least a certain amount of money. (Depending on the country, there could be a minimum of $1,000.) That hurdle disappears when the investor is part of a pooled bond fund where the investor can enter the fund with as little as $100.

---

189   "Savings in Unit Trusts, Mutual Funds Rise but Withdrawals Also High," Jamaica Loop News, November 10, 2019, https://jamaica.loopnews.com/content/savings-unit-trusts-mutual-funds-rise-withdrawals-also-high.

190   "Number of Mutual Funds in the United States from 1997 to 2020," Statista, May 2021, https://www.statista.com/statistics/255590/number-of-mutual-fund-companies-in-the-united-states/.

The pool is usually managed by a fund manager. These professionals must meet high standards of conduct as stipulated by the regulatory authorities such as the Financial Services Commission in Jamaica, the Financial Conduct Authority (FCA) in the UK, or the Securities and Exchange Commission in the U.S. Fund managers are usually compensated by being paid a percentage (1–3 percent) of the value of the pool of funds they are managing.

There are different types of unit trusts. The difference between each type is generally the underlying investment in which each trust invests. Some types invest only in shares. Other types of unit trusts include those that invest in bonds only, money market securities only, and even real estate only. There are unit trusts that invest in a mix of bonds and shares, or any other conceivable combination of securities, called balanced funds, offering another layer of diversification.

Why invest in unit trusts?

Apart from some of the reasons outlined above, a fundamental advantage of investing in a unit trust is that you will benefit from diversification of your money. Remember the saying "Don't put all your eggs into one basket?" A unit trust allows you to follow that wise advice by spreading the money over a wide range of shares in different industries and even different countries so that if a particular industry sector is not performing well, the downturn is offset by another sector that may be doing well. Unit trust managers often limit how much of the pool of funds they invest in a particular company and so on.

Perhaps one of the greatest advantages of unit trusts is the liquidity factor—the ability to draw down on your investment at relatively short notice, up to one or two days for most unit trusts. You simply complete an encashment form or equivalent, and the funds are in your personal account within a short timeframe—not so with a real estate investment, which could take months or years to be liquidated. Even an investment in a single stock could take days or weeks to sell. Note, however, some unit trusts require you to keep your money untouched for a period of three months before making any withdrawals. Prior to that period, withdrawals usually attract a penalty of up to as much as 3 percent, which encourages discipline among investors to keep their money working for them.

A possible disadvantage with unit trusts is that, if the fees charged by the fund manager are high in relation to the returns, the fund manager is able to deliver from the portfolio they manage. As I stated, some funds charge up to 3 percent of the value of the pool of funds they are managing. For example, if your fund manager charges 3 percent of the value of the funds per year, and over the years they can't deliver growth in the portfolio of greater than 3 percent per year, then you need to hunt for a new fund manager. You must find one that can deliver a return higher than the management fees that are charged and ensure the net return (after management fees) is still attractive when compared to similar or comparable forms of investment, all other things remaining constant.

How do I make money off unit trusts?

You make money on your unit trust holdings similarly to how you would from buying an individual share or stock at a certain price and selling at a higher price. So, if you bought units at $100 per unit, and the unit price goes up by $10 in a year's time, you would have earned $10 (10 percent). The rate of return is going to be based on the type of unit trust and the investment therein. Like most investments, unit trusts that invest in more risky investments will, in the long run, give a higher return. Similarly, unit trust prices can also go down, given that the behavior of the unit price will be linked to the nature of the underlying securities.

Index Funds

An index fund is an example of a mutual fund, except that instead of a professional fund manager picking the underlying investments, they are picked by reference to a market index (e.g., the S&P 500 Index in the U.S., which I introduced earlier, or the FTSE 100 index in the UK, which is made up of the 100 largest companies on the London Stock Exchange).

Index funds are also referred to as passive funds, given that the underlying management of the investment portfolio is not managed by a fund manager.

Why invest in index funds instead of traditional mutual funds or unit trusts?

One of the key advantages of investing in an index fund is lower management fees because index funds are not actively managed by professional fund managers. There are index funds with management fees less than 0.5 percent[191] compared to the typical mutual fund or unit trust with fees ranging from 1-plus percent.[192]

Given the benefits of lower management fees and the argument that index funds generally outperform most actively managed funds,[193] two of the world's greatest investing minds—Jack Bogle, who has been credited with starting the first index fund at the Vanguard Group, and Warren Buffett—believe that the average investor should invest primarily in index funds.[194] The argument is that these investors usually don't have the skills to pick individual stocks, and they would pay much lower management fees while enjoying returns that are as good as or better than most actively managed funds—recall I mentioned earlier that the S&P index averaged a return of 10.5 percent per year over the 64-year period to 2021[195]—this demonstrates the consistency and power of investing in index funds.

Vanguard and Fidelity are two of the key entities in the U.S. that offer index fund products. Getting started is as simple as logging onto their web-

---

191   Dori Zinn, "The Best Index Funds with Low Expense Ratios You Can Invest in Right Now," NextAdvisor in Partnership with *Time,* February 15, 2022, https://time.com/nextadvisor/investing/5-best-index-funds-low-expense-ratio/.

192   Michael Weiss, "What Constitutes a 'High Fee' for a Mutual Fund?," Investopedia, last modified January 31, 2022, https://www.investopedia.com/articles/mutualfund/07/stop_fees.asp.

193   Greg Iacurci, "Some Mutual Funds Are Pricier Than Others. Here's When They May Benefit Investors," CNBC, November 24, 2020, https://www.cnbc.com/2020/11/24/heres-when-active-mutual-funds-tend-to-outperform-index-funds.html.

194   Elizabeth MacBride, "A Stubborn Investing Rule, Shared by Jack Bogle and Warren Buffett," CNBC, April 17, 2017, https://www.google.com/amp/s/www.cnbc.com/amp/2017/04/17/a-stubborn-investing-rule-shared-by-jack-bogle-and-warren-buffett.html.

195   Maverick, "What Is the Average Return."

sites, creating an account, and providing the required personal information and banking details. Vanguard and Fidelity typically have branches in other parts of the world, or you may have your local equivalent to them.[196] In Jamaica, index funds are not very popular, but at least one investment management company has developed index funds that track the performance of companies in the manufacturing and financial services sectors. If you believe you have a mutual fund or unit trust fund that has a track record of outperforming the major index funds in your country, then maybe you should consider that particular mutual fund or unit trust.

Before investing in a mutual fund, index fund, or unit trust (1) look at the returns that they have provided in the last 10–20 years, (2) consider the management fees charged, and (3) seek financial advice and then make your decision in keeping with your risk appetite and investment goals.

Investing in a Business

Instead of putting your money into shares, real estate, bonds, unit trusts, index funds, or mutual funds, you could invest in a private business. Yes, the modern conveniences (cars, planes, elevators, etc.) that we enjoy today are a result of someone using their money to start a business built on the back of an idea. Such visionary ideas have helped to make the world a better place today. Consequently, there is a logic for investing in a private business, which can potentially make you far more money than if you invested in stocks and bonds. For example, some importers of certain niche products in Jamaica generate investment returns in the region of 30–40 percent per year—far above the 10 percent average of traditional forms of investment such as index funds (shares based). Note, however, there are big risks (new competitors, changes in government laws and regulations, pandemics) and big time commitments that are required in running a business, such as dealing with suppliers, customers, banks, and other stakeholders. In the end, the question is "How do you compare dealing with the heartaches (risks) involved in running a business and the time required

196   Jean Fogler, "Vanguard vs. Fidelity Investments," Investopedia, last modified May 17, 2022, https://www.investopedia.com/vanguard-vs-fidelity-4587961.

versus putting your money on, say, an index fund where you literally don't do anything or much and still make a decent—albeit, smaller—potential return of 10 percent?" Your risk appetite and investment goals will determine your answer. You can even enjoy the best of both worlds by investing some surplus profits from the business in traditional forms of investments, for example mutual funds or shares. Again, the choice is yours.

Angel Investors

Angel investors are private individuals who have the capacity and the funds (high net worth individuals) to take an ownership stake in usually a start-up company that is being run by someone else. Some angel investors have a passion for giving back to the community and fund start-up projects that align with their passion. Other angel investors are strictly entrepreneurs who are seeking investment opportunities that are better than those provided by the traditional investment types.[197] Examples of angel investors are Jamaica's first angel investor network, FirstAngelsJA, and the investors on the TV program *Shark Tank*. On *Shark Tank*, the investors (the "sharks") listen to the pitches of the business ideas, and then they try to outbid each other for ownership stakes in these companies.[198] Therefore, if you don't want to spend a lot of time running a business yourself, being an angel investor is another opportunity for you to consider.

Return on Investment (ROI)

Private businesses measure the return on their investment by dividing the net profit generated by the business by the capital invested in the business ($250,000 invested in a business that made a profit of $25,000 is 10 percent ROI). You are now able to compare that return with other forms of investments (bonds, shares) to see how your business investment compares.[199]

---

197   Akhilesh Ganti, "Angel Investor," Investopedia, last modified March 22, 2022, https://www.investopedia.com/terms/a/angelinvestor.asp.

198   Max Nilsen, "Here's What 'Shark Tank' Looks Like in 9 Different Countries," Business Insider, November 12, 2013, https://www.businessinsider.com/shark-tank-international-versions-2013-11.

199   Andrew Beattie, "A Guide to Calculating Return on Investment (ROI)," Investopedia, last modified June 3, 2022, https://www.investopedia.com/articles/basics/10/guide-to-calculating-roi.asp.

Important Investment Keys

I will close this chapter by addressing some key things to bear in mind as you enter the world of investing.

Diversification

I spoke about diversification earlier, which essentially means not putting all your eggs in one basket. The principle of diversification is especially important for persons who are closer to retirement and would not have the time to build back their financial base if they were to lose it all.

Diversification Mix

How should I spread my money across the different types of investments? There is a wide cross section of views and theories on this subject. I will give you some general principles on how to spread your money around.

There is the rule of 100 that states that you should subtract your age from 100, and the figure you get should be invested in high-risk investments such as shares, and the rest you invest in less risky investments such as bonds and or money market securities. Angela, who is 22 years old, would therefore be encouraged to invest 78 percent of her money in higher risk investments such as shares, and 22 percent in lower risk investments such as bonds. The rule of 100 is technically sound, given that it suggests that the younger you are, the greater the portion of your money you should invest in more risky investments, as you would have time to watch these investments grow and to deal with the ups and downs of the market.[200] Given that persons are living longer, some now argue for the rule of 110, allocating even more money to riskier investments.

I like the rule of 110 better, as it recognizes that people live longer, so they are able to maximize the performance of their investment portfolios over a longer life span. These rules are good guides, and they don't necessarily mean that each year you have to literally change your portfolio mix by 1 percent as you get older!

Ultimately, the final portfolio mix that you choose should be linked

---

200   "What Is the Rule of 100?," IAMS Wealth Management, August 2020, https://iamswealth-management.com/wp-content/uploads/2020/08/Rules-of-100.pdf.

to your risk profile and the timelines you have for your investment goals.

Remember that it is important that you find the right portfolio mix of risky and low-risk investments to ensure your investment grows at a reasonable rate to reach your goals. The rules of 100 and 110 exist to help you accomplish exactly that! A portfolio that is too conservative is unlikely to generate a return that consistently beats the rate of inflation.

An investment adviser will also be able to help you devise the optimal investment mix based on your risk appetite, your age, and your planned retirement date.

Portfolio Rebalancing

Over time, as your portfolio grows, it will move in a manner that goes out of line with your desired portfolio mix. For example, if your target for the next three years is to have a portfolio that has 75 percent shares and 25 percent bonds, it is likely after year one that the value of the portfolio mix, on its own, could have moved to, say, 80 percent shares and 20 percent bonds based on the performance of each. In that case, you will need to sell some shares or buy more bonds to get back to the 75:25 ratio. That tactic is called rebalancing your portfolio. Some persons routinely rebalance their portfolios once per year. There is no magic formula, really, and the key is to monitor your investments at least every month, from which you will sense when you need to rebalance. At a minimum, however, you should take a formal look with the specific objective of rebalancing your portfolio at least once per year.

Ponzi Schemes

You should avoid Ponzi schemes like the plague! A Ponzi scheme, like the one operated by Bernie Madoff, typically claims exceptionally high investment returns when compared to traditional or other forms of investments. Ponzi schemes are essentially marketed as get-rich-quick schemes, with little transparency about the underlying investments that are generating the high returns. The potential to acquire massive wealth in a short period of time creates a lot of excitement on the part of the prospective investors and provides incentives for them to invite other investors into the scheme, which keep such schemes going. According to Investor.gov, Ponzi schemes offer little or no legitimate earnings, and they require a constant flow of new money to survive. When it becomes hard to recruit new investors, or when large numbers of existing investors cash out, these schemes tend to collapse.[201]

The lure and the excitement of high returns and the prospect of a rich lifestyle in a very short period of time causes many people to invest all or a lot of their money, much more than they can afford to lose, and often they get burned. I recall years ago a lady called me to ask what I thought about certain investment schemes. I told her that for schemes that sound too good to be true—which this one was—that the caution is to put in only what you could afford to lose or just don't invest at all. I personally don't invest in these schemes at all! Some months later I got a call from the person who put in practically all of their life savings and lost it all when the scheme exploded. I said, "Why did you put in so much?"

The person indicated that when she saw that her friends were getting consistently high returns over a number of years, she felt as if it must be real. But in less than a month or two after she participated, the scheme crashed.

Before entertaining any investment offering returns that seem too good to be true, you should perform the following checks:

- Check if the investment company or person is regulated by the relevant authorities (the U.S. Securities and Exchange Commission, the Bank of Jamaica, or Jamaica's Financial Services Commission). If they are not regulated by the particular authority responsible for that particular type of investing activity, then you should run for your financial life. The 1990s and 2000s saw a wave of Ponzi schemes across the Caribbean, many of which collapsed and

---

201   "Ponzi Schemes," Investor.gov: U.S. Securities and Exchange Commission, accessed June 14, 2022, https://www.investor.gov/introduction-investing/investing-basics/glossary/ponzi-schemes.

brought untold financial stress and grief to thousands.[202] To warn the public not to invest in unregistered operations, the FSC in Jamaica published a list of unregistered investment schemes in 2009.

- Ask for audited financial statements. Reputable companies engage an independent set of professional auditors to review the financial records and comment on whether things are real or false. Investment companies that refuse to offer these or the name of their independent auditors are big red flags.

- Research the owners and principals of the investment company to learn about their background and reputation. Oftentimes, the principals have criminal records relating to fraud or financial crimes, and they move to different locations or states to lure unsuspecting victims to their nefarious schemes. Doing a quick Google search could save you a lot of heartache and pain.

- Check if others have had difficulty in cashing out or receiving investment returns on expected dates. Ponzi schemes require a constant stream of new persons to fund payments to prior investors; therefore, pulling out cash is a threat to the scheme's ability to make payments on time.

Dealing with Investment and Financial Advisers

Investment and financial advisers are professionals who are licensed by the regulators to give financial advice on securities and to give specific recommendations on how you can invest your money, allocate your portfolios, and so on. They, and the companies by which they are employed, are monitored by the regulators in order to protect the public's interest. I include life insurance agents, wealth advisers, and similar professionals in the category of financial or investment advisers.

Please ensure that your adviser is not just giving you commands and instructions—make sure you understand what you are investing in. You

---

202   "FSC Publishes List of 40 Unregulated Investment Schemes," Radio Jamaica News Online, February 16, 2009, http://radiojamaicanewsonline.com/business/fsc-publishes-list-of-40-unregulated-investment-schemes.

must read and understand the details and the fine print, and you should only invest after you have a comprehensive understanding of what the underlying risks, rewards, and other details are.

Too many times individuals with whom I talk about their investment portfolios can't answer basic questions about what they have invested in. You must only invest in what you understand. Your financial adviser should educate you based on your options, but you must do your own independent research, and then you—not your adviser—should decide where your money will go.

Sadly, not all advisers have their clients' best interests at heart. We know it because there have been so many heartbreaking stories of sports stars and others who have been robbed of millions by their advisers. Tim Duncan, a National Basketball Association star, reportedly lost approximately $20 million in 2013 due to the actions of a dishonest financial adviser.[203] It was reported that the adviser coerced Duncan into investments that he, the adviser, had a financial interest in but that he never disclosed to Duncan and that ended up losing value.

Another way to reduce the risk and the potential losses of being defrauded by dishonest financial advisers is to spend time checking in on your money. Too many times people hand over their hard-earned cash to others to handle without staying close! We must find time for the management of our money; otherwise, before we know it, our money might fly away with wings like a dove!

Keeping an Eye on Your Money

To illustrate the point (albeit, now with a slightly different perspective) further about staying close to your money, I was talking to someone in his early 50s who told me he had been paying money toward a certain investment at a financial institution every month for over five years. When he eventually called them up one day, he learned that he had much less than what he first invested—more than 50 percent less! They explained that ad-

203   Andrew Goodman, "What Athletes Can Learn from Tim Duncan's Alleged $20M Financial Loss," *Forbes*, November 11, 2015, https://www.forbes.com/sites/agoodman/2015/11/11/what-athletes-can-learn-from-tim-duncans-alleged-20m-financial-loss/?sh=68735e502204.

ministrative charges had to be deducted based on his age (the product had an investment and an insurance component), among other reasons. The key point here, though, is that if a basic check had been done online or via phone at, say, the end of year one of the investment, he would have seen that "di likkle money did a dwingle" (the little money was going down) and a decision could have been made about whether to keep it or pull it out. I check my investment accounts multiple times per month. For example, when I transfer funds to investment account A, I always send a message to say, "Hey, I just transferred $$ to my account, please confirm." Then I log in and check. In addition to the foregoing, I log on just to see how things are going multiple times per month. You should follow a similar practice.

I want to make a special appeal again for you to keep your eyes on how your pension plans/retirement funds at work or in your individual retirement accounts/investments are progressing as well. One of the easiest ways to keep watch is to ensure that you get your annual pension/retirement fund statements or to log on to the pension manager's website to track how your pension is doing. The statement or online account should show all the money you and your employer have been contributing to the plan as well as the investment rate of return. You must check regularly because you want to know if the money is growing at a rate that will generate enough monthly income when you retire. As discussed in chapter 10, if you see that the investments are not likely to give you the income you want in retirement, then you will need to start thinking of saving more, working another job, or taking some other action to ensure you have the additional funds that you will need to have set aside. Don't wait until you are almost retired to start taking action. Don't be like the person who called me to say, "Bruce, I got a letter from HR to thank me for my many years of service and that my retirement will be starting in one month's time." Yes, this person didn't realize that his retirement date was right at his door. Can you imagine the stress and distress from such a discovery! Don't end up in that position.

Investing for Your Children's College Education

Parents, I will close this section with a special word for you to remember when you're thinking of investing toward your children's college education. What do you do if you can barely survive making the minimum pension contribution in your approved retirement scheme, but you have a four-year-old daughter, and you haven't yet started to put aside money for her college fund? Do you stop your pension contribution and put that money in a college fund for your daughter ? Depending on whom you talk to, the answer will vary.

Some persons who are in this position will say, "Look, I love mydaughter, but one day she will be 18, an adult, and have her full life ahead of her. She should be able to get a scholarship or work a couple years to save and go to college. I am 44, and I don't have a lot of time to get ready for a dignified retirement, so until I can afford to make my maximum pension contribution, I will not be able to put a fund in place for her."

Is this parent cruel or practical? I believe this 44-year-old parent is practical and wise! The arguments are sound, and I would do the same thing. Fortunately, I don't have that dilemma, thank God. What you do will be based totally on your views, desires, and beliefs.

What I would say, though, is that every parent's aspiration should be to push to be in a position to take care of both their pension and their children's college funds. College funds would help your children avoid the burden of student loans, which is a gift that will last for a lifetime—in fact, for generations. The children will be able to get to financial freedom much faster in that they would be able to start to save and invest earlier without a loan to repay! So many youngsters today are not in a position to avoid student loans, and that debt sets them back years before they can start a family, be able to buy a house, and so on because often times their starting salaries are not enough for them to save meaningful amounts.

Children, you have a role to play too. You should do everything possible to reduce the burden of the financial cost of your education on your parents. Think about scholarships, and research to try to be decisive about your major or areas of study so that you don't have to switch degrees. Your wise or foolish actions will mean more or less money for your parents to find. Don't waste your parents' money. They have already sacrificed a lot for you, so say thank you by doing your best at school and acting responsibly toward your own education.

It is not to be seen as anathema or so far-fetched for children to help toward paying for their own education. They can work and study, or they can delay by a year to work and save (careful here as some people never go back to studies once they get swept up in work life). I worked and studied. It was hard, but it is what I could afford as I didn't have the money to go to university full time after leaving high school.

Your Money Journal Assignment: Invest Surplus Cash, Leaving a Legacy

WORKING ADULTS: 18 YEARS & OLDER

Are you ready to start investing?

- Indicate *yes* or *no* to each of the following:

  o Do you have an emergency fund (three to six months' worth)?

  o Have you paid off your high-cost debt (credit card and unsecured loans)?

  o Have you bought your primary residence—a house or an apartment (whether cash or mortgage)?

  o Are you contributing to a pension or retirement fund (ideally the maximum allowed)?

  o Do you have surplus cash per month after taking care of all the above items?

- If you answered *yes* to all the above, I believe you are now in a position to start investing the surplus cash in one or more of the following to grow your wealth and to achieve total financial freedom: shares, bonds, real estate, mutual funds, index funds, private businesses, or other forms of investments under the advice of a financial adviser.

- If you are looking for a passive form of investment for the long term (10 years and over) to either (1) grow your net worth, (2) put aside funds for your children's education, or (3) simply have additional money to supplement your retirement accounts, then you should, like Marcia whom we discussed in this chapter, (see table 11.2 above), consider the following:

  - Invest an amount consistently each month in a stock-based unit trust or mutual fund (this includes index funds) that has a good track record of growth (for the U.S. and Jamaica markets, this would be an average annual growth rate of 10-plus percent per year) and reasonable management fees.

  - Your investment adviser will advise you on the proportion of your money you should put in this stock-based unit trust or mutual fund—this will be driven by your age, financial objectives, and risk appetite.

  - As with Marcia, the law of compound interest will work for you (as long as you stay for the long term and don't panic during market downturns and turmoil) to grow your money exponentially over the years. Of course, again, speak to your financial adviser before you pursue this investment strategy.

  - In my view this is the simplest way to grow your money—where your money and your investment managers do all the work, while you use your time to do what you want to do.

Full-Time Students: 14–24 Years

Start your investment journey by thinking about the career path you wish to pursue (I will show how this connects to investing shortly) by exploring internship opportunities, holiday jobs in related fields, finding mentors in the area, and researching scholarship opportunities.

- Yes, this is the start of your investmentjourney—these moves will help you to secure a good-paying job (or to start a successful business) after high school or college, from which you can save and invest.

- Remember your income is your best wealth-building tool.

chapter 12

STEP 9: PAY YOUR TAXES AND ENJOY TAX BENEFITS

Benjamin Franklin said, "In this world nothing can be said to be certain, except death and taxes."[204]

Mr. Franklin's words about taxes continue to be true centuries after he uttered them. We all have to face taxes in one form or another regardless of the country we live in. Taxes represent the principal manner in which governments earn money to run their respective countries, whether it's building schools, roads, hospitals, or similar projects. There are obligations that each country must fulfill, and taxing the population and companies continues to remain a major source of funds to pay for these expenditures. Governments impose a range of taxes including, but not limited to, tax on income earned from employment (income tax), tax on investment income, and tax on the profits made by businesses.

Given that taxation is an obligatory expense, you should seek to manage it just as you would your mobile phone or food bill. In fact, in Jamaica,

---

204 Benjamin Franklin, *The Private Correspondence of Benjamin Franklin, v. 1* (London: A.J. Valfy, 1817), 266.

income tax can be as high as 30 percent, and therefore easily falls in the top three biggest expense items for many people.[205]

An important part of growing your money, therefore, is to fully understand the various taxes you must pay and to find legal ways to reduce your tax expense. Careful management of tax expenses is part of the reason why the 1 percent (the superrich) are able to keep more of their money in their pockets, further preserving their wealth.

Did you know, for example, that in 2010, Warren Buffett, who ranked in the top 10 of the richest people in the world with a net worth of more than $100 billion, paid less taxes as a percentage of his taxable income (not that he paid a lower tax amount) than his other employees, including his secretary? His effective tax rate for federal taxes paid in 2010 was 17.4 percent, while that of his secretary was 35 percent.[206] How could this be? Well, Mr. Buffett makes the vast majority of his income frominvestment income i.e., qualified dividends and long-term capital gains (I explain these terms later in this chapter), which are taxed at a much lower tax rate than salaries, which is earned income.[207] That's just how the tax code works, and he managed to arrange his income so that more of his income comes from qualified dividends and long-term capital gains.

Many people in the general population will cry out against the superrich's lower tax rates relative to the average citizen. The response of the superrich is that the tax code permits them to organize their affairs in a manner to pay less tax and that there is no moral obligation for anyone to pay more taxes than is legally required. The question, then, should be "What can the average person do to also legally minimize their tax expense?"

---

205   "Jamaica: Individual—Taxes on Personal Income," PricewaterhouseCoopers, Tax Summaries, last modified February 18, 2022, https://taxsummaries.pwc.com/jamaica/individual/taxes-on-personal-income.

206   Reuters, "In Response to Lawmaker, Buffett Claims 17.4% Tax Rate," New York Times, October 12, 2011, https://www.nytimes.com/2011/10/13/business/in-letter-to-congressman-buffett-claims-17-4-tax-rate.html.

207   Maurie Backman, "Why Does Billionaire Warren Buffett Pay a Lower Tax Rate Than His Secretary?," The Motley Fool, September 25, 2020, https://www.fool.com/taxes/2020/09/25/why-does-billionaire-warren-buffett-pay-a-lower-ta/.

Before we answer this question—which will be at a high level, as I am no tax expert—we need to define and discuss some key terms and to set the stage as to how you can also legally reduce your tax expense.

Two Types of Income

1. Earned Income

Earned income, as the term suggests, is what you are paid in salaries from your regular jobs. In Jamaica, individuals pay personal income taxes on salaries ranging from 0 to 30 percent, depending on their income bracket. At the time of this writing, if you earn less than $10,000 (JA$1.5M) in Jamaica, you do not pay income tax as the tax-free threshold is $10,000. People earning more than $10,000 are taxed on the difference above the $10,000 up to $40,000 (JA$6M) at 25 percent, and earnings in excess of $40,000 are taxed at 30 percent.[208] A similar system exists in the U.S., where the tax rates are higher the greater your taxable income is.[209]

2. Investment Income

In most countries, investment income (money that is made from holding and selling various types of investments) is split across the following categories and will usually have different tax rates.

Capital Gains

In the U.S., *capital gain* refers to the gain that is made when you sell a capital asset. A capital asset is a fancy way of describing those pieces of assets that have the potential to increase (or decrease) in value over time—shares, bonds, and real estate are good examples.[210] Let's say you bought shares in Amazon for $2,000 and then sold those shares two years later for $3,000. Assuming no transaction fees, the capital gain would be $1,000. In the U.S., a capital gains tax is applied to such gains.

---

208   "Jamaica: Individual—Taxes on Personal Income."

209   Matthew Frankel, "Effective Tax Rate vs. Marginal Tax Bracket: What You Need to Know," The Motley Fool, updated January 22, 2019, https://www.fool.com/taxes/2017/04/08/effective-tax-rate-vs-marginal-tax-bracket-what-yo.aspx.

210   Jason Fernando, "Capital Gains Tax," Investopedia, updated June 21, 2022, https://www.investopedia.com/terms/c/capital_gains_tax.asp.

If you hold a capital asset for one year or more, selling such an asset would result in a long-term capital gain.[211] In the U.S., the long-term capital gains tax rate in 2022, ranged from 0 to 20 percent.[212] If the asset is held for less than one year— this would result in a short-term capital gain, and would trigger short term capital gains tax which is generally taxed at the same rate as ordinary income, which for the average U.S. citizen is between 10 to 37 percent (2022)[213]. As discussed earlier, herein lies how people like Warren Buffett end up with a lower effective tax rate than the average U.S. citizen. The wealthy tend to make more of their money from long term capital gains, which as I just demonstrated, are taxed at a lower rate (0 to 20 percent), than the tax rate the average U.S. citizen pays on ordinary income which is 10 to 37 percent. The earnings of the wealthy tend to also include long term qualified dividends (dividends paid on shares that are held for the long term[214]), which are also taxed at the lower long-term capital gains rate.

In Jamaica, there is no capital gains tax—instead there is a transfer tax that is charged on the consideration received by the seller or the market value of the asset sold. The assets that attract transfer tax in Jamaica, like in the U.S., also tend to be of a capital nature, such as stocks, bonds, and real estate. Listed securities transferred on the Jamaica Stock Exchange (JSE) (including the Junior Stock Exchange) are exempt from transfer tax.[215]

At the time of writing, the transfer tax rate is 2 percent. There is also stamp duty (a form of tax) that is levied on the legal documents that effect these transfers. The current stamp duty amount is at a flat-rate maximum of $33 (JA$5,000), and so the amount is relatively immaterial.[216] Later on

211   Nadia Ahmad, "2021 Capital Gains Tax Rates by State," SmartAsset, October 26, 2021, https://smartasset.com/taxes/state-capital-gains-tax.

212   "A Guide to the Capital Gains Tax Rate: Short-term vs. Long-term Capital Gains Taxes", TurboTax, accessed 31 October 2022, https://turbotax.intuit.com/tax-tips/investments-and-taxes/guide-to-short-term-vs-long-term-capital-gains-taxes-brokerage-accounts-etc/L7KCu9etn

213   Ibid

214   Backman, "Why Does Billionaire Warren Buffett Pay."

215   "Jamaica: Individual—Other Taxes."

216   "Frequently Asked Questions," Real Estate Board, accessed June 10, 2022, https://www.reb.gov.jm/nmcms.php?snippet=faqs&p=faqs&viewall=1&fn=3.

I will discuss how you, too, like the super rich can take advantage of these relatively low tax rates (transfer tax in Jamaica or capital gains tax in the U.S.) and end up saving money!

Dividend Income

Another source of investment income in most countries is dividend income. Ordinary dividends paid by Jamaican tax-resident companies to Jamaican tax-resident shareholders are taxed at the rate of 15 percent.[217] You should see immediately that this rate of 15 percent is relatively low compared to the income tax at 25–30 percent. It should be noted, however, that in most countries, dividends are paid by companies out of after-tax profits (company profits are taxed at 25–33.3 percent in Jamaica, and dividends are generally not tax deductible). To impose tax in Jamaica at a further, say, 25–30 percent on the dividend when it is paid would result in excessively high effective tax on distributed profits—hence the reason tax on dividends is at a relatively low rate of 15 percent, when compared to income tax on salaries. Therefore, there aren't many opportunities to reduce tax expenses on dividend income itself in Jamaica. However, as discussed earlier, the capital gains or transfer tax charged when the underlying shares are sold tend to be relatively low when compared to income tax on salaries. See also earlier discussion on the relatively low tax rate paid on qualified dividends, compared to that paid on salaries.

Interest Income

Tax is paid on interest that is earned on savings accounts, bonds, and similar interest-bearing items. In Jamaica, interest is taxed at the source (i.e., deducted before the net interest is paid to the investor) for individuals at 25 percent, but it is to be added to the taxpayer's income. Then the tax is paid at the applicable rate of 25–30 percent, depending on the taxpayer's overall statutory income (combined income from all sources after taking out appropriate allowances).[218] Here you should see that the tax on interest income in Jamaica (as well as other types of investment income such as

---

217 "Jamaica: Individual—Income Determination," PricewaterhouseCoopers, last modified February 18, 2022, https://taxsummaries.pwc.com/jamaica/individual/income-determination.

218 "Jamaica: Individual—Income Determination."

rental income and royalties) is not as friendly or low as tax on long-term capital investments discussed above. There is at least one exception in Jamaica where you can earn interest income tax-free on what is known as a tax-free long-term savings account under certain conditions, one of which is that the principal sum should remain in the account for a minimum of five years.[219] Most financial institutions in Jamaica offer this product. I believe you should be able to find other tax-exempt interest-bearing products in your country including certain government bonds that may not attract tax as a way of making them more attractive.[220] You should bear all the aforementioned factors in mind when you are thinking about putting your money in an interest-bearing investment.

You should aspire to enjoy lower tax rates too.

Given the discussion up to this point in the chapter, you should also aspire to legally pay lower taxes, especially if most of your income is from salaries (earned income). I have outlined three basic ways for you to consider.

Maximize the use of pension or retirement fund contributions.

As already noted, the Jamaican government gives at least two tax benefits to individuals who participate in an approved pension plan. The benefits can make a big difference to your overall tax expense.

Most companies in Jamaica that have pension plans require that their employees pay a minimum of 5 percent of their gross income to the plan, and usually the employer offers something of a matching contribution. The government allows the pension contributed by the employee to be deducted from the employee's gross salary before income tax is computed, meaning that the employee would pay less income tax. Let's illustrate this further.

---

219   "Long-Term Savings," C&WJ Community and Workers of Jamaica, accessed June 30, 2022, https://www.cwjcu.com/long-term-savings.

220   How Government Bonds Are Taxed," Investor Vanguard, accessed June 30, 2022, https://investor.vanguard.com/investor-resources-education/taxes/how-government-bonds-are-taxed#:~:text=Income%20from%20bonds%20issued%20by%20state%2C%20city%2C%20and%20local%20governments,where%20the%20bond%20was%20issued.

If you earn $3,500 gross per month ($42,000 per year), and you contribute 5 percent ($175 a month) to a pension plan, you save 25 percent of $175 or $44 per month in income taxes. Over 30 years this $44 would accumulate to $15,840. If this $44 was being invested over the 30 years at 9 percent, the total would be $75,433. It gets even better, because the Jamaican government allows you to contribute up to 15 percent of your gross income toward your pension assuming your employer is contributing 5 percent—up to $525 per month using my example—for a monthly income tax savings of $131. Over 30 years, this would amount to $47,160. If this $131 per month was being invested over this 30-year period at 9 percent, it would grow to $224,584.

In the U.S., employees can enjoy similar income tax savings when they contribute money through their employer-sponsored 401(k) retirement account. For the traditional employer-sponsored 401(k) account, a tax deduction is received similar to the one described above for Jamaican pensioners when retirement contributions are made to the plan—however, when withdrawals are made from the plan in later years, these withdrawals are taxed. For the Roth employer-sponsored 401(k) account, contributions made do not receive tax deductions; however no tax is charged when withdrawals are made.[221] You should check for similar tax incentives for the retirement plan options for your country.

I am, therefore, encouraging all to consider increasing your pension or retirement fund contribution to the maximum allowed in your respective countries as soon as you're able to. You may not be able to do it immediately as you may need all of your cash to pay down expensive credit card debt, for example, but please keep it as one of your goals!

It gets better, though—in Jamaica, when the actual pension contribution itself ($175 per month at 5 percent, or $525 at 15 percent using my example above) is invested by the pension fund manager, the investment income that is earned on this money is not taxed. Yes, it is not taxed![222] Thus, your money will grow faster because the amount that would have

---

221   Yochim, "What Is a 401(k) Plan?"

222   Yochim, "What Is a 401(k) Plan?"

been taxed stays within your pension account and helps to grow the balance even faster. The U.S. has similar tax benefits for 401(k) retirement accounts where the growth in the investments in the accounts over the years is not taxed. The tax implications for withdrawals are the same as previously described above.[223] To learn more, speak to your financial adviser.

As mentioned in chapter 10, self-employed people and people whose employers don't have an employer-sponsored retirement plan also can enjoy similar tax benefits to those received in employer-sponsored plans by opening individual retirement accounts. [224]

Diversify your investment portfolio.

Another thing you can do to enjoy tax breaks is to diversify your investment portfolio to include more tax-friendly investments like the super rich. To do this, keep pressing on your total financial freedom journey and as you journey along, move to hold more of those long-term capital investments (real estate, shares) that enjoy relatively low tax rates (compared to salaries) when they are sold (capital gains tax in the U.S. or transfer tax in Jamaica) and when qualified dividends are paid in the U.S., as discussed earlier. I personally apply this strategy by investing in unit trusts (in Jamaica) that hold the majority (minimum of 51 percent) of their underlying investment in shares. The gains made on these units held are not subject to tax.[225] These lower tax charges will certainly keep more money in your pocket and will therefore accelerate the growth of your investment portfolio, as is the case for the superrich! Take note that these shares-based unit trusts, to which I made personal reference, are high risk (given that shares are considered high-risk investments). You must, therefore, have that aggressive investor risk profile, be prepared to invest for the long term (over 10 years), and be guided in your decisions by your investment adviser. If your risk appetite is on the conservative to moderate side, you can consider tax-exempt interest-bearing products like I mentioned earlier (tax-free

---

223   Yochim, "What Is a 401(k) Plan?"

224   Yochim, "What Is a 401(k) Plan?"

225   Oran Hall, "Taxes and Investment Income," *The Gleaner*, September 27, 2014, https://jamaica-gleaner.com/gleaner/20140427/business/business81.html.

long-term savings accounts and tax-exempt government bonds) to minimize your tax expense.

Other Opportunities

In the U.S., opportunities exist for individuals and households subject to certain conditions to deduct mortgage interest paid on their residential mortgage as a tax deduction (this is not available in Jamaica) as well as donations to certain approved organizations.[226] Donations to certain types of organizations in Jamaica are allowed as a tax-deductible item.[227]

Speak to your financial and tax advisers before you apply any of the suggestions discussed above.

Tax Evasion Versus Tax Avoidance

We really have been talking about tax avoidance above, where companies and individuals use legal means to reduce their tax expense. There is also tax evasion, which is where persons use fraudulent means to pay less taxes—for example, not reporting portions of their income, overstating their deductible tax expenses, or simply not filing or paying taxes at all!

Earlier in this book, I spoke about people using only honest means to grow their wealth and how destructive it can be when fraudulent means are used. I cited Bernie Madoff who operated a fraudulent Ponzi scheme and who was sentenced to 150 years in jail as an example of someone who made money dishonestly. Note, however, that tax evasion is another example of an illegal means to try and save money, which will eventually catch up with the guilty parties and usually ends up badly. For example, there have been some famous names who have gotten into difficulties in the U.S. for tax evasion, such as Wesley Snipes. Mr. Snipes is an actor, and in 2008 he was fined $5 million for willfully failing to file millions of dollars' worth of past

---

226   Backman, "Why Does Billionaire Warren Buffett Pay."

227   "Jamaica: Individual—Deductions," PricewaterhouseCoopers, Tax Summaries, last modified February 18, 2022, https://taxsummaries.pwc.com/jamaica/individual/deductions.

tax returns.[228] He also served a three-year prison term in 2008. Evading tax is simply not the way to grow your wealth. It usually ends up decreasing your wealth and tarnishing your reputation.

National Duty to Pay Taxes

Someone tried to trap Jesus by asking him if the Jews should pay taxes to Caesar, who was seen by the Jews as their oppressor. Jesus then asked them to look at one of their coins to see whose image was on it. They said it was Caesar's image. Jesus went on to say, "Render unto Caesar the things which are Caesar's; and unto God the things that are God's" (Matthew 22:21, KJV). His statement is a reminder that we should pay our taxes, as that is how governments run their countries. Even if the government is oppressive—which they were to the Jews—all were still encouraged to pay what was owed to Caesar. We should pay in accordance with the rules set by the government of the day—and so we, too, should pay our taxes. Of course, don't get me wrong here. If we see injustices in the tax system, we have a right to cry out and push for change, especially to protect the weak and vulnerable who may not have a voice to push for changes themselves. However, pushing for change can't be an excuse for us not to pay our taxes. I am not preaching here—I am just saying that we all must pay our fair share of taxes given that we all use public goods and services, which are funded by taxpayers' dollars.

In closing, the main message of this chapter is that tax is one of the biggest expenses you will have in your personal finances. With the right tax planning within the boundaries of the law, however, you can pay less tax and have more left over for you to build your wealth. Maximizing your pension contributions and diversifying your portfolio to enjoy more returns from investments in long-term capital assets (subject, of course, to your risk appetite) are quick ways to reduce your tax expense.

---

228   Benjamin VanHoose, "Wesley Snipes Says He 'Came Out a Clearer Person' After Serving Prison Time for Tax Evasion," *People*, November 2, 2020, https://people.com/movies/wesley-snipes-reflects-prison-time-tax-evasion/.

The Goldsons

The Goldsons continue to make great progress:

- They have now paid off the loan shark debts as well as their car loan, which was accomplished over a two-year period. They paid a total of $35,333.

- They now only have $8,000 to pay on the credit card, which is the last debt outside of their mortgage.

- The increase in the rate of their debt repayment was made possible as Mr. Goldson got the new job he had planned for, and his online teaching business pivoted to another level.

- Mr. Goldson now has an assistant helping in the online business to ensure he spends enough time with his family.

- The Goldsons now expect to finish paying off the credit card debt in the next four months.

- They then plan to build a robust three- to six-month emergency fund afterward, as they now only have a one-month fund.

- The Goldsons then plan to open individual retirement accounts (IRAs) and aim to contribute up to 10 percent of their income for the first two years and then increase it to 15 percent, as they would only be paying their mortgage and would have built up their emergency fund to cover three to six months by then.

- They then plan to start investing 5 percent of their income in a low-cost index shares-based fund.

I encourage you to continue to be inspired by Mr. and Mrs. Goldson as you, too, journey toward financial freedom.

We have covered the nine steps in the section of the book that deals with growing your money:

- Understanding your current financial health by looking at 10 financial indicators

- Setting financial goals that are meant to turn around your financial indicators

- Understanding your money personality

- Budgeting to save

- Building an emergency fund

- Managing debt

- Planning for retirement

- Investing surplus cash

- Managing taxes

We must now learn how to protect this money we would have worked so hard to accumulate. Protecting your money is the subject of the next section of this book.

Your Money Journal Assignment: Enjoying Tax Breaks

WORKING ADULTS: 18 YEARS & OLDER

- If your country gives tax breaks based on the amount of money you contribute toward your pension savings, you should consider increasing your pension contribution to the maximum allowed in order to take full advantage of these tax savings.

- Look at your investment portfolio and work with your tax and financial advisers to figure out how you may structure your portfolio toward more tax-efficient long-term capital investments (shares, bonds, and real estate) or tax-exempt interest-bearing investments without going outside of your risk profile. If you can achieve that balance, then you will reduce your overall tax expense and, therefore, have more money to save and invest.

- Speak to your financial advisers about opportunities to reduce your tax expenses by taking advantage of deductions relating to interest you're paying on your residential mortgage (U.S. readers only or where this applies) and donations made to charities or not-for-profit organizations.

FULL-TIME STUDENTS: 14–24 YEARS

I want you to be reminded that when you start to earn, paying taxes is a national duty, and therefore, you should remember two things:

- Apply only legal means to reduce your tax expense.

- Do not be overly aggressive in applying tax rules.

part 3

PROTECT YOUR MONEY

chapter 13

STEP 10: GET INSURANCE PROTECTION—
THE STORMS OF LIFE WILL COME

In this chapter, I deal with three specific tools that you can use to protect your hard-earned wealth: having adequate insurance, establishing proper estate planning, and protecting your financial records. I will first deal with the subject of insurance protection.

Insurance as a Means of Protecting Your Wealth

Insurance in all its forms will protect you from some of the dangers that we all have to face. Whether it is sickness, death, or natural disasters, troubles abound, and that's part of what it means to be human. Job, who is renowned for his patience and his sufferings, said, "Man that is born of woman is of few days and full of trouble!" (Job 14:1, KJV). Trouble will come to your doorstep and to my doorstep one day—not if but when—and when it comes, one way to protect or mitigate the impact is to have insurance in its various forms. The various types of insurance that I will discuss are life insurance, health insurance, property insurance, and disability insurance.

These four classes of insurance should be considered needs when preparing your budget, given the potential adverse impact if you don't have them in place. Let's now examine each of these types of insurance in more detail.

Life Insurance

This is protection that your beneficiaries get in the form of a cash payment by a life insurance company upon your death. In order to get coverage, you are required to pay what is called a premium. The amount of premium that you pay is linked to the state of your health (if you are in good health, you pay less), your age (the younger you are, the less you pay), and the amount of coverage or protection you want (more coverage means higher premiums).[229]

Who needs life insurance?

The question, then, is "Who needs life insurance?" Life insurance is typically for people who have dependents who would suffer severely if the breadwinner were not there to provide support anymore.

There are a number of life insurance companies in Jamaica, and they are listed on the website of the Financial Services Commission, the entity that regulates insurance companies in Jamaica. You can find the equivalent listing on the website of the regulator in your country.

If you are the main breadwinner, or one of the main breadwinners in your family, and you were to die earlier than expected, how would your family replace your income to continue to enjoy a decent standard of living? How would your children go to school? How would the rent or mortgage be paid? If your answer is "I don't know," or "We would be in trouble," then life insurance is a tool that you should consider. If you are a student, and you are not yet working, or you may be working but you have no dependents, please soak up this knowledge as one day you will need to put it into practice.

How much life insurance coverage do you need?

Personal finance experts recommend at least six to 10 times your gross

---

229   "How Much Does Life Insurance Cost?," Progressive, accessed June 10, 2022, https://www.progressive.com/answers/how-much-is-life-insurance/.

household income as a quick benchmark as to how much coverage you need.[230] The idea is that the life insurance proceeds when invested should be able to generate or substantially replace the lost annual income.

Although the monthly income generated from investing the life insurance proceeds may be good enough to continue to pay all expenses and debt obligations each month, it is not uncommon for some people to ensure that the life insurance coverage also includes amounts to settle their major debts, which would ease the burden on their loved ones.

Additionally, I should point out that most mortgage companies insist that you take out a life insurance policy and assign it to them for mortgage loans over a certain amount. Assignment is the legal process of giving over the rights and benefits of your policy to another. It means that if you were to die, the mortgage company would use the insurance proceeds to settle the mortgage that you owe them, and then pay over any remaining balance to your family or estate. In that case, you would already have one of your major debt obligations covered, so please take it into consideration as you think about the total coverage you need.

Term Life or Whole Life Policies

The next question, then, is "What are the basic solutions that life insurance companies offer to manage the risk of you dying while you have dependents?" There are two basic types of insurance policies or contracts that the average person buys to get the coverage they need: whole life policies (also known as permanent life insurance) and term life policies. Whole life policies provide protection for as long as you live (as long as you continue to pay the premiums), and a cash value (like a savings account) is built up over the years.

Term life policies, however, only provide protection for a specified period or term, ranging from 5 to 30 years. There is no cash value or savings built up over the years—therefore, the premiums are much less expensive.[231]

You will generally find that it is less expensive to get the total coverage that you need to protect your family with a term life policy than a whole

---

230   Beattie, "How Much Life Insurance Should You Carry?"

231   Kurt, "Term vs. Whole Life Insurance."

life policy. I will illustrate this point with a story. (If you live outside of Jamaica, you may not be able to relate to these numbers given that insurance rates and coverage will differ based on each country's demographics and social context. However, I believe you will still get the principle being presented.) I know a 43-year-old office manager from Kingston, Jamaica, who earned $38,000 (JA$5.7M) per year. He was paying over $330 per month (JA$50,000) for whole life insurance premiums for which he was getting coverage of $150,000 (JA$22.5M). But when he estimated the insurance coverage that he needed using 10 times his gross salary, it was $380,000 (JA$57M), which was far above the $150,000 (JA$22.5M) coverage he was getting for the $330 (JA$50,000) per month. He was able to restructure his policies and shifted them all to 20-year term life policies with the help of his agent and increased his coverage to the $380,000 ($57M) while paying a premium of $130 (JA$19,500)!

Before you choose a term life policy, determine if you have any medical conditions or known family diseases that could come upon you later on or could get worse with time. With the aforementioned history, if you went with a term life policy, then when the term of the policy expires you could face a great increase in your premiums as you would be older and your medical condition could have become worse. Recall that the price of your premiums is linked to the state of your health and your age.

Given the reality of these variables, you will need to carefully assess with your insurance adviser if you need term life, whole life, or both.

Health Insurance

Health insurance can be defined as "compensation you receive in the event of an undesirable medical event happening." The inability to pay medical bills is the number one reason for personal bankruptcy filings in the U.S. Many people get sick, don't have the insurance protection to deal with the bills, and their finances get wiped out. Therefore, one of the key types of insurance protection we need is health insurance.

How much coverage do you need and at what cost?

The main concerns with health insurance are similar to those of getting life insurance coverage: how much health insurance coverage do you need to protect yourself and your family, and at what cost?

I try to figure it out by calculating the cost if one of my dependents needed major surgery or organ transplant. I also look at the cost of the coverage for postsurgical care. Are there known family diseases that I need to especially monitor? Once you have the answers to those and similar questions, then you can talk to your insurance agent about the policies that match your needs and the likely cost.

Critical illness policies are also a potential tool you can include in how you manage your health insurance needs. These policies pay out lump sum amounts if you are diagnosed with one of a list of critical illnesses, such as a heart attack or stroke. I then use all the above information to narrow down my policy options and check if a local or overseas insurance company or both can meet these needs—again, I do all of the research under the guidance of an insurance agent. It's best to enter these conversations with your insurance agent with some knowledge and awareness of how health insurance policies work.

Deductible

You will also need to understand the concept of a deductible, which is the amount of an insurance claim that you have to pay before the insurance company becomes liable for the rest of the bill. For example, if you have a health insurance policy with a deductible of $1,000, and the medical bill is $3,000, you have to pay the $1,000 first before the insurance company will pay the balance. Know what your deductibles are and always have at least that amount ready so that you can quickly access the medical care you need. Here you should see another powerful reason why you need to have an emergency fund, as this is one of the best sources to cover deductibles.

Coinsurance

Some health insurance contracts also require that the insured pays a portion of the medical bill even after the deductible has been taken out, which is known as coinsurance. It is usually a fixed percentage (usually around 20 percent but can be as high as 50 percent) of the bill that you pay, and the rest is covered by the insurance company. If the coinsurance in my example was 20 percent, then the insured would have to pay an additional $400 ($2,000 × 20 percent) toward the bill.

You must, therefore, make sure that you understand which medical procedures or activities have coinsurance on them so that you can plan and have the funds ready in advance. Your choice of insurance provider will, therefore, be influenced by how much of a deductible and coinsurance you have to pay. Please consult your insurance adviser before you make any decisions on this very important subject.

Pre-authorization of Medical Procedures and Health Care Providers

Understanding which doctors, surgeons, or other providers you can use and any extra cost for using medical professionals not on the approved list of health care providers under your insurance company is extremely critical. Why? It will allow you to manage how you choose the health care provider that you believe can help with your medical condition. Most of the health care providers are generally good, but before you finalize appointments, you may want to check first if a specific practitioner or hospital that you prefer is on the list of approved providers for your insurance company.

I know of a case where a man, let's call him Bob, had a very specialized and complex medical procedure, but the surgeon that he wanted to do the surgery was not on his health insurance company's list of approved providers. Fortunately, Bob found out before the procedure and was able to make alternative arrangements. Imagine if Bob hadn't spoken to the insurance company before engaging the surgeon—he would have a serious medical bill as the insurance company would not have honored the claim.

Health Care Provided by Your Government

Governments in many countries also provide health care benefits in one form or another to their citizens. In the U.S., there is Medicare and

Medicaid. In Jamaica, the National Health Fund (NHF), a government agency that is funded by contributions from payroll taxes (NIS contributions) paid by employers and employees, also provides support to persons in the form of prescription drugs for a list of chronic illnesses. Do not let pride get in the way of your accessing these benefits. Some people believe government-funded programs are only for low-income people. You are already paying for the benefit through your payroll or other taxes, so why wouldn't you claim the benefit?

I know of people who are quite financially well off, and yet they still access the health benefits of the NHF in Jamaica. Perhaps that's why they achieved their level of financial comfort—understanding the system and taking legal advantage of relevant benefits. Accessing NHF benefits will save you a lot of money. If you have a similar body like the NHF in your country, please research and access these benefits as well.

Property Insurance

Yet another undesirable event is property damage. For example, your car may sustain damage in a collision, or your house may be badly damaged by a hurricane, flood, fire, or lightning. Our homes generally represent the single largest investment we will ever make. Imagine your house going up in smoke after nine years into your mortgage payments. How do you get back to another house at that age? One way is to have what is known as property insurance.

There are three parties in a typical property insurance relationship. The first is you, also referred to as the insured. The second party is the property insurance company that would provide the coverage or cash payout in the event of an accident or loss. The third party usually, as the term suggests, is a stranger or someone outside of the contractual relationship with the insurance company and is involved in some way with the property loss or damage.

There are two types of protection that you get from a property insurance company: (1) protection against physical damage to your property or theft of your property, and (2) protection against liabilities you may face because you may be responsible for someone's injury or harm. Instances might be someone getting injured at your house as a result of your failure to execute all safety measures on your property. You may hit someone with your car, and you may be sued for the individual's loss of income or for pain, suffering, and the like. A court judgment could require a massive payout from you, and if you don't have adequate insurance coverage (for liability and physical damage), this could wipe you out financially. It is, therefore, extremely important that you have adequate insurance protection in place.

I will continue the discussion on property insurance but restrict the discussion to your house and auto, two of the most valuable items most persons will ever own.

Insuring Your Automobile

It is a legal requirement to insure your car in most countries,[232] and property insurance companies offer two main products that will allow motorists to meet the requirements of the law:

1. Comprehensive insurance contracts: Such coverage protects against property damage and liability exposure whether you are at fault or not.

2. Third-party insurance contracts: The insured only gets protection for property damage and liabilities owed to third parties. In other words, the insured gets no compensation for damages to their own car. Such policies are usually taken out on older cars (anything beyond 10 years where the value of the car is low). Given that the benefits are fewer than with comprehensive policies, this type of policy is usually much cheaper.[233]. You can pay extra premiums on either your comprehensive or third-party policies and enjoy additional benefits on top of the standard benefits. Think of it as a "compre-

---

232   "Auto Insurance in Different Countries," International Driving Authority, April 17, 2017, https://idaoffice.org/posts/auto-insurance-in-different-countries-en.

233   "Difference Between Comprehensive and Third-Party Insurance," Digit, accessed June 10, 2022, https://www.godigit.com/motor-insurance/car-insurance/difference-between-comprehensive-and-third-party-insurance.

hensive insurance plus" contract or a "third-party insurance plus" contract. For example, although your standard third-party insurance contract does not cover you if your car is stolen, if you pay extra, you could have that benefit added to your policy. The option may be wise if you have an older car and it is your key means of transportation or earning.

Auto insurance premiums—how much should you pay?

The amount that you pay in premiums is dependent on a range of factors including, but not limited to, the following considerations:

1. You want a comprehensive or third-party contract.

2. You are an experienced or inexperienced driver. New drivers, with licenses for less than two years, will generally pay more given that they have less experience on the roads and are more likely to have an accident.

3. You have anti-theft devices in your car, which reduces the chances of your car being stolen.

4. You have never made a claim or not made a claim for a certain period of time. Your claim history would qualify for what is called a no-claim discount, which is a way the insurance companies reward you for being a good driver.[234]

You should keep these factors in mind as you figure out and negotiate your insurance premium rates.

Don't just focus on the annual premium.

I find that many people place too much focus on the annual insurance premium cost during the negotiations of their premiums, while ignoring other critical details about their car insurance. For example, many people don't discuss and assess the adequacy of the liability protection—for example, the personal injury protection coverage—before finalizing their policies. For years I used to be so focused on trying to get the best premium

---

234   "What Factors May Affect Your Car Insurance Premium," Allstate, last modified December 2017, https://www.allstate.com/resources/car-insurance/what-affects-premiums-and-rates.

and deductible amount, without considering how adequate the personal injury coverage is based on, say, the number of persons that I tend to carry in my car and so on.

Personal injury coverage is important as it covers medical bills for you and your passengers and related legal expenses including lawsuits if you are sued because you caused injury to others during an accident. Do you know how much personal injury protection you have on your car insurance policy? Monetary awards due to injuries can be large and could seriously erode your financial resources if you don't have enough coverage.

Getting the Best Deal

In terms of getting the best deal on your basic annual premium, I encourage you to shop around and consider using an insurance broker in this process. Brokers can quickly tell you the costs and features of the insurance products for different insurance companies, which will save you a lot of time and, possibly, money. Some insurance companies now sell directly to policyholders without the use of a broker, and you should investigate this option and weigh what's in your best interests.

Other ways to bring down your premium include the following:

1. Negotiate for a discount if you insure more than one vehicle with the company.

2. Combine insurance products. Many companies will give you a discount if you give the company other business such as your home insurance.

3. Get insurance through a group scheme at your company or through your professional associations, as they can negotiate better rates, given the number of persons in these groups.

4. Increase your deductible, which means you would have to pay more toward a claim, but you would pay less annual premium as a trade-off. The savings in the premiums over the years could add up to a tidy sum. If you have a good track record as a driver and a good emergency fund, you could end up saving a lot of money

while having the peace of mind that if you did have an accident, you would be able to deal with the deductible from your emergency fund.

5. Pay annual premiums in full if your cash flow allows, rather than paying monthly or quarterly, which usually results in a greater overall payment for the year than paying the total up front. If you can pay the annual premium quarterly or monthly without interest, then you could take advantage of that possibility and reduce the pressure on your cash flow. Don't be afraid to ask about these options—you may be surprised.

Insuring Your Home

This is another major property that must be protected, as I alluded to briefly earlier. The key thought here is first to ensure that you have property insurance on the physical building as well as the contents of your house. If you have a mortgage, you are usually forced to insure, at minimum, the physical building. Even after you pay off your mortgage, please continue to insure your home! I mean insure it against physical damage due to a hurricane, flood, fire, lightning, and similar events. Most, if not all, insurance companies in Jamaica will provide 100 percent coverage in the event of physical damage due to most of these loss events. In the U.S. "act of God" events (events outside of human control) are usually excluded.[235] Check your policy, therefore, to make sure you understand any exclusions.

The next thought, then, is to ensure that your home is not underinsured. The best way to prevent being underinsured is to check, annually, that your coverage is based on the replacement cost, which is what it would take today to replace your home if it were to be totally destroyed, not the market value at which someone would be willing to buy the home. Those values are distinct amounts. If you fail to insure at the replacement cost and you submit a claim for damage, you will only get a percentage of your claim and not for the total damage, which is known as the average clause.

---

235   Laura Green, "Act of God," Investopedia, last modified March 7, 2022, https://www.investopedia.com/terms/a/act-god.asp.

Let's say the replacement cost of your beautiful three-bedroom house in Montego Bay, Jamaica, was $600,000, and you insured it for $400,000. Your house would be underinsured by $200,000 (33 percent). If you suffered a loss of $60,000 due to a tropical storm, unfortunately you would only get 67 percent of the $60,000 ($40,000). You would have to cover the $20,000 difference! So, underinsuring your house is not a joke and could expose you to serious losses!

Finally, in addition to taking out coverage for physical damage to your property, ensure you have adequate liability coverage in the event of your negligence that leads to bodily injury to others or their valuables. This could wipe you out financially!

How much premium should you pay?

The premium you pay will be driven a lot by the replacement cost of your home as that cost is usually one of the primary factors used in its derivation. It means, then, that the bigger your replacement cost, the higher your premium is likely to be. The age of your home, construction material used, and environmental factors (such as the risk of fire, flood, or hurricane) all will influence the premium. In most countries you should be able to negotiate with your insurers based on your awareness of how your home stacks up against the aforementioned factors. Of course, principles relating to increasing the deductible and bundling your auto insurance and using a broker are additional strategies you can use to help lower your annual premium.

Content Insurance (Renter's Insurance)

Being similar to but different from homeowners' insurance, content insurance is bought by tenants to protect them from losses if they suffer damage to their property (e.g., furniture) as well as liability protection if due to their fault they cause harm or injury to someone else at the rental property. Renters should definitely include this insurance in their monthly budget because it could save you from major losses or liability claims. Also, it is usually a lot cheaper than homeowner's insurance given that the scope of coverage is much less. Homeowner's insurance is generally for the actual property plus the belongings or contents of the homeowner versus renter's insurance, which only covers the contents.

Disability Insurance

Finally, one more likely event is losing the ability to work due to sickness or injury, which could mean no income until returning to work and the related adverse implications. The potential for illness and injury introduces us to disability insurance, which is one way to manage this risk.

Disability insurance provides replacement of income (or a portion of it) in the event of a physical disability that disrupts your ability to work. Disability can be for a short period of time or permanently.

Factors Affecting Disability Insurance Premiums

Your disability premiums are linked to a range of factors:

1. Are you in a high-risk or hazardous job (e.g., construction worker) that increases the chances of your becoming disabled?

2. What amount of income would be lost if you became disabled? The higher the income, the more expensive the premiums will be.

3. What is your age? Younger workers generally enjoy a lower premium.

How much disability insurance coverage is needed?

Short-term disability insurance can replace up to 70–80 percent of your income, with the period that defines *short term* usually being less than a year. Long-term disability insurance covers between 40 and 60 percent and can go on for many years. [236]

Should you buy disability insurance?

Everybody needs disability insurance! Studies show that if you're under age 35, chances are one in three that you will be disabled for at least six

---

236   Tanza Loudenback and Ronda Lee, "Short-Term Disability Insurance Can Replace Up to 80% of Your Salary, but Experts Say It's Usually Not Enough," Business Insider, November 3, 2021, https://www.businessinsider.com/personal-finance/what-is-short-term-disability-insurance-explained.

months during the course of your career.[237] Additionally, three in 10 workers entering the workforce today will become disabled before retiring.[238]

You may say, "Bruce, I'm young, and my job is not hazardous. I work in an office and not in the gold mines where there is more physical danger."

The truth is that our lives can change in a second with an adverse medical diagnosis or an injury (e.g., a fall, a car accident), and neither of those two examples have anything to do with a hazardous work environment. It should be clear that if your income drops because you are unable to work due to a disability, that situation would be a very serious threat to your financial stability. While your emergency fund will provide you with some protection in the short term, upon a permanent disability, those funds will soon run out, and your financial condition will deteriorate rapidly. The conclusion, therefore, is yes, you should buy disability insurance.

Budget for Insurance Premium Payments

Remember the discussion earlier on budgeting and where I argued that you should include your insurance premiums as an indispensable part of your needs in your budget? The advice was to provide the protection you may need that would otherwise be financially destructive. Let me qualify this by saying that if, after you consider your absolute must-haves (i.e., food, transportation, utilities), no money is left over, you would be forced to live without insurance coverage because you must first take care of the absolute must-haves; however, you should proceed to plan to include your insurance premiums as soon as you can find the needed funds.

The Role of Employers in Providing Insurance Protection

Some employers provide health, disability, and life insurance coverage to different degrees. You should happily sign up for all available options once you are given the opportunity as doing so will save you some premium payments while giving you coverage. Please, however, always keep the fol-

---

237   "Disability Facts and Statistics," LifeInsure.com, accessed June 15, 2022, https://www.lifeinsure.com/disability-facts-and-statistics.

238   "Disability Facts and Statistics."

lowing two points in mind.

1. Do your overall assessment to check if what your employers offer for disability, health, and life coverage meet the overall insurance needs for you and your family. If not, you will need to buy additional coverage.

2. Remember that in most cases these benefits are discontinued once you leave your employer, so you would be exposed to some or a large degree of risk. Before you decide to leave your current employment, you should start arranging replacement coverage.

Non Financial Considerations

In choosing an insurance company for your home, car, or life (apart from the financial considerations of deductibles, coinsurance, replacement cost, and annual premiums), the following nonfinancial factors should be examined.

1. How quickly will the companies settle insurance claims to allow you to repair or replace your damaged car or house?

2. What is the quality of their customer service and add-on benefits? Some companies offer annual reminders of when your car registration or health checkups are due in addition to emergency support on the scene of an accident.

3. To what extent do they use technology to simplify access to policy information, claims submissions, and communications with them? For example, many insurance companies now allow you to get an initial quote for your annual premium on their website as well as pay your premiums by credit card or direct bank transfer rather than needing to visit their offices in person.

In this chapter I have covered the first of three protective measures that you can take to protect your money, all built on different types of insurance coverage. The next chapter will address another protective measure, which is the very uncomfortable but important topic of estate planning.

Your Money Journal Assignment: Preparing for the Storms of Life

WORKING ADULTS: 18 YEARS & OLDER

Life Insurance

- Check if your current life insurance coverage is about six to 10 times your gross salary.

- If it falls short, talk to your insurance agent about getting a term life policy to help close the gap. (Term life policies can be from three to 15 times cheaper than whole life depending on your country.) Remember not to stop or cancel any policy until the new policy comes into force.

Health Insurance

- Does your current health insurance coverage protect you or your dependents from major medical issues such as major surgeries, strokes, or heart attacks?

- If not, talk to your insurance adviser. Get some quotes, and work out a strategy to increase your coverage. It may take some time to get to the level of coverage that you really need for you and your family, but not having proper coverage could send you into medical bankruptcy.

- Discuss with siblings and agree on a plan to deal with medical expenses of elderly parents. Failure to do so could create rifts and divisions in your family.

Property Insurance

- Check if the property insurance on your house includes the replacement cost. If it does not, set up a plan to insure at the full replacement cost to avoid being paid on the average clause basis if you had a claim.

- Check the personal liability coverage on your car policy. Consider adjusting that amount if it is too low (based on the advice of your insurance agent), given that being underinsured would expose you financially if you were at fault in an accident. Also check the adequacy of the liability coverage on your home policy.

FULL-TIME STUDENTS: 14–24 YEARS

- Find out whether your family (talk to your parents or guardians, but approach this with a spirit of humility) is appropriately covered in all insurance types.

- Use the knowledge you garnered from this chapter to share how important it is for the family to develop a plan to get the appropriate coverage where necessary.

- Encourage your parents or guardian to then speak to an insurance adviser on how to increase or adjust the insurance coverage (where necessary) for the family.

chapter 14

STEP 11: PLAN YOUR ESTATE BEFORE SOMEONE ELSE DOES

We have now come to the uncomfortable, but very important, subject of estate planning, which is another method that you can use to protect the wealth that you have built with your blood, sweat, and tears!

Estate Planning Defined

Estate planning is, essentially, planning for the timely and efficient transfer of assets after death while minimizing taxes and expenses associated with the transfers. Estate planning also specifies who will ensure that your wishes are carried out and who is to take guardianship of your minor children.

What Does Estate Really Mean?

The word *estate* means the listing of assets and liabilities that you have at the time of death. It includes your home, furniture, jewelry, cars, debts, and so on—things that you own and owe. That definition shouts that we all must put deliberate plans in place as to how we are going to ensure that our loved ones access our assets in the quickest and most efficient manner so that they don't have to worry about it while they are grieving. Yes, there are things that you and I must deliberately do today to ensure the smooth transfer of these assets.

Proper estate planning also allows you to identify and transfer your assets to persons (beneficiaries) who will be responsible enough to respect and manage your hard-earned assets in a way that ensures that those assets are not wasted but instead are invested and provide financial security for future generations in your family.

Four Ways to Transfer Your Assets

There are at least four ways to transfer assets to your loved ones:

1. A will

2. Ownership structures

3. Naming of beneficiaries and joint account holders

4. A living revocable trust

The Use of a Will

Writing a will is one of the most important aspects of planning your estate. So, what is a will? It is a legal document that explains, among other things, how a person wishes to dispose of their assets after death and to whom these assets should be transferred (i.e., beneficiaries). Culturally, in Jamaica and elsewhere in the world, there is a belief that just by talking about preparing a will, you will be calling down death on yourself. This superstition is believed to be a contributing factor to why so many people die each year without having a will. (They die intestate.) In the U.S., 68 percent of people die without leaving a will.[239] I believe the statistics are very similar in Jamaica, based on the large number of cases the Administrator General's Department (AGD), which administers intestate estates, has to deal with each year for persons who die without a will. According to an article in the *Gleaner*, $80 million (JA$12B) worth of assets belonging to people who died without a will was being managed by the AGD in

---

239   Reid Kress Weisbord and David Horton, "68% of Americans Do Not Have a Will," The Conversation, May 19, 2020, https://www.google.com/amp/s/theconversation.com/amp/68-of-americans-do-not-have-a-will-137686.

2016.[240] Those are large numbers for a developing country with a small population of approximately three million people. We often read about the tension and strife in families over the assets of loved ones who died without leaving a will. Leaving a will creates fewer problems as it generally costs less and takes a shorter time to transfer the assets of a deceased person to the beneficiaries named in the will of the deceased, relative to the time and cost needed to transfer the assets of an intestate person to beneficiaries that are determined by the courts .[241]

Yes, I repeat, if you die without leaving a will, the courts will generally kick in, and will determine how your hard-earned assets are allocated instead of through your direction![242]

In Jamaica, the Intestates Estates and Property Charges Act is the specific piece of legislation that determines how the assets or estate of an intestate person gets allocated. The Act has a table of distribution that dictates how your assets would be allocated after deducting certain expenses such as administration expenses (for the persons administering your assets or your estate), funeral expenses, debts that can be verified as bona fide, and other liabilities incurred.[243]

If you look at the table of distribution, it will certainly inspire you to make sure you get that will in place. In general, it gives priority to your spouse or common-law spouse (first in line for your assets), then your children (second in line), your parents (third in line), your other relatives (fourth), and then the government (fifth).

Here is an example of where it gets tricky when you don't have a will. If you are separated from your spouse but not divorced, and you die

---

240   "Administrator General's Department Closes 425 Intestate Cases—Chuck," *The Gleaner*, May 4, 2022, https://jamaica-gleaner.com/article/news/20220504/administrator-generals-department-closes-425-intestate-cases-chuck.

241   Lisa Smith, "What is a Will and Why Do I Need One Now?," Investopedia.com, December 23, 2021, https://www.investopedia.com/articles/pf/08/what-is-a-will.asp.

242   Smith, "What is a Will."

243   "Intestates Estates and Property Charges Act," Global-Regulation, accessed June 6, 2022, https://www.global-regulation.com/law/jamaica/2938384/intestates-estates-and-property-charges-act.html.

without a will, the table of distribution would still allow your wife to get a decent share of your estate (up to 66 percent if, say, you only had one child who is alive at the time of your death) as the first in line. Even if the two of you were for all practical purposes "done and dusted" and have basically moved on, but the divorce just was never finalized, would the spouse from whom you have separated still be first in line? Yes, indeed, that is the law.

Parents of the deceased could also get some of your assets even if there is a surviving spouse and there are no children involved. What if you never had such a great relationship with your father or mother, and for whatever reason you would not necessarily want to give them that much? They would still share in your estate. Yes, indeed, they would! The same kind of possibilities mentioned for spouse and parents exist for those persons who would be third in line, etc. I am not finished yet. There is also the possibility that you have no spouse, children, or relatives. If so, then guess who could get your assets? Yes, the government!

Look, the point here is for you to stop whatever you are doing right now and make a note in your diary to get your will in place.

There are many stories of famous people who died without a will. In each case, it created undue delays and pressure on their loved ones. For example, the legendary soccer player Diego Armando Maradona did not have a will in place,[244] and neither did superstar singer Prince,[245] which no doubt will make the whole process of asset distribution take much longer.

The best practice is that if you have a relatively small estate and only one or two adult beneficiaries, you could get a simple will form at your local pharmacy (at least this is the case in Jamaica) or use an online service and get it done. If you have one or more of the following circumstances, then you should seek the help of an attorney to help you to get a will done

---

244   Tali Weinberg, "What Not Having a Will Means for Maradona," *Safewill* (Blog), last modified August 9, 2021, https://safewill.com/blog/posts/what-not-having-will-means-diego-maradona.

245   Jessica Wang, "Prince's Estate Worth $156.4 Million in Final Valuation," *Entertainment Weekly*, accessed 31 July 2022, https://ew.com/music/prince-estate-final-valuation/.

properly: lots of beneficiaries, minor beneficiaries, assets in multiple countries, or use of different vehicles of ownership of assets.

Writing a Valid Will

Preparing your will properly is extremely important. Key features of a properly prepared will include but are not limited to the following:

1. It must be in writing and easy to read and understand, whether typed or written.

2. It must be signed by the testator (person writing the will).

3. It must be dated.

4. Beneficiaries should be named.

5. It must be witnessed by at least two qualified witnesses.

6. It must or should name at least one executor (a person whom you can trust to administer your estate and ensure that the transfers of your assets are done as smoothly as possible).[246]

Failure to perform one or more of those six steps could either make the will invalid or cause delays in it being probated (the process of taking it to the court for it to be accepted as valid before the assets can be transferred to your beneficiaries).

Additionally, once you get married, the will that you had before the marriage is no longer valid, and you will need to do another one.[247] Imagine a scenario where John gets married but didn't update the will he had before marriage, and then he dies. That situation would mean that John would have died intestate. The surviving spouse and family members would then have to deal with all the inconveniences that come with someone dying intestate. Married people reading this book, please check if your will has been updated since your marriage!

---

246 Mary Randolph, "Settling an Estate: Does the Will Appear Valid?," Nolo, accessed June 10, 2022, https://www.nolo.com/legal-encyclopedia/settling-estate-will-appear-valid-32437.html.

247 "Does Marriage Affect Your Will?," AMD Solicitors, accessed June 10, 2022, https://amdsolicitors.com/does-marriage-affect-your-will/.

In order to transfer your assets (bank accounts, real estate, or stocks and shares), the will must be probated, and a Grant of Administration obtained from the Supreme Court of Judicature of Jamaica. Obtaining the Grant of Administration authorizes the executors named in the will to act on behalf of the deceased and take the necessary legal steps to administer the estate and do all the things that the deceased outlined in the will.[248]

Be careful, therefore, to only choose executors who are willing and able to take on this critical task of managing your estate—failure to do so could mean long delays in your assets being transferred to your loved ones.

Taxes

In Jamaica, stamp duty (a form of tax) must first be paid before an application can be made to the Supreme Court for a Grant of Administration.

The stamp duty rate, as mentioned earlier, is fixed at a maximum of $33 (JA$5,000) regardless of the value of the assets in your estate.[249]

After the payment of stamp duty, there is also transfer tax that must be paid (generally) on the market value of real estate and shares that are owned by the deceased at the date of death. Taxes paid in relation to an estate are sometimes referred to as death taxes.

At the time of writing, the transfer tax rate in Jamaica is 1.5 percent.[250] The good news is that there are certain items that can be offset against the assets in the estate before the transfer tax rate is applied. These items include but are not limited to mortgage debts and funeral expenses. It gets better because, if the value of the estate after all these deductions is less than $67,000 (JA$10M), no transfer tax would be payable.

Do you know the threshold for which an estate would be taxed in your country? Do you know the applicable taxes and expenses that you are likely

---

248 "How to Probate a Will in Jamaica—From the Perspective of Property Lawyers in Jamaica," FTCW Law, August 6, 2018, https://ftcwlaw.com/property-lawyers-in-jamaica/.

249 "Get the Facts—New Tax Initiatives," Jamaica Information Service, May 10, 2019, https://jis.gov.jm/information/get-the-facts/get-the-facts-new-tax-initiatives/.

250 "Frequently Asked Questions."

to pay? If you don't, you should find out what these are as it will help you to plan how much cash your estate will need to pay the required taxes.

Legal and Other Fees

You will need an attorney to assist with the probate process and to provide other legal advice at a fee, which generally falls in the range of 3–5 percent of the value of the estate in Jamaica. The executor also has the right, under law, to charge up to 6 percent in administration fees. If you do not leave a will and the Administrator General has to administer your estate, the Administrator General will charge the estate the 6 percent fee.[251]

Funding Estate Expenses

Life insurance proceeds that are paid directly to an estate or a trusted individual can be used to pay estate expenses. Using a trusted individual will allow for quicker access (as this would escape the probate process) to cash that will be needed to pay up-front expenses, such as stamp duty and transfer tax in Jamaica. Term life insurance should be considered, as this is relatively inexpensive. Many estates don't have enough cash to deal with these expenses, which has resulted in untold hardship on the named beneficiaries,[252] given that, as mentioned earlier, these expenses must generally be paid before assets can be transferred to the named beneficiaries. Speak with your insurance adviser or attorney for further guidance.

Use of Ownership Structures

As mentioned previously, estate planning is about how you organize your estate in order to efficiently transfer your assets. Apart from using a will, you can also transfer certain assets via the method that you chose to own them.

Real Estate

If you own real estate in joint tenancy—for example, with your

---

251   "Administration of Estates," Administrator General's Department: An Executive Agency, accessed June 10, 2020, https://agd.gov.jm/services/administration-of-estates.

252   Francine Derby, "Reduction in Death Duties May Breathe Life into Probate Practice," April 28, 2019, https://www.lexology.com/library/detail.aspx?g=cfd02554-635d-402f-bdfd-c6294e9807c3.

spouse—your ownership interest in the real estate will automatically be transferred to your spouse if you die first. It is not to be included in the list of assets available for distribution in your will. Joint tenancy is a very cost-efficient and fast way to transfer real estate. If there are people to whom you want to give a certain piece of real estate, then you could consider owning such assets in joint tenancy before you die.[253]

Shares

You can also choose to own shares jointly with others. For example, you could own shares jointly with your son, and if you die first, or your son dies first, the entire shareholding goes to the surviving person automatically and would not be included in the assets available for distribution in the will of the person who died.

Naming of Beneficiaries and Joint Account Holders
Life Insurance Proceeds

Life insurance proceeds are paid out to the named beneficiaries on a life insurance policy when the insured dies. The beneficiary could be an individual (a family member) or the deceased person's estate. You should, therefore, double-check at least once per year if you are still comfortable with the named beneficiaries on your life insurance policy. Let's say Martha got married to James, but prior to her marriage, her mother was her sole beneficiary on her $500,000 life insurance policy. Martha should now consider splitting the proceeds with her husband, given her changed marital status. If Martha forgot to adjust the names of the beneficiaries, and she were to die first, then guess what will happen? All of the funds would go to Martha's mother, and her husband, James, would not be entitled to any. Can you also imagine if Martha's mother and James were not enjoying a good relationship? It could be a toxic showdown!

Investment, Bank, and Pension Accounts

The same principles discussed above for life insurance would apply for

---

253   "What Is the Difference Between Joint Tenancy and Tenants-in-Common?," National Land Agency, accessed June 10, 2022, https://nla.gov.jm/content/what-difference-between-joint-tenancy-and-tenants-common.

those assets as well. You should update the names of beneficiaries and joint account holders on those holdings periodically, as your life goes through different stages.

In the event that you die before one of the named beneficiaries or joint account holders, the surviving people whose names are on the account will get the money. Such accounts would generally bypass your will (except under certain exceptional circumstances that your attorney can highlight).

Use of a Living Revocable Trust

A living revocable trust is a legal vehicle that allows your beneficiaries to benefit from your assets without them having outright control or legal ownership of those assets. You would transfer ownership of your assets to the trust during your lifetime—these assets would not be available for distribution to the beneficiaries named in your will. They would therefore escape the probate process, hence the time and cost involved with that process—this is one of the major advantages of setting up a living revocable trust.[254]

You can also use a living revocable trust to protect the interest of your minor children (those under 18) after you die, especially in cases where you may have concerns that your surviving spouse may not support or show kindness to some or all of your children, particularly those children from another relationship. How would a living trust provide this level of protection? The trustees (the people with the authority to manage the affairs and assets of the trust) could, say, upon your death, be required to pay certain expenses, such as college tuition or housing, for your minor children until they reach adulthood, at which time specified assets or moneys could be distributed to them. You can also use a living revocable trust to give money to your adult children over a period of time if you believe giving them too much at once may be unwise. The use of living revocable trusts is not only for the rich and famous. Speak to your attorney to determine whether you should consider or avoid one based on your unique situation.

---

254   Barclay Palmer, "Should You Set Up a Revocable Living Trust?," June 15, 2022, https://www.investopedia.com/articles/pf/06/revocablelivingtrust.asp.

Guardianship of Your Minor Children

Children under the age of 18 are considered minors, and unless you name someone to be their legal guardian, your children could become wards of the state or bounce around from house to house with strangers or family members who may not necessarily have the children's best interests at heart. A legal guardian would effectively play the role of parent in your absence— generally, the guardian would only step into this role if both parents are not around. Think about how important this is. Please think of at least two people, in order of preference, who you believe would do an excellent job of stepping into the guardianship role. Then proceed to ask the first person if they would be willing to accept that role and brief them on what is involved. If that individual is not willing, you can move to your second choice.

Once you have secured an agreement, then include this guardianship role in your will in the section provided.

Knowledge about estate planning and the associated consequences will protect your wealth and ensure that it goes to the people whom you care about and who will be good stewards of the money you worked so hard to accumulate. The wise King Solomon expressed concern about leaving wealth to those who may waste it when he said, "I came to hate all my hard work here on earth, for I must leave to others everything I have earned. And who can tell whether my successors will be wise or foolish?" (Ecclesiastes 2:18–19, NLT).

Your Money Journal Assignment: Plan Your Estate Before It's Too Late

WORKING ADULTS: 18 YEARS & OLDER

- If you don't have a will, you should seek to prepare one as soon as possible. A quick way is to go online (there are several websites that will help generate a will quickly and inexpensively) or get a will form from your local pharmacy (in the case of Jamaica). Check the rules in your country or start talking to an attorney about putting a will in place. Also, make a list of your assets and where they are located for easy access by the executors administering your will. Keep the list with your will, and tell your executors where to locate your will.

- Identify and name guardians for your minor children in the event you and your spouse or partner should die early. Ensure you get agreement from these guardians before including their names in your will.

- Go through all your bank accounts, investment accounts, pension accounts, life insurance policies, and any accounts where you have beneficiaries named, and check if, based on changes in your life circumstances, you still want these persons to benefit from your assets if you were to die. Make any relevant changes where necessary.

Be sure to also have a broad conversation with your attorney about the best combination of vehicles discussed above that you could use to transfer your assets at death. For example, you could have a discussion as to whether a living revocable trust is a vehicle you should consider or avoid based on your specific circumstances.

FULL-TIME STUDENTS: 14–24 YEARS

- Find out whether your parents or guardians have their wills in place. Approach the topic with love and a sense of humility.

- If they don't, explain the importance of writing their wills by sharing at least three reasons you learned from this chapter.

chapter 15

STEP 12: PROTECT YOUR FINANCIAL RECORDS—THEY WILL PROTECT YOU

Imagine that you are just about to close a deal on a car that you have been trying to sell. After advertising it for the last six months, someone is finally ready to buy the car. You really need the cash from this car to help you finalize an offer on a home on which you have already put in a competitive offer to the sellers. The buyer is on your veranda with a cashier's check or bank check ready to pay for the car, but after one hour of waiting, you emerge with a very deep look of sadness, because you couldn't find the title of the car. You explain that you turned the house upside down, making it look like a junkyard, but there was no title.

Needless to say, the buyer leaves in frustration, and you didn't get to sell the car. Getting the new title would take a number of weeks, and so the deal was a missed opportunity.

That simple scenario makes the point very clear how extremely important it is to secure our financial records to allow for speedy retrieval when they are needed.

The challenge of securing our financial records has become more complex, given that we now often get receipts and financial records (e.g., life insurance policies, loan agreements) via email and other electronic means.

You should store key financial records securely in a safe, a fireproof cabinet, or a secure online location.

It is quite common for people to forget to collect titles (car, house) from government offices or financial institutions. At your earliest convenience, you should collect all outstanding titles from all financial entities and government agencies.

Key documents that you should be able to access readily include but are not limited to the following.

Titles (Car, Home, Land)

An inability to quickly access these can create delays in using the assets for a secured loan or to complete a sale. Titles that are not readily accessible after your will has been probated would delay the transfer of ownership to the beneficiaries until the titles are located.

Loan Agreements

Loan agreements carry very important terms and are needed especially if there is a default and if the lender is trying to repossess your asset. It is important to quickly have access to these agreements so that you can huddle with your legal advisers to interpret the conditions under which the lender could repossess your asset. In cases where there is a dispute about how interest and fee charges are calculated, it is the loan agreement that will allow you to determine what the actual formula for the calculation is supposed to be. Loan agreements also provide evidence that a transaction actually occurred, which is especially important when individuals lend money to other individuals. Many times, because of friendship, people don't make a written record of the loan term, the amount loaned, repayments, and other relevant terms.

Critical Contracts

Employment contracts and lease agreements for real estate transactions are critical to determining final payments where a lease or rental has been terminated or when an employee separates from an employer. Such contracts should be readily accessible and be reviewed so that you can accurately anticipate routine and final payment amounts in order to plan your cash flows accordingly.

Will and Related Records

Your will and a list of your assets and their locations should be easily accessible. The names of the financial institutions, the branches, account types, and account numbers should be kept together with your will in a safe place. Many people let their attorneys keep a copy of their will, which is wise. Failure to find a will will result in your being treated as having died intestate with all the implications discussed earlier. Even a will that is not necessarily your last will and testament is the one that will be used to determine how your assets are distributed rather than an updated but misplaced one. Clearly, an outdated will is not desirable because your final wishes might not have been reflected in the earlier will.

Birth and Marriage Certificates

Birth or marriage certificates that can't be found could delay the payment of the life insurance proceeds, so their storage is critical. For example, marriage certificates are needed to prove that you are the lawful spouse of an intestate spouse. The intestacy laws in Jamaica puts the spouse first in terms of distribution of assets, and if another person is claiming to be the spouse of the deceased, your marriage certificate will quickly settle any doubts that you are the actual spouse.

Passwords and Combinations

Safes and email accounts containing very important information, such as electronic receipts, contracts, and other critical documents, need to be accessible by persons whom you absolutely trust to avoid delays and major inconveniences in finalizing your estate. Therefore, make arrangements to share passwords and combinations with these trusted individuals.

The Goldsons

The Goldsons continue to execute well, and their latest progress is as follows:

- They paid off the last $8,000 of credit card debt as planned. Now, their only debt is their mortgage.

- Having paid down so much debt, they went on to build a full three-month emergency fund (approximately $14,000), which took about five months after having paid $2,225 of consumer debt ($1,873) and their car loan ($352).

- They opened their IRAs and are now contributing 15 percent of their income.

- They accomplished this goal faster than they had anticipated because Mr. Goldson got a promotion at his new job and his online business continued to do well.

- They executed their other plan of investing 5 percent of their income in a low-cost index fund via automatic deduction each month.

- They now have a will, have named guardians for their two minor children, and have all their financial records safely secured in a safe at home and at their attorney's office (will).

Following is a summary of the outstanding achievements by this hard-working couple:

- They had negative savings of −17 percent, and now their savings rate is a positive 20-plus percent per month.

- They had a debt-to-income ratio of 62, and now their DTI is below the benchmark 43 percent. They have paid off $60,666 worth of debt.

- They once had a negative net worth of $33,999, driven largely by heavy debt, and now their net worth is over $250,000.

- They now have life insurance, health insurance, and a will among other important achievements.

They took more than seven hard years to accomplish their successes, but they are now well on their way to total financial freedom. Congratulations to the Goldsons! You, too, can achieve similar levels of success with the same kind of attitude and resolve!

Your Money Journal Assignment: Discovering and Protecting My Financial Records

WORKING ADULTS: 18 YEARS & OLDER

- Take stock of all your important records (titles, loan agreements, investment records, share certificates, insurance contracts, passwords, marriage certificate, birth certificates, etc.) and ensure that they are safely secured. Protecting those records is vital to your future and will save you time, money, and stress.

FULL-TIME STUDENTS: 14–24 YEARS

- Speak to your parents about the location of your birth certificates, passports, school transcripts, and other records that directly relate to you.

- Ensure that all of those items are kept in a safe location. Each is an important life record, and not being able to quickly access them could cost you a scholarship, grant, or the ability to travel at short notice, not to mention affecting your ability to directly or indirectly earn money!

part 4

SOW YOUR MONEY

chapter 16

STEP 13: LOVE THY NEIGHBOR

Love Thy Neighbor

This is one of the shortest chapters in this book but perhaps the most important. You will see why as we go on.

"Sow your money!" It's a powerful statement that embodies the idea that you must first have something to sow or give, which is why we could not put this chapter earlier in the book. Many people in their hearts wished they could have helped their mothers more, their churches more, and their children more. I believe in the 14 GPS your money principles in this book. When you put them to work (yes, you must take action to change your direction—faith is not just believing in your mind; it is also moving your feet), they will eventually help you to get surplus cash so that you can have something to sow, something to give.

The story of the Good Samaritan, told by Jesus in the Gospel of Luke, would not be remembered nor would he have been described as *good* unless he had some goods. He had resources and assets, plus a heart of compassion. It is not good enough to just have a heart of compassion. To bring about real change in some situations will require compassion plus using some of your assets. The scripture says, "Suppose you see a brother or sister who has no food or clothing, and you say, 'Good-bye and have a good day; stay warm and eat well,' but then you don't give that person any food or clothing. What good does that do?" (James 2:15–16, NLT). It does little or zero good.

What do we really mean by sowing our money? Where should we sow our money? And the biggest question of all is "Why sowest thou thy money?" After all, you worked so hard to become financially independent.

"Mr. Scott, you're now telling me to sow my money. Really, why? Where were all these people and places among which you are likely to tell me to sow my money, when I was working like a horse, toiling through the night, pouring out sweat and tears, dripping like a marathon runner! Isn't this money for me and my immediate family to chill, 'braff,' flask, and enjoy?"

The answer to all of those questions is a resounding no. In fact, the standard to help others is very high. We are expected to help others even before they ask. The standard in the words of scripture is "if we see our brother in need and close our bowels of compassion from him, how can we say the love of God dwells in us?" (1 John 3:17). It is not the easiest thing to do, but that is the standard.

Imagine what our communities and the world would look like if we all helped others in need even before we were asked. Offering help where we see the need is precisely what the story of the Good Samaritan is about. One human being saw another human (not seeing color, gender, age, or anything else) in need—lying, bleeding, or dying on a lonely and dark Jericho road—and he gave of his time. He stopped his busy schedule to tend to him and take him to the hospital. He gave up his assets—his oil to bind the wound, and his donkey to take him to the hospital. He gave him compassion; he didn't merely throw some dollars at him and speed past in his shiny SUV jeep. He stopped to check on his condition, took him to the hospital, and promised to follow up with a visit. The Good Samaritan saw a need, not the race of the wounded man. The man was almost dead; he could not actually ask for help with words. However, he was shouting for help, speaking through the language of his almost lifeless body on the dark, lonely Jericho road (Luke 10:25–37).

I believe I have started to answer the question "Why should we sow our money?" My arguments so far have said, very simply, to help those in need based on the dignity of their humanity and not based on color, age, and so on! I have said, in effect, we should love our neighbors, which means to focus on those in need, not just ourselves and immediate family members. I will come back to the *why* question later.

I believe it is time to define the word *sow*. The word *sow*, according to the *Merriam-Webster Dictionary*, means "to plant seed for growth especially by scattering."[255] The definition reminds me of the words of Jesus when he said, "Except a corn of wheat fall into the ground and die, it abideth alone: but if it die, it bringeth forth much fruit" (John 12:24, KJV). The seed must be released, it must fall, and it must be planted. To plant means we have to be prepared to identify a spot of ground to put or release that seed, a spot of ground that will be good so that the seed can grow into a strong fruit-bearing tree. This definition means the sower represents you and me, the ones who have surplus resources (some "goods"). It means we must find worthy causes to put some of that surplus to benefit others, to benefit our communities. Earlier in this book, I talked about one of the reasons financial freedom is a big deal. It is because it helps us to change our communities. Yes, it does. If you have some seed (surplus money), find a spot of ground—a community project—and release that seed so it may grow. So that the "yute dem" (the young people) may grow, so that some teachers at a school may grow, so that Mr. Brown's board house that was ravaged by a fire may grow back.

I thank God for the many community projects into which I have been blessed to sow using the three goods that he has given to me—my time, my assets, and my mind. I'm referring to these projects only to drive home the

---

255   *Merriam-Webster*, s.v. "sow (verb)," accessed June 6, 2022, https://www.merriam-webster.com/dictionary/sow.

point of how much of an impact we can have when we release those seeds.

This step is called "Love Thy Neighbor" because we can and should be good neighbors. We can choose (it is a choice) to use our assets or goods or surplus cash for good or bad. The same cash in the bank can be used to buy a bullet or a bulla (a Jamaican pastry) for a hungry, inner-city youth. It is a choice. Our individual actions help to shape our communities and, hence, our countries.

We can't rely on our governments alone to solve all the problems in our communities. Yes, the government has a role to play, but if each of us decides to make a difference in helping just one person in a real way (giving our goods and our compassion as a nice package), imagine the chain reaction and the explosive global and community impact it would have!

Regarding the impact that we can have when we decide to love our neighbors and by extension be good neighbors, I think of the small inner-city Church of God of Prophecy at 19 High Holborn Street Kingston, Jamaica, that hosted a Vacation Bible School (VBS) when I was growing up in Southside, Central Kingston—the church hosting VBS was indeed doing a good neighborly act! It was at VBS at age 14 that I made the most life-changing decision of my life when I decided to become a Christian and hence became a follower of Jesus Christ. The decision has been the foundation for every success I have had in my life. That small church, therefore, now has a big stake in all the persons and projects I support because it played a major role in my decision to become a Christian. So, I encourage you, too, to be a good neighbor and, therefore, become a partaker in changing our communities and generations to come.

Your Money Journal Assignment: Love Thy Neighbor as Thyself

Working Adults: 18 Years & Older

- Think of ways you can bless someone in need, without putting you and your family at financial risk, and even without your being asked by the person for help. It could take the form of sponsoring lunch money, tuition fees, gifts to charities—the list goes on. Sow seeds and enjoy true happiness!

FULL-TIME STUDENTS: 14–24 YEARS

- You don't need money to be a good neighbor. You can start now.

- Do you have an elderly neighbor who needs some help around their house now and then or needs someone to go shopping for them?

- You can join a youth club that does charitable deeds. There are many opportunities to sow your talents—you must seek them out.

- In addition, most universities favor those students who can demonstrate a habit of voluntarism when assigning scholarships.

chapter 17

STEP 14: LIVE THE GOOD LIFE

Live the Good Life

Ecclesiastes 5:19 says, "To every man whom God has given wealth and possessions, he has also given him the ability to eat from them, to receive his reward, and to find enjoyment in his toil; these things are the gift of God"(NET). Here, the wise and wealthy King Solomon, teaches that we should learn to enjoy our hard earned wealth.

Therefore, in addition to being a good neighbor, you should also live some "good" life with your money in the here and now, on this side of eternity. Have you ever seen a U-Haul behind a coffin that is on its way to the cemetery? No, you haven't. We cannot take our material wealth with us. So, while you are being a good neighbor, live some good life, and be good to yourself. Take that vacation, buy that gadget, or spoil yourself a little. However, live your life in such a way that you don't erode your underlying investments generating the income that has given you financial freedom.

Your Money Journal Assignment: Live the Good Life

WORKING ADULTS: 18 YEARS & OLDER

- While blessing others, also take time to enjoy the fruits of your labor by planning and doing amazing things you dreamed of—the overseas travel to faraway places, the home improvement project, the golf vacations, or whatever it is for you. We only walk this road of life once. But don't get carried away and land yourself into or back into high-cost debt and living beyond your means.

FULL-TIME STUDENTS: 14–24 YEARS

- For my college and high school readers, the idea is really about living "the balanced life" and not so much about the good life at this stage.

- Now, you must decide to work hard to get the best education so you can live a really good life after finishing school.

- But you should still have some fun while you push for the best school grades.

- So, take those fun breaks (watch a ball game, go to the movies, go fishing), but don't overdo it. Your grades are your main priority right now. You will have your entire life later!

chapter 18

CONCLUSION

First, let me extend heartiest congratulations to you for navigating through these 14 life-changing steps to financial freedom. I trust you found the book empowering, inspiring, and entertaining.

The Foundations

By now, you should have grasped the foundations on which the house of financial freedom is built. They include having a clear understanding of what financial freedom is. You should have grasped that financial freedom has at least three layers:

1. Total financial freedom (Your money works for you—i.e., you only work if you want to).

2. Partial financial freedom (You are able to save, and you are on top of your debts—but you can't live solely off your investments at this stage).

3. Financial bondage (You live from hand to mouth and or have a mountain of debt).

Another foundational truth you should now know is how to avoid the four horsemen (cultural influences) of the global savings crisis:

1. A culture of "How much is the monthly payment?" rather than looking at the total cost of purchasing an item including the interest cost

2. A culture of keeping up with the Joneses by people spending what they don't have to keep up with their neighbors online and on their streets

3. A culture of instant gratification that promotes consumerism, an archenemy of saving money

4. A culture of a lack of financial intelligence (money-management skills) among generations that have already left high school and college and those who are soon to leave high schools and colleges

The main impact of those horsemen is that they rob people of their ability to save money. Saving, as has been hammered home with every word of this book, is the lifeblood of becoming financially free. It is the seed portion of your income that you cannot afford to eat, but that you must use to pursue financial freedom mercilessly. Remember, no savings, no financial freedom!

The House of Financial Freedom—GPS Your Money

You should now be more than familiar with the 14 steps that are split across the three iconic themes of grow, protect, and sow (GPS) your money—these steps are the blueprint for building your house of financial freedom.

Grow Your Money: Nine Steps

You should now know the following:

1. How to complete your financial health check by preparing and analyzing your statement of net worth, your statement of income and expenses, and your 10 financial health indicators.

2. How to set financial goals. They should be designed to specifically address the financial indicators that you are struggling with. You know the importance of being obsessive about achieving your financial goals.

3. How to identify your dominant money personality and the safeguards you need to put in place to manage the weaknesses that are inherent in your dominant money personality.

4. The importance of living on a budget and how to save like the ants. You know how to allocate your income between needs, wants, and savings. You now know how to track, trim, and chop your expenses (to save money) and are aware of the multiplicity of ideas on how to increase your income (so you can save even more money).

5. The importance of (1) having an emergency fund, (2) how to build one, and (3) the fact that the lack of an emergency fund is the main route through which many people end up with a mountain of high-cost debt and financial sorrow.

6. How to calculate your debt-to-income ratio, the importance of using debt wisely, and the risks and rewards of borrowing. You also know the different ways of attacking your debt mountains (i.e., debt snowball, debt avalanche, debt consolidation, and strategies to restructure individual debts).

7. That most people are at risk of not having enough money when they retire, simply because most employers have switched to defined contribution plans (e.g., the employer-sponsored 401(k)s in the U.S.), which don't guarantee a set amount of income when you retire. You also know strategies to help overcome that risk, which include maximizing your pension contributions as soon as you can and signing up for a retirement account or plan at the earliest possible opportunity.

8. That wealth creation is not just about saving money, as money left in a savings account or under the bed will be eaten away by the

termite of inflation. You understand that in your fight against inflation, investing your savings is your number one tool.

9. That there are legal ways to reduce your tax expense by including for example, more long-term capital investments in your portfolio and maximizing your pension or retirement contributions.

Protect Your Money: Three Steps

You should now also be aware of the following so you can protect the money you have accumulated through blood and tears:

1. Insurance in its various forms, such as life, health, disability, and property, are four key tools to absorb potential adverse events that could wipe you out financially.

2. Good estate planning is important to ensure the most efficient and timely transfer of your assets to your beneficiaries when you die (hard to say, but such is life).

3. Securing and protecting important financial records in both hard and soft copies is significant—records such as your will, titles, listing of your assets, passwords to key bank accounts—and there are steep consequences if those documents are not readily available when needed.

Sow Your Money

You should now understand the following:

1. Your wealth is to be sown and shared with the needy, broken, naked, and hungry.

2. You are blessed to be a blessing.

3. While you must help others, you must also live and enjoy the fruit of your labor and the good life.

A Challenge to You: Kick-Start Your 14-Step Financial Freedom Journey Today

If you are 18 years old and above and are working, I challenge you to pause right now and do the following:

- Complete the financial health check at the end of chapter 4 (if you have not yet done so), or access it at www.14stepstofinancialfreedom.com to determine the state of your current financial health.

- Reflect on how far you are from your mandatory or voluntary retirement date, and then visualize what you would like the quality of your life in retirement to be like.

- Reflect on your financial health check results, and then make an honest assessment of whether your retirement will be what you envisioned it to be if you continue living without making any adjustments to how you manage your money. If the answer is that you must act and do something different, then move to the next point.

- Write down at least one specific financial goal that will turn around each weak area based on your financial health check results.

- Paste these goals on a wall that you must pass every day in your home, and then each day do something that takes you closer to achieving each financial goal. Before you know it, you will be well on your way to the land of financial freedom.

If you are between ages of 14 and 24, not working, and are in high school or college, I challenge you with the following:

- Believe me that you do have time on your side, and every dollar you save and invest will have a lot more time to work for you—at least 40 years. So, you should always be aware that you are well poised to get to financial freedom with some simple steps by the time you are 55 to 64 years old.

- Remember the story of Marcia and how she started to invest a relatively small sum every month right out of college, from her first job, and was able to retire at age 62 comfortably? Decide today that you, too, will be like Marcia.

- Close your eyes and visualize what it would mean to be able to choose to work if you want to when you get to age 55 or 65.

- Do you like what you see? If yes, then let this visual be your lighthouse that guides you safely to the land of financial freedom using the principles taught in this book.

These are the types of actions you must take to change your financial direction. You must invest not only in stock and bonds, but also in yourself. Please find some time for yourself. This is intergenerational stuff we are talking about in this book. It is not good enough to just read books like these; you must take some action. There is an ancient Chinese proverb that says, "If you do not change your direction, you will end up directly where you are headed."

A Testimonial

I close with a testimonial by someone in Jamaica who took action after attending my financial freedom course, which covers the same content as this book.

I attended Bruce's "14 Steps to Financial Freedom Course." This course was a "Damascus Road" experience for me. In talking to Bruce and reflecting on the course content, I realized that I was heading for a big financial crash. I took the grow, protect, and sow (GPS) your money principles from the course and then executed a plan of paying off my credit card (48 percent interest rate) and moved to clearing up all my loans. I also rearranged my insurance coverage, both life and health insurance. I'm now adequately covered in both areas while paying out less money. This course is a must do. I guarantee it will change your life wholeheartedly!

—Christopher Wright, principal, Holy Family Primary and Infant School, Kingston, Jamaica

Go and be like Christopher Wright and take some action that will change your financial direction and destination!

appendix

ACKNOWLEDGMENTS

Thanks to God for giving me the passion, wisdom, and strength to write this book.

Thank you to my dear wife, Suzette, and our three sons, John, Justin, and Jared, for painfully suffering through being the first sounding board on the content of this book.

Thanks to my late grandmother, Ms. Olive Shepherd, and my mother, Ms. Janet Shepherd, for your love and for giving me a godly upbringing. These values have given me the self-confidence and belief needed to succeed in every sphere of life.

Thanks to all my siblings, uncles, aunts, cousins, and all other family members for your role in shaping me into the person I am today.

Thanks to my PwC family for your sterling contribution to my professional development.

Thanks to my church families over the years for your contribution to my spiritual upbringing.

Thanks to all professional associations, institutions, and colleagues that gave me the opportunity to serve and, in the process, have helped me to grow professionally.

Thanks to Ms. Maxine McDonnough for your fine editorial work on the first draft of the manuscript. Your diligence and hard work are deeply appreciated.

Thanks to Ms. Julie Broad and the entire Book Launchers team for your technical input and guidance on all stages of this project, including getting my book into the hands and hearts of readers. You are indeed a world-class organization!

Thanks to Ms. Dionne Golding for your detailed and insightful review of a draft of the manuscript

Thanks to my technical content reviewers who gave invaluable insights on the chapters dealing with taxation (Mr. Brian Denning, tax partner), estate planning (Ms. Camille Facey, attorney-at-law), property insurance (Ms. Sharon Donaldson-Levine, general insurance executive), and retirement planning (Ms. Shannique Chang, pension specialist). I take full responsibility for any inaccuracies found in these chapters.

Thanks to all the organizations and schools that gave me a platform to talk to your audiences about financial freedom—these sessions have helped to shape the idea for this book.

Thank you to the teams that helped to bring awareness and publicity to the book—

I truly appreciate your efforts.

Thanks to all my financial mentees for the opportunity to coach you, and thanks to all my well-wishers and everyone who has spoken a kind word of encouragement to me personally or on the book project.

ABOUT THE AUTHOR

Bruce Scott is the territory leader (senior partner) at PricewaterhouseCoopers (PwC) Jamaica, a member firm of PricewaterhouseCoopers International Limited, one of the largest professional services networks in the world. He is a chartered accountant (Jamaica), a licensed certified public accountant (CPA) in the State of Colorado (U.S.), and a chartered certified accountant (UK).

He holds a master of business administration (MBA) in finance from Manchester Business School (UK) and completed executive education at the world-renowned INSEAD Business School (France). He became one of the youngest Jamaican and Caribbean chartered accountants ever at age 21, notwithstanding the challenges he faced while growing up in humble beginnings in the volatile inner-city community of Southside, Central (Downtown) Kingston, Jamaica.

Bruce wrote this book and developed a course on the same content to empower others on how to achieve financial freedom and to break intergenerational poverty.

Bruce passionately believes that financial intelligence leads to financial independence. He has presented and taught his 14 Steps to Financial Freedom courseto a wide cross section of audiences including teachers, students (high school and college), working adults, retirees, and just about every kind of person across Jamaica, the U.S., the Caribbean, Canada, and the UK.

He is a proud past student of Jamaica College (JC)and Holy Family Primary and InfantSchool in Southside. Bruce went back to his alma maters and taught his financial freedom course to teachers and students. His financial freedom course, which is taught by Bruce, is now an optional course for fifth (11th grade) and sixth formers (12th and 13th grade) at Jamaica College.

He is a past president of the Institute of Chartered Accountants of Jamaica (ICAJ) and a former technical adviser (six years) to an International Federation of Accountants (IFAC)board member. He is a Christian (since age 14) and likes to share his faith, especially in a cross-cultural setting. He plays golf in his spare time, as well as football (soccer) with his youngest son (eight years old), and is a budding piano player. Bruce used to play a lot of football (soccer) back in his younger days during which he represented JC in the under-age-13 and under-age-15 categories and played in community leagues (Santos for under-age-16 and True Love in Southside for under-age-14). Bruce also played cricket for JC (captain of the under-age-14 team).

He is married to Suzette, and they have three sons: John, Justin, and Jared.

Lightning Source UK Ltd.
Milton Keynes UK
UKHW011940030223
416465UK00009B/83